MW00965981

QUESTING FRANCE:

DEEPENING THE SEARCH FOR MY HOLY GRAIL

Personal Growth Through Travel ©

By
Marilyn Barnicke Belleghem, M.Ed.

Quest Publishing
2005

Quest Publishing
Post Office Box 1640
Burlington, ON, Canada
L7R 5A1

Quest Publishing is a division of
Marilyn Belleghem Consulting Inc.

Published 2005

2005 Marilyn Barnicke Belleghem M.Ed.

Library and Archives Canada Cataloguing in Publication

Belleghem, Marilyn Barnicke, 1943-
Questing France : deepening the search for my Holy Grail :
personal growth through travel / by Marilyn Barnicke Belleghem.

ISBN 0-9734129-2-5

1. Adultery--Psychological aspects.
2. Marriage--Psychological aspects.
3. Self-actualization (Psychology)
4. Belleghem, Marilyn Barnicke, 1943- --Travel--France.
5. France--Description and travel. I. Title.

BF637.S4B4386 2005   158.1   C2005-904321-0

Compositor: Carol Magee

Created in Canada

In appreciation to my children, Julia, Katherine and Matthew, who have shared both my joys and sorrows. They have struggled through some very difficult situations with me. Their support and acceptance of my work, is a testimony to their strength of character.

To my sister Joan, who has supported me in the most trying times as well as the most victorious, I give my heartfelt thanks.

My deepest respect and appreciation is for Brian Coleman who believed in my work and never faltered in his encouragement.

With special thanks to Lucia Kulpa Baraniecky, my paternal grandmother, who was a source of strength and inspiration as a role model for courage and fortitude, long after she left this world.

I want to also thank Jack Belleghem, my first real romantic love, the father of my children, and the one person who shared my growth from innocent adolescent school girl to self responsible adult woman. Without Jack and my relationship with him, I would not be the woman I am today.

Disclaimer

I have used the real names of some people in this account. I have also changed the names and personal characteristics or left off last names of some, to give them privacy. It is not my intention to tell the version of events that others might have, but to portray people as I experienced them at the time. Most of the conversations are made-up and based on the original records to make the point I want to convey and to develop the characters as I saw them.

About the Author

Marilyn Barnicke Belleghem M.Ed., is a Registered Marriage and Family Therapist and has a master's degree in adult education and applied psychology. She is a clinical member of the Ontario division of the American Association for Marriage and Family Therapy. She has a private practice in Burlington, Ontario, Canada. Her solution focused approach has made her a sought after counsellor, consultant, speaker, and guest in both national and international media.

GLANUM

Saint-Rémy-de-Provence

TABLE OF CONTENTS

PREFACE

Some of our journeys are taken by choice. Some are taken by chance. Others are ones where the choices other people make change our course.

I am about to tell you a story that covers several years of my life and travel to a variety of locations. Travelling is a way to experience new and interesting places. Travelling can also present opportunities for personal growth. We can move through physical space and we can move intellectually, emotionally and spiritually. How we are on the outside is a mirror of our inner Self. While looking outward, we can also learn to look inward and discover our Self.

My purpose in telling you my story is to share what I have learned. Learning is part of our life journey. I have used notes, journal entries, correspondence and photographs to create this story.

I have included life skills that I have learned through my experiences and my professional training. I want to help others recognize the characteristics in their relationships—both those they have with others, and their relationship with themselves. We can learn from our history and make changes to our ways of relating, so our future is one of choice not chance.

Emotional intensity can distort memories and put greater meaning into them for the person most affected, while others who were present may not even recall the specific incident. I know some facts are lost. Some may appear exaggerated. This is my story.

In order to tell this story, I need to include other people and my version of the relationships I have had with them. This is not about their versions of events. It is about my experiences and my honest interpretations of what happened. It is my truth.

I went to England and Ireland and returned to write Questing Marilyn. I challenged my conditioning—the beliefs instilled in me. I learned to think for and about my Self. I came to know myself at a deeper level. I found my Holy Grail.

In Questing France, I write about the process I have been through as I worked toward creating an honest loving marital relationship. I want to intimately share my life with my husband, conquer the hurdles and challenges of our lives, and create a bond based on honesty and mutual respect. I seek to have an adult/adult relationship as the core of my life, where we each strive for personal fulfillment as loving people. A romantic tour of France, celebrating twenty five years of marriage, was an important time for working toward this goal. Hence I have chosen the title Questing France.

Over the years of this story, I also worked to grow with my children as a responsible parent. I seek a lifelong relationship with them and to teach by my examples. Even though children grow into adults, there are many areas where they turn to their parents for guidance, support and love. Travel provides opportunities to strengthen parent/child relationships.

I also believe we grow in depth through loving. Being able to not only find, but also to hold onto my Self, while in committed intimate relationships with others, demands that I deepen the search. The Holy Grail that is my Self is richer and more varied when I share it with love.

Everyone experiences similar events in different ways, depending on who they are and what they have done. There are common threads to all of our human experiences. If these threads have not woven their way through your life, I'm sure you will find some experiences that have woven through the life of someone you know.

In my work as a therapist, I have taken many journeys with my clients. Rather than tell stories of other peoples lives, I have chosen to tell my own life as it is the one I know best.

Enjoy!

Marilyn

CHAPTER ONE

IT'S GOOD TO BE HOME

A Return to Familiar Territory and Seeing with New Sight

May 1986

Returning home from my reflections over a coffee by the lake, I am on time for my twelve year old son Matt to cycle home from school for lunch. I scavenge through the fridge to make us something to eat. As we chat he tells me about his news and his contributions to The Book. I hadn't seen The Book before in all the excitement of returning home.

It is a large ledger intended for some legal purpose—perhaps when file notes were all taken in longhand. It has a hard cover, green leather binding and about an inch thick of lined numbered legal size pages. Matt hauls it from the kitchen desk and tells me his dad had brought it home the day I left and told our children they had to make an entry for every day I was away. It was kept in the kitchen and Jack supervised their entries. This was to be the record of what they had done while I had traveled on my Quest to England and Ireland.

I focus on Matt and leave The Book to read after he returns to school. Once he has gone, I undertake the daunting tasks of regaining order in the house. I move swiftly, loading the dishwasher, unpacking my dirty clothes and starting the clothes washer, assessing what part of each child's responsibility for their own belongings to challenge them on first, then find something in the freezer to prepare for dinner. I plan a barbecue meal. Many of our meals on the trip were vegetarian. I missed barbecued meat. I take a break with a glass of lemonade and sit down with The

Book to see what has happened while I've been away for three weeks. Our dog Pickles stays close to me. He jumps on my lap and paws at me to be petted.

There are lots of anecdotes from my daughters about a school project or test, something they have done with their friends and what Dad made them for dinner. My letters home are tucked in the back. It starts out as a fun read.

As I progress, I see that one of my friends, Beth, has been to visit on a Saturday afternoon with her daughter. She has two children from her first marriage, a daughter sixteen, the same age as my second daughter Kathy, and a son who is two years older than Matt. Her son and present husband are not mentioned. They must not have been with her. Our children have known each other all their lives. We have skied together in winter and hiked throughout the year on the Bruce Trail. Pot luck dinners, shopping excursions and meals out have been shared. Everyone gets on well, although my eldest daughter Julia feels left out at times. She is eighteen months older than the other girls.

Kathy wrote about the visit and how the three girls went wandering about Oakville in my car. They were apparently delivering packages. *What were Jack and Beth doing while the kids were away? Where were the boys?* A slow burn starts behind my chest bone and my jaw clenches.

I also see Kathy went to stay at Beth's for the long weekend. Jack and Matt had been there for dinner when they went to pick up Kathy. Julia notes in large block letters that she didn't go and insisted her father drive her home to Oakville on their way from the cottage. Oakville is considerably out of the way on that route.

She was obviously upset. The subject is not made reference to again. I'll have to ask her about that.

Had I heard mention of this when I was away? Perhaps some tension in the tone of a phone conversation had alerted my sub-conscious. *Did one of them tell me and I blocked it?* Funny how things we do not want to accept actually register in some region of our brains to resurface later. *Had I been called home early?*

When Beth had asked me how she could help my family while I was away, I asked her to stay away and let my children have some time with their father. From past experience, I knew she was likely to show up with dinner prepared and a bottle of wine. She would come in like Jack needed rescuing. He did not.

I hoped that he would understand the challenges of getting all our children off to school while getting himself ready for work, supervising their coming and going, preparing meals, shopping for groceries, and packing them all up for weekends at the cottage. I wanted him to miss my efficiency and companionship. It is im-portant that teens have supervision and structure, so their school work is kept current and they do not get into mischief. The girls also had the use of my car. I hoped it was being supervised. Rules are necessary for smooth family functioning. Children need guidelines. *Where was Jack?*

I'd wanted my husband to miss me and welcome me home with open arms. I hoped he would have a new appreciation of how much effort it took to keep the house running smoothly. I'd hoped he would appreciate me and all the effort I put forth for our family. Instead he had avoided my arms when he met me. He physically distanced himself every time I tried to get near me. He didn't even want to snuggle in bed.

My heart is pounding, my palms are sweaty and my mind races. I do not like the implication of the words I am reading. *Is this something else I heard over the long distance wires with my mind's ear that didn't consciously register?*

Reading between the lines, as I scan the remaining pages, I see my daughters had ordered in pizzas with friends over. Matt was away overnight at one of his chums. A comment insinuates the girls were left alone until very late one night. They were not sure when their father got home. I must be aware of my feelings but not let them control me. I must not just react. I must keep my thinking brain in gear before I act.

This woman has been a problem between my husband and me in the past. She is very flirtatious. She finds ways to be with him when she knows I am committed elsewhere. There has been embarrassing gossip about them over the years, but I have been assured they are just friends. My mind in a whirl, I return to responsibilities.

By late afternoon, when my children come home from school, I am feeling familiar again with the routines of my household and beginning to feel some semblance of control. I have used my anger to fuel my actions. I tackled chores with a vengeance. If I cannot control some things—like my husband's behaviour and my emotions—I must control the physical things or I fear I will go mad. Any outward sign that I have been absent has been packed away. My newfound inner confidence in my own abilities is raging. Thankfully, I have the weekend to get over the time differences and get a grip on myself before I have to return to work. I do not feel like the happy relaxed woman I wanted to be on my return from an overseas vacation.

I decide to keep quiet about the contents of The Book for now. I will avoid a conflict. I want to enjoy being with my family again. My children are full of stories and questions. I am so glad to be home. We eat outside in the warm spring evening. I watch Jack and he seems nervous and distracted. I wasn't expected home until tonight. My early return caught him unaware. I wonder what plans he had for last night. As I wander the garden, I try to act as natural as possible. Anxiety grips my heart. Exhaustion weighs heavily on my body. I am not yet back on Eastern Time.

Unhappy family interaction is hard on the mental health of all family members, but especially children. They are powerless to change their environment. If, when the parents are in conflict, the child is made the confidant of either or both parent, they are burdened emotionally beyond their ability to cope. They are in loyalty conflict. Children who witness behaviour that they feel they must keep secret from the other parent stress their psyche. They want to believe, love and trust both parents.

Problems with eating, sleep, bed wetting, compulsive behaviours, withdrawal, aggressive behaviour and lack of ability to form relationships can result. The concern for adult problems can also affect concentration and academic performance.

Some children learn roles to cope with family conflict:

Gatekeeper – controls communication, passes messages between their parents.

Joker – acts foolish and distracts from the tension.

Record Keeper – keeps score and holds memories.

Mind Reader – interprets what others meant to say, explains motives and feelings and tones down the emotional intensity through telling that things will improve or aren't that bad.

Scapegoat – attracts attention away from parental conflict by inappropriate behaviour so the tension between the parents is deflected.

PICKLES

CHAPTER TWO

ACCEPTING RESPONSIBILITY FOR A PROMISE

Leftover Questions About Intent

I wait for an opportune moment. The children are busy elsewhere. I am prepared. I feel strong and sure of my direction, knowing my facts are firmly in place. I must also be concise and get straight to the issue I want to address. Being apologetic and hesitant will give him openings to distract me. I want to sound confident without being too forceful.

As Jack sits reading in the family room, I slide the tape he made for me to take on my Quest into the tape player. In as even a tone as I can muster, I say;

"I want you to listen to this and tell me why you made it."

I keep my eyes firmly fixed on his face to see his reaction. I want to bring the message he has implied out into the light of day so we can face it and openly accept there is a problem.

As the sound of Pickles barking, birds singing and communication between my children and I, plays through the speakers, I see a look of what I infer as embarrassment. I know him well. He looks like he's been caught with his hand in the cookie jar or worse. Pickles comes running into the room looking confused.

"Do you remember me asking you if I could borrow one of your classical music tapes for me to take to England? I wanted something to play when travelling, while wandering in cathedrals or trying to get to sleep."

I see him warily nod his head in assent.

"Do you remember volunteering to make me one as it could be longer than the pre-recorded ones?"

I hear his voice, suddenly hard.

"Yes."

"Do you remember taping this?"

"Yes."

His answer comes just as his voice sounds through the speaker asking one of our children a question.

"I wonder why you recorded something that would so obviously evoke feelings of homesickness."

As I look at his face, his look challenges me. I must not start to chatter on. I tend to do that when I am nervous.

"So, are you saying I made you homesick? You cannot blame that on me."

I am unhappy with his tone and feel my anxiety increase. I doubt that I am going to get an honest answer from him. He is acting as if he had done exactly what I wanted. He is likely to say that I am the one who had not adequately explained the specifics of what I expected. He has this way of turning things around so he looks as if he is totally justified in what he has done, and I am somehow dumb, sick, stupid or crazy.

I know this is a situation where I cannot win my point as he will not accept responsibility for making a promise and not keeping it. I know if I pursue the matter further, he will turn it into a fight. I want him to accept that he knew he didn't give me what I asked for. I want to know why he did this. I try to summarize the situation. I want to make sure we are talking about the same memory.

"I recall driving home from a Toronto Symphony concert and remarking on how some of the pieces played would be very enjoyable to listen to on my Walkman while travelling in England. I asked you if you would lend me one or two of your tapes of classical music that might be enjoyable to me. You suggested you would record one for me that is longer than the pre-recorded ones and you would choose pieces you know I like. Do you remember that?"

"Yes, that's what I made you, or started to, but ran out of time."

I look straight into his deep blue eyes and then ever so slowly shift my gaze to his eye brows so the intensity of his return stare does not affect me so deeply. I continue to look at him. I try to do so without blinking. I want him to know that I am fully aware that he knew what I wanted, and purposely gave me something else.

The tape was deliberately made in a way that was too different than what we had spoken about. This is typical of how he uses a switch and bait tactic. Switch the content of what I say to bait me into complaining or correcting, and then refuse to admit to his part in it. He tells me I said something I never even thought, let alone would say. When I tell him that is not what I just said—it isn't what I intended or meant—he comes up with something new, slightly different but further from my original point. The original point or request is left in the dust of confusion. This might work for him in winning his cases as a lawyer in a court of law, but it is deadly to a relationship. This isn't about winning; it is about accountability and being trusted to keep a promise. It would be easy for me to blame myself and say I should have listened to it before I left to make sure it was what I wanted or I should have made it myself. But he offered and he committed to doing this for me.

I lower my gaze, remove the tape from the player and shut off the machine.

"Does this tape sound like what you now admit I asked of you, and you agreed to do?"

"I thought you'd like to....."

Being able to ask for what I want is a skill I have learned. Just like many people, I was trained not to ask for things specifically, because that would be rude or selfish. We are to take what is offered and be grateful. Assertive, adult communication, involves accepting responsibility to get one's wants met. Therefore, being able to ask is an important part of an adult to adult relationship.

Listening is also a skill. Some people make up what they think others want, instead of finding out what they actually want.

Gift giving is an example of this. In situations where a gift is expected as part of the relationship norm, giving the other what they ask for can be seen by some as giving away personal control. Giving someone something close to what they have asked for, or something completely different, may feel like the giver has maintained personal control. Their philosophy is I will give what I want to give not what you tell me to give. They fear being controlled.

The givers always have the right to refuse the request. They might choose to say something like: "I'd rather we shopped for that together." Or "That is too expensive for me right now." This gives a clear message and does not set up expectations that will not be met.

In some relationships the giver is supposed to guess or know what the other wants. Little clues may be left about and hints may be given, but a direct request is not made. Sometimes people see the attention to the hints as a sign the other is really interested. Many people hate gift giving because they feel powerless to please the other and are not aware of the hints. They fear being wrong and facing criticism.

Some people think that if someone loves them they will know what is best for them. This is a childlike method of avoiding asking for what they want. It is shifting the responsibility for their wants onto someone else. They may never have learned to ask for their wants or never trusted anyone would give them what they ask for. Asking for what we want and trusting that someone is listening is part of a functional relationship.

Some people fear letting others know what they want, as it allows them to get too close. It can also lead to disappointment if the other person is uncaring or manipulative. They would rather not ask for what they want than risk having their expectations go unmet.

Many traditional gift giving occasions end up being disappointing because a clear understanding of the reasons and expectations for the gift giving have not been negotiated. This same principle applies to sexual interaction. Being able to ask for what we enjoy and trusting the partner will at least consider the request is part of an adult relationship.

Of course there is always the joy of receiving an unexpected gift that fits with our likes and pleasures. For me this is flowers. I love receiving unexpected plants and bouquets. I'd hate to have a standing order for something from a florist though. It is too pre-dictable.

I want a relationship where we can speak about our wants and expectations. I want to be heard. I want the promises others make to me to be kept. If they do not want to give me what I ask for, they should say so. Then I can deal with the issue myself. I do not want my words twisted and ignored, and then when I complain, be told I am the one who was unclear. I want good communication. I want to be able to show appreciation and show disappointment. I want to be understood and to understand the people in my life.

"Does this tape sound like what you now admit I asked of you?"

When there is no response, I repeat my question with slow delib-erate wording. I make eye contact with him again and say;

"Never mind. This isn't going anywhere." *What did I hope to prove?*

I wanted to prove he knew what I wanted. I wanted to see his face, read his reaction and judge his intent for myself. I wanted him to listen to me with a desire to understand rather than avoid my feelings. I know he is playing mind games with me. My heart sinks and to hide my tears of frustration and rejection, I leave the room. There must be a load of laundry to fold or a child that needs my help. *Keep busy! Don't think. No. Yes. I must think!*

I am pleased that I kept my cool. I maintained control over myself. I worked so hard while I was away just focusing on not letting what others do or say turn me into a reactor rather than master of myself.

I do not feel my husband cares about my feelings. I do not feel he cares about me. *Why is he so distant and hard?* The answer that comes into my thoughts frightens me. I focus elsewhere to try to avoid the disturbing possibilities.

The next two weeks pass in a blur of activity. The office mail and messages, professional meetings, a speaking engagement and clients fill my time. I have my hair cut. My hairdresser asks me about my trip. As I start to tell him of some of my adventures, he says that when Beth was in she said I was having a horrid time. I did send her a letter and comment on some of my frustrations but I certainly didn't expect my confidences to be spread about the town. I wasn't having a horrid time. I was being challenged and forced to adapt and change. I was finding things were not as I expected them to be. I had many great times on the trip. I feel violated and exposed.

Time for a new hairdresser.

I chat on the phone with Elizabeth about our trip. She had originally called me about the trip and I enjoyed our time together. She shares some of her experiences on the final days of the time in Ireland. She had a strong sensation of spiritual awakening that has made the trip a very positive experience for her. She described a moment of unexpected, yet penetrating insight when she fully realized our universal connection that lies beyond the boundaries of our body. I have had such experiences, although fleeting, and know exactly what she means. It is very powerful.

Unfortunately, one of the women hit her head on the roof of Newgrange, and knocked herself out. She recovered but suffered from a headache. Another caught my cold and was ill. She recounts that they had a lovely full moon for the final celebration and ritual.

I explain that my coming home early had not been expected by my husband, but was greeted with delight by my children. As we chat, I apologize for my part in not letting people get closer to me and for keeping my distance with my Walkman; the days I spent separate from the group and my final leaving. She tells me she had no problem with me and that obviously separation and connection were more my issue than hers. I wanted more free time and fewer long van rides. I thank her for letting me know about the trip and assure her that I am happy I had the experiences I did. I suggest that perhaps less time spent in the isolated nunnery and more time elsewhere—where we had more freedom to visit places of interest—could have worked better for me. I state that I will take the lessons I learned about how I like to travel into account in planning my future trips.

As we share memories, I know I am ashamed that my marriage is so unsettled. I want so much to have a happy family and a husband who wants to be with me. I hold my reserve. I say goodbye before my desire to pour my aching heart out to her takes control. She is such a supportive woman, but this is my problem not hers.

A mid-week political barbecue dinner on a lovely spring evening puts us together with friends and colleagues from all over Halton County. We have both been involved in political work, volunteering in a variety of ways and have attended many of these types of functions. I greet and hug a woman who I consider a friend. We have both known her for years and Jack has had a long time political connection with her. I know my husband respects her and we both enjoy her company.

I exclaim: "You are one of Jack's favourite women."

She replies; "I am not Jack's favourite woman." She winks at Jack and laughs to the surrounding group. For a moment I expect her to say; "Of course, you are, Marilyn." but she doesn't. I am shocked. At the first opportunity, I quietly ask her what she meant by her comment. She suggests we have lunch some day soon and a good chat. Fear grabs my heart. I tell her I will call. I wonder if I really want to hear what she would say. I ask Jack about it later. He says he has no idea what I am talking about. He claims he didn't hear the comment or catch the wink and smile.

Jack too is working long hours to catch up for the extra time he took away from the office when I was away. He has an inquest that takes him out in the evening. I feel disconnected from him. Jack and I need time together. We need to get back on track. I never expected my trip to put such a wedge between us. He was so encouraging for me to go.

I speak with another woman I met on my Quest. We had shared tea in Dublin and she was heading off to India to the Ashram of Sai Baba, before returning to Toronto. Her experience had been phenomenal, with deep awakening and spiritual connection. She shares with me some of the messages of love and the acceptance of all religions that are Sai Baba's teachings. She explains that peace starts with righteousness in the heart of each person. Honesty and sincerity lead to beauty in character. Harmony in the home results and it spreads to the community and in due course, to the nations of the world. Her enthusiasm is contagious. I ask if she has spoken with Elizabeth since her return as her words are very similar to the experience Elizabeth shared with me. I too have had a deep spiritual desire to have peace within my own home. I was able to come to a place of peace with myself in Ireland. Now my challenge is to hold on to that peace and share it.

I feel so much better after speaking to her. I recall the tune of a piece of music I learned at church and quietly sing: "Let there be peace on earth, and let it begin with me…"

I know there are experiences on my life path that I must accept and face. There is no turning back. There is no exit door. I must trust the connection I have made to my spirit, to my Holy Grail, to guide me and sustain me. I must trust my inner voices. I must find a way to be true to my beliefs and follow a path that will lead me to the life I know I am capable of having. I must find a way to bring greater peace into my home.

My marital relationship swings between times of intense intimacy with good conversation, satisfying sexual encounters and warm hugs and what feels like complete detachment. I have shared many of the experiences of my trip and felt Jack really listened to me. He laughed at the story about finding the dancing maiden circle. He suggested I tell his mom about the sense I had of the spirit of his dad being close, when sitting on the stile on the coastal path, near Lamorna Cove. Other times, I need to keep on neutral topics, not talk about my reality, and not question or chal lenge him. He has become more moody and testy. I am being more watchful and aware of how we are relating than I ever recall being before. Whatever is going on, I must not deny there is something very wrong.

Dysfunctional family interaction is linked to control and power issues. Communication is guarded, insecurity is high, trust is low, and direct confrontation is avoided. In this state, growth is blocked, productivity is frustrated, and joy and spontaneity are absent. Words are chosen for effect. Honest feelings are hidden. Emotional cut-off, distraction, communicating problems to and through a third party and stonewalling, are strategies people use when they are unable to resolve conflict. It does not solve problems. It postpones them. It can intensify emotional reactions, undermine personal confidence, lower self esteem and block intimacy.

Functional families have the capacity for change and growth. They have conflicts and resolve them, and show tolerance for individual differences with authentic interaction. They engage in open honest communication. Each member has a sense of self worth and a feeling of being a part of the family. A sense of security strengthens relationships.

One person cannot make a marriage or a family. It takes a common desire and cooperation. There must be a sense of shared purpose. Growth and change take struggle. The struggle can be confronted and resolved, or run from and avoided.

If we run from our troubles, we will continue to confront the same processes in different guises. Learning to resolve a conflict in one area of our lives helps us resolve conflicts in other parts of life. We can learn the life skills that make us happy.

CHAPTER THREE

COME FOR A SWIM AND A BARBECUE

I Must Accept What I Do Not Want to Know

June 1986

Jack tells me he has accepted an invitation to a barbecue at Beth's for Sunday. Usually we consult with each other before accepting a weekend engagement. He has also offered that we supply the steaks. When I questioned his decision in making the arrangements with her rather than first discussing it with me, he dismisses my question. When I ask my question again, he accuses me of being too controlling and trying to start a fight.

Saturday June seventh we attend a wedding of one of Jack's nephews. I reach for his hand during the ceremony. Sitting in the familiar church, surrounded by family, I feel safe and happy. We were so young when we married and we had so much life ahead that we couldn't possibly have foreseen the trials and tribulations that we would face. Trust, love, commitment and determination are needed to keep a marriage alive and functioning. I whisper to Jack that I very much want to be married to him and even though we are tied by vows we made long ago, I would want to make the same commitment again. He smiles at me and tells me not to talk in church in a mocking parental way. His teasing doesn't imply that he shares the same feelings and I sense he isn't so sure. I am disappointed. Something is amiss. This is going on too long. This isn't just a mood or him being tired. I must get him to talk to me and share his thinking.

After the ceremony we mingle with the extended family. I delight in greeting Jack's uncle Grafton who drove my school bus when I went to high school. During the evening, I dance with his brother and swap news and memories with his mother and sisters. They are eager to hear about my trip and I excitedly tell them about going to Castle Bellingham. We laugh and tease like only people who have shared life's experiences can. My children are all dressed up and enjoy time with their cousins. They dance and laugh together, sharing stories of many childhood antics. Being a part of a family who, although not in regular contact, genuinely care about achievements, sympathize with problems and accept and share is an important part of keeping life in perspective.

I dance with my husband. We dance well together and easily fall into the familiar steps. Being held in his arms in such a familiar way feels wonderful. He dances with our daughters and I dance with my son. We all do the group dances. Tired and joyful, we head for home. *I wish there were more family weddings. I had such a good time.*

Sunday the eighth of June is a beautiful warm day and our children are looking forward to a swim. Jack had insisted he go to Mari's Delicatessen to buy the meat. I had offered to pick up some steaks when I did the grocery shopping but he insisted I leave it to him. I am surprised when I see the price on the package when he puts it in the cooler with the expensive chilled wine.

"What's so special about this barbecue that you are spending so much?"

I get the "are you trying to start a fight look" and keep further questions to myself. I see he is in high spirits and anxious to be going.

Beth's husband meets us in their drive. Almost immediately, Beth, already in her swim suit, follows her children out the door. Hugs and greetings are shared and the kids rush off to change. There is an emotional charge of excitement in the air. Jack carries the cooler to the kitchen, leaving me to bring in the bag with our swim suits and towels. Beth hurries ahead to hold the door then goes on in.

I like Ted. He is warm and genuine. We have often been at social gatherings together, even back as far as when Beth was married to Jack's law partner and he was with his first wife. My how times change. He holds the door for me with a gentlemanly flourish and broad smile.

The screen door gently closes between us and I hear him say,

"I'll keep an eye on the kids while you change."

He heads across the expanse of lawn to the pool enclosure. I stand inside the door and watch him go. *What a nice man!* He picks up the end of a hose and starts to roll it away. He must have been watering the flowers.

As I move into the kitchen Jack and Beth are laughing over some thing I missed and are unaware of my presence. Their sense of intimacy charges the air. Just as I am about to speak the kids rush down the stairs, giggling and chasing and the mood is broken.

I feel terrible. I ask Beth where she wants us to change. Following her suggestion I take our bag up to the master bedroom. My sense of responsibility pressures me to get out and supervise my children. My intuition tells me no one is thinking of me. At this moment I am not Beth's friend. It should have been her and I in the kitchen with the men in the garden. No one is in the kitchen when I pass.

Beth has carried drinks and snacks out to the pool area. They are being devoured by dripping wet kids. I head directly for the steps and gently slide into the water. I do several lengths before the gang returns to jumping and splashing. There is lots of laughing. I am not in a playful mood. I pull myself up onto the pool edge with only my feet in the water, and watch.

Jack comes from the house and moves directly to the diving board. He dives in neatly. Beth follows him off the board with a near perfect dive. She comes up very close to him and they exchange warm giggly smiles. Even though I am very close it is as if I am invisible. I glance across the pool at Ted in his smart casual clothes. He looks dejected. *Does he see what I see? Is he annoyed at the kids?*

Jack and Beth are like shameless lovers unaware of others and the impression they are giving. *Am I the only one who sees this?* The other children seem absorbed in their play. Julia sits on the far edge. At eighteen she appears to be picking up on this flirtation. I catch her eye and she gives me a forced toothy smile. I slide into the pool and swim over to her. I make idle comments about the lovely garden. I know she is not fooled. *Why do my children have to see this?*

> Eyes are one of the most important flirting tools. While we take in information with our eyes they are also very powerful transmitters of social signals. How one looks at another person, meets their gaze and holds it, before looking away, determines the intimacy level between them. Prolonged eye contact indicates intense emotion and is either an act of love or an act of hostility. This is not hostility. I consider a glare of hostility toward them but know I will be ignored. They do not see me. They obviously do not care who is watching them.

I move to a chaise and Ted offers to pour me a glass of cold white wine from a bottle in an ice bucket. There is pop on ice and I call to offer one to Julia. She declines and slips back into the pool. I try to chat with Ted but feel the words that need to be spoken are out of bounds. Time drags. The fun in the pool goes on and on. I feel trapped, watching something I do not want to see.

> Romantic love, the feeling of being "in love", stirs the spirit of the lovers. It is as if they expand into a greater space that no one else can enter. Some believe falling in love is a spiritual experience that fuels the soul's journey. Others believe it is a temporary insanity that shuts down all reason.
>
> The "in love" feeling introduces the idea that this is the one and only person with whom I can be truly my Self and so I feel as if we are mating at a soul level. It stirs the primal drive of lust and possession. Passions run high and the emotional intensity is exhilarating. It sparks the thought: "This one is my one true love."
>
> This form of romantic love, once experienced, unites the lower instincts with the energy of the heart and stirs the mind, creating the idea that it is predetermined. The sense is of being meant for each other, being powerless over the feelings and that all others must be forsaken.
>
> Some people never feel this awakening, this feeling of euphoria, while others fall in love on a frequent basis. Music, poetry and literature are filled with romantic notions and idealize the joy of falling in love. People "in love" seem to recognize a deep connection in one another—a bond that joins them with the echo of timelessness that they feel will never end. It is a magical state, filled with promise and illusions. This state of being in love can be overwhelming. Sexual tension is also a major part of the attraction.

Finally, Beth gets out of the pool, making a show of drying herself off and accepting a glass of wine Jack has just poured. She does not move away from him. The physical distance between them is closer than a usual social zone. There is a personal area we all have around us and it is reserved for lovers, family and very close friends. They are standing too close. Her head tilts to the side and a flirtatious smile accompanies her words of thanks.

I feel my body tight and closed. My arms are tightly folded over my chest and my legs are tightly crossed. I purposefully fight my irritability and change my position. I try to adopt an expression of polite interest. *Relax Marilyn!*

As I watch Beth focusing her attention on Jack and ignoring me, I wonder how this can possibly be the same woman who called me, just last February, distraught, on her way to the airport. Her father had called her to tell her that her mother had just had a stroke in Florida. She asked me to support her. Once she arrived and found her mother had died while she was en route she requested that I go to Georgetown, get her children out of school, tell them that their grandmother had died, take them home and help them pack suitcases, then take them to her brother's house to make the trip to their home town. She asked me to pack her clothes and send them along as well. Her husband was on a golfing trip and would go straight to the hometown. She would be flying there with her father and her mother's body. I had cancelled my afternoon clients, something I very rarely did, to meet her request. *Where is the woman who is my friend now?*

Letting my mind wander the pain of the past, I also remember Jack asking me to tell him the story I used with our children when my father died. We had spent a lot of time with Dad as he suffered with pancreatic cancer. Our children loved and missed him. I had used the life cycle of the Monarch Butterfly as a way to explain his death. I compared our present life to that of a caterpillar that can only crawl along the ground. It then spins a cocoon and spends time as if it is dead, transforming into a beautiful butterfly. Humans turn into angels like the caterpillar turns into a butterfly. Jack had written a poem and had it faxed to a lawyer's office in Beth's home town to be printed, delivered to her brother and read as a tribute to her mother at the funeral. He had approached me as I was reading in bed with his version and we had made some final edits together. I was shocked when I heard that he had sent the poem just from him, without even including my name. He had even discouraged me from sending flowers from our whole family. It should have been an expression of sympathy to her, her children and her whole family. I also heard that Jack's poem was published in their local paper as a tribute.

Tears sting at the corner of my eyes, as I recall Jack blaming me for not doing something for Beth at that time. He manipulated the situation so I looked like a thoughtless bitch. Rage starts to grumble in my gut. I know I must move. I decide the best place to make what seems like a normal change is to re-enter the pool. As I slowly swim lengths, I dip my face in the water to hide my tears. The kids are jumping and laughing. They splash water on me and I welcome the distraction.

"Are we getting you wet Mom?" Matt asks with some concern. I laugh and splash him hoping my sorrow isn't noticed. Turning onto my back I kick my feet hard moving so I give each of the kids a good soaking. They squeal in delight and decide the new game is in good fun. Playing with the kids changes my focus. I am surprised to hear myself laugh.

Beth's voice cuts through the fun as she scolds the group in general for splashing water out of the pool. Since they are in the country, the water must come from their well or be trucked in. Catching one of the kids off guard, I kick furiously splashing a good dose of water into the air and over the edge. In defiance, almost as a dare to Beth to take me on, I cup my hand and splash water in Beth's direction.

"That's enough. You were told to stop. Don't give a bad example to the kids." His voice is stern. I am so tempted to kick and splash water in his face, but instead I give my husband a hardened grin, mocking his authority.

Cutting the tension that I feel is obviously brewing between us, he dives from the board. I want to be childish and tell him he splashed

23

water out of the pool. I see Beth head for the diving board and decide to leave the water. Time for another glass of wine.

I apologize to Ted for splashing the water. He is the one who does the pool maintenance. In a distracted off hand reply he tells me not to be concerned.

Time drags with excruciating slowness. The boys decide they've had enough and head for the house. Beth heads off with the excuse to check on dinner. Jack says he'd better get the barbecue started and follows her. *Why is he barbecuing instead of Ted?* I want to go too but there are two children still swimming. I give them the five minute warning and impatiently wait. I wonder at saying something to Ted about our spouses' behaviour, but he is chatting with Julia. Perhaps I could say something to Jack, but I am fearful of being told I have created something out of nothing with my jealous imagination. I have heard him say on other occasions that my out of control jealousy is ruining our marriage. My feelings are obviously not ruining their fun.

Sending the girls in to change, with their towels and whatever else they can carry, I stay to assist Ted in packing up the remaining trays and glasses. The silence between us is tense. I avoid eye contact. I am afraid I will cry if I dare admit my feelings and suspicions. I do not want to upset our children. I will then be accused of ruining a perfectly fine day. Damn, why am I always on the defensive?

As if he is afraid of being alone with me, Ted sends me into the house saying he can finish up what needs doing by the pool. As I step noiselessly through the back door, I hear soft laughter from the kitchen. It is so very intimate. Suddenly I feel as if boiling water flows from the ceiling scalding me. As my body flushes, my knees go weak. I quickly move into the washroom and after closing the door, slide to the floor. This is too obvious, too blatant, too much. Tears scald my hot cheeks and drop on my now shivering body. I know what is happening here. The last traces of my denial crack with an audible snap.

I know the sensation of being admired, seduced and flirted with by someone I find attractive. The mutual desire is very powerful. The energy flies around a couple as if in this state of intoxication and is obvious to anyone near who has experienced the feelings. Slowly it awakens in me that something I was repeatedly told was just a friendship is really obviously so much more. I wanted to believe them when they claimed it was harmless. I wanted to save my marriage. I do not want to see this now. The pain in my chest is as if my heart is ripping in two. I feel as if I cannot breathe. *Breathe Marilyn!*

I shudder with the silent sobs. I struggle to keep quiet. Gradually I get my breathing under control. I count each one, in and out. I feel the air go in my nose and out my mouth. I hold the air inside. Deeper and longer, one two three four, breathe in and out. I get control of what I can – my breathing.

I struggle to my feet, looking at my red face in the mirror. I splash myself with cold water to try and calm the swelling. Looking deeply at my own eyes in the reflection, I admonish myself. *Get a grip!*

I quietly leave the washroom. I can see Ted through the screen door far out the laneway. His back is toward me. I open the door and pull it closed with a loud click as if I have just come in. Jack immediately exclaims in a loud voice:

"I'd better check the barbecue."

I lower my head and pass him in the hall on my way to change. Beth starts to hum in the kitchen. *Damn.*

The evening crawls along. Ted has been cool and we have avoided each other all evening. He is tense. I wonder if he senses my agitation. Beth and Jack are oblivious to us and share long lingering looks and meaningless conversation that is too perky. Their posture shows a desire to be close with gestures that complement the movements of the other. I notice how naturally their body movements and gestures are synchronised as each lifts their wine glass at the same moment. It is behaviour evident between people who like each other and get on well together.

I feel as if I am assessing a client's level of connection, as I look for these types of behaviours with couples who come for counselling. It is most often evident in premarital couples and couples nearing the end of their counselling when they have resolved their issues and are hopeful about their future.

I attempt to get some adult focused conversation going to ease my awkwardness, once all the children leave the table. I direct my question to Ted.

"Have you ever been to England and Ireland?"

"Don't start talking about your crazy trip now Marilyn." Jack retorts.

"Why was the trip crazy?" Ted questions.

"Marilyn went off with a group of women on some sort of pilgrimage and had a miserable time. They did weird rituals out in fields full of stones and went to churches and burial sites for meditations." Beth quips in a demeaning way, as she stands gathering dishes. Jack follows her into the kitchen. I sit stunned, tears clinging to the corner of my eyes.

"When was this?" Ted questions softly. I try to explain some of the highlights of my Quest and the personal growth component. I dab at my eyes and apologize. I can see he is distracted by the giggles and soft conversation coming from the kitchen. He asks some polite questions and says he doesn't think it is crazy. He has had some significant events in his life that have involved major changes in thinking and he seems to genuinely understand the change in consciousness I went through on my Quest.

"Sometimes we have to get a different view of ourselves when life throws us curves." He replies solemnly.

I am more than eager to leave. It is a school night for the children. Jack seems to dawdle and stall. The kids are chattering about getting together again and trying to say goodbye. I watch the manoeuvring so the romantic couple can share a hug behind the car. Ted said his goodbyes inside. He is not privy to this scene unless he is looking out a window. *Do they really think I cannot see them? Do they really think it looks like just two friends saying goodnight?*

Once home, I send our children off to their rooms to get ready for bed and ask Jack if we can talk. He says no. He is suddenly very tired and heads up the stairs to bed. The last thing I can think to do is sleep. What a difference from last night. I find my journal and pour out my raging thoughts.

Keeping a journal can assist us in tracking our progress and seeing repeated patterns that we do not change. When the same issue comes up, year after year, and we complain but do not take the steps to change, we are stuck. Without the repeated words staring at us from the page we can miss how long we have avoided a situation.

Confronting what we deny can lead us to our fears. Fears can be faced and dealt with so life progresses differently or our fears can keep us in the same old rut. I have been avoiding my fears. I must now come face to face with what I know to be true.

Friends are people who choose to be in a relationship with each other. They do not keep their relationship and meetings a secret from spouses. There is no sexual implication or behaviour. A friend is someone with whom we can be ourselves without trying to get their attention, seduce them or worry about impressing them. We can tell secrets to a friend and know they will not betray our trust. We can talk about things that are embarrassing, things we have done, lovers we have had, fears, hopes, dreams and challenges. There is affection between friends as well as mutual support. Friends do not steal our belongings, ideas or spouses.

Knowing how we feel when we are with a friend we trust, recognizing how the other feels when they are with us, and openly sharing our feelings is at the core of friendship. Being with a friend is energizing, comforting, and enjoyable, and allows us to open our hearts and minds to each other. Friends are good for our mental health.

CHAPTER FOUR

WHAT THE HELL IS GOING ON?

Am I Ready to Face My Fears?

July and August 1986

Over the next few days I overcome my fear of confrontation enough to try to question Jack about my suspicions. I show him the specific entries in the green book that concern me. He deflects my questions and gives what I call a crooked answer. He turns any concerns I express into accusations. He says I am being too suspicious and making up stories. His long years of litigation experience have given him plenty of practice in debating and winning. I feel lost and frightened. I am terrified I will lose more than an argument if I push too hard without more evidence.

Thinking I might calm myself, I review my professional literature and a handout I have to give clients when they suspect an affair.

Some Signs That Show Your Partner Could be Having an Affair

- Is your partner distracted and seems off in space?

- Is there new attention to physical appearance, perhaps new clothes, extra care with grooming, new underwear?

- Have the work habits changed, a closed office door, locked briefcase, extra unexplained time away from home and the office?

- Have day-to-day behaviours changed, perhaps being more secretive and more protective of their planning calendar?

- Is a formerly messy vehicle suddenly spotless?

- Are there clues in the car? Cups with lipstick, condom packages?

- Have there been unexplained mood changes?

- Has the sexual activity changed? Some people want more because they are revved from the excitement, yet more monogamous people stop being sexual with their partner.

- Are secretive phone calls or hang up calls being made?

- Does someone's name pop up too often?

- Are there senseless fights and unreasonable criticisms?

- Are there credit card charges for places you never visit or shop? These could be hotels, restaurants, and gift and flower shops.

As I read the list, I can see there are too many indicators that my husband is having an affair with a woman I have considered my friend.

Since my husband and I share office space, and I oversee the accounting for both of our businesses, it is easy for me to check receipts and phone records. I must be patient until they all come in. Slowly the picture comes together. I am cautious to keep my fears to myself. This is lonelier than I was in Ireland. I am surrounded by friends, family and colleagues yet dare not yet say a word. I cannot turn to my husband for advice as I have done with so many challenges in the past. I must be true to my Self and have enough evidence to be sure.

Because her number is long distance from Oakville, the itemized bills show there were many calls to Beth from Jack's cell and office phones. I wonder if our bookkeeper picked this up. *Does she know?* Receipts for gas for his car and expensive meals while I was away paint a clear picture. I match the calls and invoices with comments in the green book and plot them all on a calendar.

I call Beth to try to chat. I want to see if she will casually mention that she and Jack were together while I was away. This would be in keeping with them being friends and their relationship not being a secret. Her responses to me are stilted and full of avoidance. No mention is made of their meetings.

Jack is distant and distracted, then suddenly attentive and loving. He thoughtfully tries to please me with a nice dinner or flowers, after too many of my casual questions are avoided. I feel manipulated but so want to believe he is sincere. I want to see if he will mention the meetings. He doesn't. I know I am hitting close to the mark as I see trouble in his eyes. I am not accustomed to being so calculating. My usual way would be to blurt out my suspicions and vent my feelings.

"Beth and I are just friends!"

Friends do not exhibit this glazed reaction to each other. They do not have secret meetings, ignore responsibilities and have blatant disregard for others when they are together. They do not flirt with sexual connotations, stare into each other's eyes and glow. Friends include others in their activities and talk about their time together openly.

I have known that Jack and Beth have been attracted to each other since they first met. There is such a thing as love at first sight. Our brains and bodies are created in a way that we have physical and emotional reactions to people before we even hear them speak. However, just because we are attracted, it doesn't mean we have to act on that attraction. Hopefully, we will find many people in our lives that we are attracted to and many people will find us attractive. This is part of being open and alive.

Falling in love involves a change in brain chemistry that helps the lovers focus on the positive aspects of the beloved and ignore their imperfections. The change causes a euphoric high, a feeling that everything is wonderful. When we meet someone to whom we are sexually attracted, our bodies respond by releasing chemicals that can leave us illogical, breathless, with sweaty palms, and an increased heart rate that gives us flushed cheeks. We are turned into lovesick fools.

People who fall in love are often asked "are you blind?" They really are blind, because of the brain's chemical response. The level of the chemistry can't be sustained for a long period of time, so at some point it begins to drop. It eventually becomes ineffective. We can get our brains back in gear and act with intention. We are not powerless over this change.

All I can pray for is that the chemical reaction wears off soon. A heavy dose of responsibility is often a sure way to kill the fantasy. I must be careful not to be seen as the one throwing cold water on their heat. This will spark an attack on me. I have been around this process with the two of them before. I have been through it many times with clients too. Life is so different when she is not pursuing him. *How much does he pursue her?*

On the morning of Friday June twenty-seventh, Jack waves me and our children off to our cottage in Muskoka saying he will be up in time for dinner. I share the cottage with my sister Judy and her family and it is my turn to do Friday dinner. He has asked me to make one of his favourites. I balk at the work involved on a hot summer day. I'd rather be relaxing. I decide not to say no. When I call him on his cell phone as we are waiting to eat, expecting him to arrive at any minute, he says he is still in Oakville and has just eaten take-out chicken. I am shocked. I start to protest. He accuses me of trying to start a fight and denies he asked for a full turkey dinner. I swallow my words of rage, carefully place the receiver on the hook, quietly walk to our bedroom and lie down on our bed.

Judy softly knocks on the bedroom door. I tell her to come in. I had told her I would be responsible for dinner but she couldn't believe I was doing a turkey. We usually only have turkey for celebrations. I try to tell her again and hear justification in my quivering voice.

"Jack specifically requested it and I was trying to please him", I sniffle.

She assures me she believes me. Matt told her he heard his dad even ask for stuffing. Both she and her husband had been shocked at the request. I understood, as I was too. However they were looking forward to a good meal. It was all ready but the gravy.

"Beats hot dogs!" her husband had said.

Jack arrives long after midnight. I am lying in the dark. I hear him come in. I stay silent. I am sure he knows I am not asleep, but he chooses not to ask.

The morning is new, clear and warm. I slide from the bed, grab a tee shirt from the hook on the back of the door and quietly leave the room. The cottage is silent. I love the early morning and want to be alone. I remove my swim suit from the clothes line, change in the bathroom, pick up my sunglasses and hat and head for the lake. My blue canoe slides silently into the water. I paddle through the reflective flatness, leaving tiny ripples behind me with each stroke.

I am also leaving my roles and responsibilities behind. I move quietly into a deeper more authentic part of my Self. I do not want to be with others, pressing in with their demands and expectations. I have been fulfilling my roles and keeping very busy trying to ignore my feelings. Now, I want to be alone.

The sun is dancing off the water and I pull my hat lower over my eyes to shield them from the glare. I use my paddle to turn my direction around the point of rock in Gravenhurst Bay where the red and white channel marker blazes in the direct sunlight. I paddle steadily through the narrow gap and between the islands that lead to the open water of Lake Muskoka. The sun is warm on my body as I pass the lighthouse, stark white against the intense blue sky. I hear the hum of a small motor, and then a lad suddenly appears with a fishing rod stuck out of his aluminium boat. He swishes by and we wave in casual greeting. I am gently rocked by his waves. The glassy calm returns.

Heading straight out to open water, I know that on some porch hidden in the trees, someone can see a woman alone in a blue canoe, paddling steadily. I stop and glide. Perhaps I'll tip the canoe and cool off. A dragon fly alights on my dripping paddle. I watch it with total absorption. Time has no meaning. I move from my knees to sit on the bottom of the canoe, prop a life jacket against the seat behind me and lean back. *I should have brought sun screen.*

I hear a cry above and let my thoughts and spirit soar through the clear hot sky like the swooping gull. For a moment, I let myself believe I am free.

Suddenly, an intense awareness of a heavy weight inside my chest brings me crashing down. I do not want to feel it. I do not want to think. The heaviness feels as if it is strong enough to take me deep under the water. I imagine a heavy force pulling me under, down into the deep blackness below. It is as if I am suddenly drowning. I gasp for air. Tears stream down my face and I heave with sobs. I have to deal with the newest evidence that Jack has purposefully played me for a sucker. *What an idiot I am.* I want to jump out of the canoe, out of my skin, out of my life.

I resist new self-knowledge. How busy I have been keeping myself to avoid self-confrontation. I regain the paddling position and paddle hard straight out into the wide expanse of water. My breathing is hard and fast and my arms ache.

STOP! ENOUGH!

I slow my strokes and arc my paddle to turn and head back to the cottage where everyone is most likely still sleeping.

I hear the powerful motor before I see the boat flying through the narrows straight toward me. It is ignoring the slower speed posted in the channel. *Can they see me in the glare of the sun? Is it my fate to be run down by a speed boat?* Turning the boat in a wide arc so they are heading north, the two men aboard wave in silent greeting. I imagine they are off golfing. Golfers in Muskoka take their boats to the club. It is part of Muskoka tradition.

The waves rock me. I hear them splash as they hit the shore. The waves of life affect me. I do not always see them coming. They change my balance and perception. I fight to stay level. *Could I let myself drift on those waves of life as easily as I ride the swells of water in my canoe?*

To ignore the waves made by those I love cuts me off from knowing them. To do this I must ignore their reality. Letting their waves control my life denies the heart and soul of me. Perhaps, someday when my children are older and more settled, I will be less exposed. Someday never comes. Like all the tomorrows that were going to be better, one's reality is in the consecutive moments. Now is the later of all those moments ago. If I wait until later, I will find that I have lived my whole life reacting to other people and have no life of my own.

My thoughts shift from my internal dialogue to the plants and trees clinging to the rocky shore. The birch and pines share the earth that has settled in cracks and crevices and covers the granite Canadian Shield in shallow patches. In mutual co-operation each appears to help the other hold on to life as the storms and seasons pass.

I believe Jack and I share the same foundation on which we build our lives. Our roots started intertwining a long time ago. We were teenagers then. I still cling to the illusion of being safe next to him. I have hoped that the winds of fate will blow on us more gently because we are together.

The delicate balance that holds those trees in their ledge on the precipice could so easily be upset. The roots hold the soil that gives foundation and life. *If one tree were to die, could the other survive? Would it fare better alone? It would have more space and nourishment.*

As the roots grow and sink deeper into the cracks of rock, their pressure could split the very foundation upon which their survival depends. Or as the water follows the path of the roots then freezes with the winter's cold, their safety could be shattered as the pressure of the frozen water pushes the supporting rocks off the cliff. There must be a threshold where they grow too large and either destroy the source of their life or need more nourishment than can be provided in that hollow and they die.

As I delve and dig deeper into what is happening in my life, am I in fact confronting the source where, with knowledge, I could very well shatter the foundation on which my life is based? If I die to myself, if I ignore what is happening with Jack, and go on as if everything is normal, if I stop fighting for nourishment and to live my life as an individual, would Jack develop more fully and to a greater potential? He will be free to live as he chooses if I play the suggested role of supporting and unquestioning wife. Will this allow his desired growth? Must I die as my Self to hold my marriage together? Is it even possible to hold onto this marriage? How far has their affair gone this time?

The heat on my shoulders tells me I may be burning. The morning sun has risen and the nearby cottagers fill the air with familiar noises. Boats are more frequent and my quiet contemplations are distracted. *Are my family up and enjoying breakfast?* I feel hunger and a desire for coffee.

I understand the paradox of my present position. I have been clinging in denial about my husband, fearful to prod further, fearful of shattering my safe foundations. I am hesitant to take a hard realistic look at what I am living, repeatedly holding myself back, in fear that I will lose my security. When I explore the areas of potential growth that leads me to greater heights and a fuller expression of who I am truly capable of being, I feel the withdrawal of support from my husband. I know I cannot deny that my life is changing. I'm stretching too far into new possibilities and delving too deeply into the past, asking too many questions and confronting and changing too many beliefs for my life to stay the same.

Are there enough supports, enough shelter, and enough warmth to dare to emerge from who others believe me to be? I wonder.

Jack will expect an emotional challenge but I do not want to shatter this lovely weekend for my family. The choices and the challenges are mine. *Can I survive this confrontation and flourish?* I am not a tree and I have the ability to move, to create and to express in many ways. I am the one who must be in control of my Self. I put greater force into my paddle. I am determined to put greater force into shaping my life.

One role played in a dysfunctional family is the martyr. Acting as a sacrificial victim, this person chooses last place, accepts being left behind and suffers as if it will lead them to some higher good. The higher good is often a form of power that leaves other family members feeling resentful, angry and guilty. It is a form of manipulation that draws attention to the martyr as somehow better than other people.

Giving up something we might want so others can have a turn, because it is not the most opportune time to claim our right, because of the reaction to people who have nothing to do with the problem, and to allow others to complete their agenda when ours can wait, is an act of thoughtful giving. It can also be because we truly do not want what is being offered. Being self aware helps us give appropriately so our well being is protected.

Martyrs are often cast in the role during early teaching and through family patterns. By examining our tendencies to go into the martyr role we can decide if it is our true way of wanting to relate, or a role we do not know how to break.

CHAPTER FIVE

TRYING TO GAIN CONTROL

Balancing My Inner World with My Outer World

I am not eating well and I cry easily. I finally decide to share my worries with my sister Judy. Sitting on the cottage deck, with the men off in the boat with the children, I tell her of my suspicions. She is both concerned and caught. She says she is glad I have shared this with her but it puts her in an awkward position. She and her husband have often spoken to each other about what they have seen but decided to mind their own business. Any chance of trying to talk to me was apparently blocked and she tells me it has been as if I have not wanted to know.

I have been so blind. I have deluded myself with false hopes. *Open your mind and eyes Marilyn!*

Judy overheard Jack on the phone with Beth from the cottage when I was away. The tone seemed too intimate for a man stopping by to pick up his daughter. He was careful with his dress and shaved before he left. That is definitely not the usual pattern of leaving the cottage. She has also seen and heard things in the past that raised her fears. She and I recall many circumstances over the past fifteen years where Jack and Beth have been obviously more than friends.

"Do you remember when...?"

The painful memories flood over me. She triggers thoughts of so many times she has seen situations when I was embarrassed and hurt by Jack's and Beth's behaviour. I wanted to block her words and deny my memories. I have not wanted to admit that my husband could lie to me so blatantly. I have deluded myself by choosing to ignore what at some level I have known for a very long time. *Why can I not face the truth and act on it?*

I have been living in a fantasy world wanting to believe that their flirtations are harmless. Seeing them gravitate to each other over the years—at parties and fundraising dances, getting the same chair lift and skiing on the same ski hills, sitting beside each other at business dinners. They seem to light up when they see each other. Their long lingering looks and slow warm smiles always tore my heart out. When I spoke about it, I was accused of reading too much into an innocent friendship. Jack would argue that I have told him men and women can have friendships and business relationships without it hurting the marriage.

There have been many break ups and reconciliations in our relationship over the years. They started before we were married. He would always return and tell me the others were meaningless and then romance me away from my reservations and fears. *Oh, he can be so convincing!*

When I raise my concerns in general ways with colleagues and women friends, the most common advice I receive is to ignore this behaviour because men are like that. They need a lot of ego stroking but rarely give up their homes and families for a mistress. It isn't only his ego I think she is stroking.

"Let him have his fun. He will get bored with her and either move on to another or decide the danger isn't worth it. Just make sure there is lots of sexual activity at home. Give him what he wants even if you have to fake it! You could also discreetly find yourself a playboy then you won't be jealous. Marriage is different than romance."

Some women even recount stories of their husband's women and laugh. They show expensive pieces of jewellery and tell stories of expensive spa trips or shopping excursions they have enjoyed as a result of the husband's guilt.

Yes, I have been attracted to other men. Especially the seductive ones who sensed my desire to be held by a man who wanted to hold me. Their whispers in my ear on a dance floor or personal comments with sexual innuendoes stirred my desires. I wanted to feel valued, respected and loved. Their flirtatious lines and suggestive ways tempted my fantasies. *Did they see how needy I was for affection and attention?* But I want my husband to want me. I want to be his only woman. I want his eyes to light up when I come into a room and the smile to dance on his lips when he looks at me. We have times like that and then there are times when he treats me as if I am unwanted and he'd be happy if I just went away. *Was he happy I went on my Quest so he could romance Beth without having to deal with me?*

Excitement can be kept alive in a marriage but it takes time away from responsibilities. It takes commitment to the marriage from both partners. It cannot happen when there is a third person in the marriage relationship. I have been more committed to this marriage than he has. His words from long ago echo in my head. He had joked that he couldn't imagine being married to the same woman for twenty-five years as he was sure it would be boring. *Our life sure hasn't been boring.*

I decide to cancel my invitation for Beth and her children to visit us in Muskoka. Jack is angry when I tell him. I assure him I can cancel my own invitation to the cottage if I want. He wasn't even going to be there as he said he had to work. *Was he planning on coming up when she and her children were there?*

I cannot sleep. I've been tossing and turning for two hours. Jack told me Beth came into Oakville to get her hair done and they had lunch and went for a walk. I was at the cottage. *Why does he have to do this in my space? Did she come to our office? Is he using this to show how angry he is with me? Does he care who sees them?*

I am glad I know she was here. If anyone says anything to me, at least I know and will not be caught off guard. *I hate this!*

His moods change and the expressions on his face give him away. I just keep putting one foot in front of the other as if on automatic pilot. I continue to track his calls and spending. I have not told him what I know from looking at the accounting records and his appointment book. I must have my details clear before I speak to him. There is too much for them to be "just friends."

Kathy and Matt are off to camp the last two weeks of July. Julia is working in the evening, so we have uninterrupted time to really talk. I pick a private time to confront Jack with copies of all my notes and his bills. They provide a paper trail of his actions. I make sure the originals are back in the office files and I have duplicates well hidden, in case he attempts to rip them up. At first he is furious and accuses me of snooping and invading his privacy. I assure him I am trying to protect my family from a predator who wants to destroy our marriage for her own gain. He tells me I am too harsh and defends her. This surprises me. Perhaps I should have expected this.

I specifically ask pointed questions about the number of phone calls to her home and school and their proximity to expensive meals. He admits the dinners were with her, but claims again that they are just friends. I ask why they were kept secret. He says because I would give him trouble over them. He insinuates I am too controlling and want to stop him from enjoying life. I ask him why, if they are just friends, she would not meet with me? He tells me to ask her.

I produce the letter from Beth explaining why she cancelled a lunch date we had made. Perhaps she never intended to meet me.

I hear his angry words. He states that she is a newly married woman and accuses me of having a problem with suspicions and jealousy. I ask if Ted was invited to those dinners. I ask if Ted knows about the meetings and calls. He tells me I had better get some professional help as I am ruining our marriage with my accusations. There is no acknowledgement of his behaviour being more than one would expect of two friends. Fortunately, I do not get distracted defending his criticisms of me, my motives or mentality. I stay firm in my resolve to get whatever is going on out in the open.

Finally he shouts at me: "OK, do you really want to know the truth? Do you?"

I look deeply into his angry eyes and tell him I am ready to hear what he has to say. He glares back at me. After a tense silence he finally tells me he is in love with her. Like flood gates opening on a huge dam, he pours out a stream of suppressed anger toward me. It has obviously built up over years of resentments. Some of the issues are small, while others are huge. They have to do with money, parenting differences, me getting my master's degree while he was turned down when he applied, my change as I became more confident and successful and old suspicions about my sexual and romantic behaviour, both before we were married when we were not even dating and suspicions he has had since our marriage. For someone who accuses me of ruining our marriage with my jealousy, he sure is carrying a lot of it himself. I am shocked by the depth of his feelings. I am amazed that he carries issues that I thought were resolved long ago so close to the forefront of his mind. It is as if he has been rehearsing his accusations of me for just this moment.

"Is this what you have been confiding in with her about all these years?"

"Yes, she listens and really cares about my feelings. We have both been lied to and betrayed. We have a lot in common. We both want an honest relationship. I cannot have that with you."

I am stunned. There seems to be little logic in his words. I am not the one who has been lying. I ask questions, sincerely trying to understand what he is talking about. He refers to conflicts we have had that go back years and years. I listen, keeping myself as composed as possible, while each accusation stabs me like a knife. I feel as if my innards are spilling onto the floor.

He goes on and on and on, like a steam locomotive blowing an immense pressure from its bowels. I understand his hurt, his pain and know that we have both expected many things from the other in this marriage. We have both been disappointed in all that marriage really meant. Many of our expectations were unrealistic. Each of us tried to create the life we wanted. Sometimes we went his way and sometimes we went mine. I thought we were compromising. Now I hear he resented the times I got my way.

Many of our ideas about marriage were based on romantic fantasies, on fears of what the other might be doing. At times, both of us went elsewhere to get our needs met. He tells me he has felt that he could never make me happy. He says I do not make him happy.

No one can make anyone happy but themselves. We can do things the other asks of us, things we know they like, but it is their responsibility to be appreciative and joyful or critical, always expecting more. His statement that he could never make me happy ignores this. His lack of acceptance that he must find his own sources of happiness ignores this. Life is filled with challenges. We need to accept that some of them will result in conflict and strife. Some will cause us to feel sorrow and pain. That is the nature of life.

"What is it that blocks your ability to find happiness with me?"

He tells me he cannot imagine staying married to me, as our life is always changing. In my heart I feel that he has repeatedly run away from accepting responsibility to make his life the way he wants. He has not made a mature commitment to work together to find a lifestyle where he can be happy. He has run to Beth with his disappointments and made up stories about getting rid of me to find happiness with her. She has befriended me to know how I was thinking, when I would be occupied elsewhere and she has moved in to areas where we should have resolved issues, not run from them. I have a burning resentment for her falsehoods but know I must focus on our marital relationship now. We are in a very deep crisis.

"Do you want to work on getting our marriage healed?" I ask with great trepidation.

"I do not know. I cannot go on like this. I want the pain to stop. More than anything, I want to raise my children in a stable home, so they have a good chance at making the best life possible for themselves. I love them more than myself. I will even suffer living with you, to make that happen."

"Do you think you can ever forgive me for all the ways I didn't meet your expectations?" I whisper.

"I may never forget, but the pain gets less as time goes on. I will never love you like I once did. I see you as the mother of my children, but not much more."

I decide this is not the time to talk about stages of marriage development and that when the responsibilities of life are part of a romantic relationship, the "in love" feelings fade and the reality of adult life takes over. Marriage is not about going around in a state of lustful bliss. While many people get married to save on living costs, to have regular sex and feel settled, there are a lot more facets to marriage than that. I want to tell him a lot about

45

my hurts and unmet expectations, but I keep my mouth shut. This is not the time.

One way I deal with stress is to try to make some sense of it and to talk it through. Some say I talk issues to death. Perhaps that is true.

When I play out a problem over and over in my head until the pain stops, I can disconnect from my feelings and think about the situation more clearly. I flood my consciousness with various possible ways out of the situation and over talk it. I find possible solutions and follow the thread of each to a possible conclusion. This is not the time to get my need for that met, but to think carefully and stay quiet. *Listen Marilyn!*

I believe maturity is the ability to accept the consequences of our thoughts, words and actions. I want to be very careful what I think, say and do right now. I need to stay focused and present my case for working on our marriage carefully. I want him to get back into his head from the emotional state he is in, and look at the devastation a divorce will bring on us and our children. We have worked so hard to build the life we have. I do not want him to throw it all away.

My desire to become a marriage and family therapist was based on my desire to have a happy family and a lasting committed marriage. I wanted to know how to stay happily married. Both of my grandfathers left my grandmothers and they suffered greatly by that abandonment. My father and mother never seemed to be on the same track and their marriage was destroyed by their anger over the unmet expectations each of them had for the other. Mom wanted some intellectual self-fulfillment and independence. Dad wanted someone who would always be there for him, focusing on him and his needs and wants. He wanted all the loving care he couldn't get from his mother when he was forced into the parentified child role after his father and older brother left. He became the father figure to six younger siblings. Mom just couldn't fill that void in him.

Over the years of my graduate courses at university, I was told that I was too serious and didn't know how to play. I learned that not everyone took responsibility as seriously as I did. By understanding how I create a "What if something bad happens?" scenario in my head, I worked at accepting there were lots of possibilities for good things to happen as well. I worked to be more daring on the ski slopes. I tried not to worry about how my responsibilities would be handled if I was to break a leg or worse. I watched other women having fun and I really wanted to learn how to just relax. I kept an eye on my kids and envied their daring. It was a challenge to just let go and really enjoy whatever I was doing. I had been taught ladies didn't laugh out loud. I wanted to free myself to really enjoy myself and to be able to laugh at myself.

I also learned during my training that I was called the over re-sponsible partner in my marriage. While my husband worked very hard he also knew how to play. I would resentfully cut the lawn while he golfed or shovel the snow and care for our children when he had ski days. I wanted to leave a party when he wanted to party on. I did leave one time and he came home about six in the morning. I wanted to know how far it had gone with the women he was dancing with when I left. He told me I was a party pooper and jealous for no reason. I had doubted myself. To avoid confrontation, I sometimes swallowed my pain. Other times I cried and pleaded, demanded and criticized. I could be a real bitch. I didn't know how to ask for what I wanted and needed, and often didn't even know myself what it was I was missing. I wanted him to know how to help me feel better. He just wanted to get away from me. He wanted me to be happy.

I know from years of marital work that Jack's fantasy of a life with Beth is not the reality he will experience and that their relationship will also go through the stages from fantasy to reality. The responsibilities will only increase with trying to support two families emotionally and financially. The demands will be enormous.

Sunday July 20, 1986

I want to do something where I can generate some good feelings. I need to find some joy to counter balance the intensity of my pain. I decide to head off with my camera to the Royal Botanical Gardens in Burlington. Since Jack has been so withdrawn I'm not sure he wants to spend time with me. I prepare myself for rejection and tell him of my plan. He seems pleased with the idea and suggests we have lunch out.

As we wander through the rose arbours the buzz of the bees and the scent of the blooms in the summer sunshine nourish my soul. I snap pictures and examine the many varieties and shades of roses. Our pace is leisurely. We climb the rambling steps of the rock garden that is built in an old quarry and the tumbling water speaks to my heart. I stand watching the grasses sway in the current and remember the fun I had as a child playing in the Credit River. My toes curl. I imagine stepping into the stream, feeling the slipperiness of the rocks and the cool temperature of the water.

I look across the expanse of garden and see Jack looking thoughtful, in a world of his own. My heart lurches with an ache that runs through my body in a shiver. I long to run to him, hug him and laugh together. I hold my reserve and wander toward him. He looks up and our eyes meet and hold for a fleeting moment. *This whole situation is really quite bizarre.*

"I love this place. I love the way the different gardens have such a different feeling." He smiles and agrees with me that gardens can bring peace to the soul.

The purple cone flowers blaze in masses of colour in the perennial gardens. I take more flower pictures and one of an empty bench. Jack wanders off. I let my fantasy imagine us sitting on that bench, embracing. I want to hug him and hold him and never let him get away from me. I silently laugh at myself. I must keep control of my impulses. I have no control over him. I do not want to risk a blatant rejection. He must choose to be with me. He can choose to come to me. I have not pushed his advances away. I must wait. I must accept his choice.

For now, I am content to wander in silence, knowing that my emotions are calmed and my anger and despair are gone. They have been tempered by doing something I love and being with someone I love. He cannot stop me loving him. Bittersweet feelings slowly flow through me. I know my future will be mixed with many emotions as I live the years ahead. I have great hope for my work that has no real dependence on Jack. I know my sadness is not a clinical depression because I can feel hope and love. In deep depression feelings are not felt. I feel.

Self awareness leads to self expression. I am learning to know my Self and to express my Self, even though I fear rejection and criticism. I know I can survive criticism. I certainly have had enough of it in my life.

My mind turns to the tasks I have ahead on my work schedule. Time slides past in a meaningless flow. Eventually, the private reflections that have been separating us dissipate and we find each other again. We hold hands as we return to the car and decide to go out to dinner.

Each of us has the right to control access to our physical, emotional and intellectual space. Whatever our age, we sometimes need solitude to develop our uniqueness. Having the confidence to take private time is part of being mentally healthy.

Privacy protects us from intrusion and is not meant to hide anything, or avoid relationships. Privacy involves things others could know, but do not have a need to know. Being alone allows us to think our own thoughts, decide our own wants and explore new ways to be ourselves. Sometimes we need time to relax and be quiet. We can use time alone to focus on ourselves, meditate, pray, sleep, exercise, read, cry, or regain emotional control.

Secrecy is keeping information to ourselves that we do not want others to know. Having secrets with others develops intimacy, builds opportunities for surprises, and is normal in relationships. When a secret is kept in a situation where if the secret was told the people involved would make different decisions, the secret has power. Informed decisions based on facts are not possible.

An affair gives the couple in the intimate relationship a sense of power. Their secret creates a sense of excitement between them. Fear of discovery and the efforts made to keep the secret, give emotional intensity.

Once an affair is discovered, the power it held can be dissipated by the sharing of the secrets. Once the details of the relationship are open knowledge, the power is lost.

When an affair is over the secrets need to be told to the spouse to shift the loyalty away from the lover and back to the marital partner. While it can be very painful to hear about what our spouse did with someone else, it allows for problems to be identified and resolved. If secrets are withheld, the intimacy between the lovers is not completely severed.

Sharing information at a deep level, builds intimacy.

CHAPTER SIX

HOW DO I FIT IN THIS NEW REALITY?

Do I Change my Self?

I dream I'm in Georgetown. I am all dressed up wearing fancy red sling back shoes with very high heels and gold trim. They are too big for me. I keep trying to move forward to be with some other people who I cannot see. I keep the shoes on, but my feet slide sideways. I am having trouble walking. Finally, I start to cry in frustration. I feel foolish. I try to find a tissue. The only ones I can find are for sale. I have no money. I awake feeling frustrated and sad. I am crying. I reach for a tissue from beside my bed and blow my nose. *Why was I too small for my shoes? Why didn't I just take the shoes off? Why did I have no money?*

I call Beth and try to meet with her. She gives me what seem like lame excuses why she cannot. I want to tell her to stop her flirtatious behaviour with Jack as she is attacking my marriage. I know it is not innocent fun as they have claimed in the past.

Since Beth will not meet with me, I decide to write her a letter. I cry as I write the words to the woman who I had once believed was my friend. We had met when she came to Georgetown with her husband. He was the newest lawyer joining the law firm. I had made a special effort to help her meet people and feel included. We had shared picnics in the park when our children were toddlers, taken them to swim classes, cross country skiing in the ravine, tobogganing at the golf course and shopped for clothes together. We often had pot luck dinners and did our Christmas baking together. We'd use her mother's recipe for white fruit cake and my mother's one for dark, and then split the batches. We did this with cookies and squares too so we had a larger selection. I had been there for her when her husband left her. I listened to her cry and rage about the position she was left in as a single mother. *Can she not see her time with Jack is destroying our friendship? Is her relationship with me not worth preserving?*

Many women fake a friendship with a woman in order to seduce the husband. I have been used. *Why have I been such a dope? Do people know and laugh at me behind my back?* Humiliation fills me and I fear I will throw up.

After clearing up the lunch dishes, I see Jack sitting glumly in the back yard with downcast eyes. I must not lose this moment. I approach him and ask for a hug. It takes a few moments but he rises and we embrace like good friends. I want to lean into him and ask for reassurance and support but he pulls away. He tells me he needs to move and is going for a walk. I ask if I can join him. He smiles and says "Sure."

We walk and walk covering streets we have never been on before. There are long silences. Each intersection provides us the chance the head back home, separate or continue on. As if in total sync, we instinctively make the choices that keep us wandering together. It is easy to talk as we walk. Sometimes we laugh and hold hands and other times we cry. We have known each other since we were awkward teens. He was my high school hero. He is the love of my life.

I know that Jack has triangulated Beth into our marriage instead of sorting out our disappointments with each other. He had used her as a confidant and they built a case against me. She used the confidences I shared with her to seduce him! They have developed a bond with me as the enemy. They have both been two faced with me and I trusted them. I thought they cared about me, but they have been building a relationship with each other. I hold my thoughts quietly in my head. My pace quickens as my anger surfaces, and then slows as I feel defeated. Jack matches his pace to mine.

This is so typical of behaviour that blocks marital intimacy. When one partner in a marriage has their primary loyalty outside the marriage, the marriage cannot grow as an intimate entity. Sometimes, it is the daughter's confidences she shares with her mother, or her reporting all her feelings and marital events to a sister or friend that puts a wedge between the couple developing trust. How many times have I had clients say to their spouse "I don't want you telling _____ so much about our relationship."

Couples need a boundary around things that really only affect them—like sex, money, and what they may disagree about, like the way they raise their children. They can ask for advice, but the final decision about what to do is theirs to share. Telling others too much about private matters kills the marriage. A marriage needs both partners working on solving problems and not building supportive armies to prove one of them is right and the other wrong.

The phone call from Ted surprises me, but also is a welcome relief. He is unsure at first of my reaction. I assure him I am only too glad to share our information. He recounts a day his instinct nagged him to go home in the middle of his work day. He tells me he never goes home mid day but he felt something was wrong. He found Jack and Beth sitting by their pool sipping wine. I share with him all my information about their meals and meetings and he tells me of some dates he felt they met. He is as devastated as I, as we put the pieces of the deceptions together to tell a wretched tale. Any remaining denial is finally broken with our words.

We both want to save our marriages and agree to try to stop the romance. We also both know we cannot control our spouses and that they must make the choice to stop their relationship. We will all live with the consequences.

When Beth goes north with her children to vacation at her family cottage, Jack seems to settle down. We have many more long talks and start to wade through the pain and sadness of our marriage. I get out the photo albums and we recall so many great times. Both of us, however, have had an undercurrent of distrust of the other. Lack of trust poisons a relationship.

I know I love Jack by the definition of love being "the ability to have an intense interest in his welfare so he can thrive and grow, only depending on me when he is in need." He has also professed his desire for me to live and grow and promised he will be there for me when I am in need. When I wanted to return to work as a teacher, he asked me to stay at home and cover the domestic responsibilities so he could focus on his career. He promised he would always ensure I was looked after. He promised his career goals were for our future.

Tuesday August 5, 1986 1:42 am – the cottage

I am writing this down to try to make some sense of it. I am in bed alone with strange feelings and thoughts. This past weekend with my sister and her family, I had a sense of emotional tension that is not usual. They left early yesterday to avoid the heavy holiday weekend traffic. I know she wanted to stay up but I want some time here alone with just my family. She has been here all of July.

Jack has gone on home as he has to work today. I will go down Wednesday morning. It is our month to use the cottage and I wanted some time to relax. I booked my first client for Wednesday at one.

August 15 1986

I had a dream about a cat suddenly scratching me after it appeared to be friendly. I must take a closer look at who I trust and what I trust them with. Who is appearing to be friendly but is setting out to hurt me?

In thinking about the images of my dream, I wonder if Jack's secretary is deceiving me. Her loyalty is really to Jack, her employer. They have worked together a very long time. She must know about Jack calling Beth and his meetings with her. I cannot connect a cat with her, but I must be careful with her.

His bookkeeper would have seen the expensive meals on the credit cards as she posts his expenses to various accounts. She would be in a position to see all the details I collected if she looked with awareness. She might also know that I was looking. I must be careful with her too. *Who can I trust?*

The only person I know who has a cat is Beth. I do not trust her. It saddens me to accept this as I feel I have been good to her and to her children. *What a mess!*

I am careful not to express any of my suspicions in the office. I do not want to mix our professional lives with our personal issues. One of the easiest ways to destroy good working relationships in a family business is to get the staff feeling they need to take sides. There is tension in the office. I notice attitudes are more reserved. I am as business like as possible and avoid opportunities to expand on queries about my personal life and my children. Perhaps they think I am being less than friendly, but I must be careful with my

professional stance. I must appear capable and confident especially if there are suspicions that our marriage is in trouble. The office is the last place that I want to share my concerns.

I turn down a job to teach assertiveness training at night school in Bramalea starting in September. I have other priorities. I have enjoyed teaching night school in the past as it is very different than doing therapy. I've met some interesting people and gained new contacts. There will be other opportunities.

I have a dream where I go into a fancy reception with lots of wonderful food. It is in a prestigious wood paneled room, crowded with many well dressed people. I feel happy and hope some of my friends will be there. As I am starting to help myself to some of my favourite things, I realize that I have only a blanket over my shoulders covering my underwear. The blanket keeps slipping. I know I am inappropriately dressed. It is as if I can not reach for what I want because if I do, I will be exposed in my underwear. In so many ways, I feel as if my life is even better than I hoped it would be. *Am I really ready to enjoy the party? Am I not part of the group? Am I going to be exposed as someone not worthy of my place? I wonder how the message that I am not dressed for the occasion fits with my life.*

The last week of August is quiet. I am at the cottage with my children. It is a time for rest and a chance to refocus before the hectic back to school preparations and return to routines. The weather is cool and there's no motor on the little boat. Matt has been bored and impatient. I thought Jack was going to be here all week but he returned to Oakville saying he had urgent issues.

I've had a lot of time to think. Part of me wants to confront "The Other Woman" to vent my anger. I know that will not help anything. She went through the pain of a marriage break-up when her first husband left her. I cannot believe that knowing what she experienced then, she would ever become involved with someone else's husband, especially the husband of a friend. I wonder what she might say to me. She could be very hurtful. If the meetings between them continue, perhaps I should meet with both of them. I wonder if her husband would be willing to do this with me.

One of the workshops I attended at a conference spoke about arranging for meetings with all four people in a situation like this. The amazing thing that happened in the meetings was that the stories of the two having the affair had told about their marriage were filled with lies. People having regular sex with a spouse told the lover they had a sexless marriage. Having to look at the spouse and deny their intimacy, and be exposed for the lie to the lover, had very powerful effects. One man had told his lover his wife was terminally ill and they were really separated, even though they still lived in the same house. The healthy wife was horrified. When the stories were confronted openly, anger was evident. In some cases it was the first expression of real anger between the lovers.

In the videos that were used in the presentation, it was interesting to watch the seating as the lovers tried to explain to their respective spouses why they wanted to end the marriage and be with their new love. Over the time of the exposures of the lies the distance between all four people widened. It was as if each person needed to look out for themselves. Their new awareness that someone they love and trusted lied so blatantly to their face and about them to the other person, had them reassessing their personal situation.

57

As I contemplate this as a suggestion, I know that it would take all four adults to agree to this. I wonder who I would want as the therapist. It would have to be someone strong and who believes in this process. I'll have to suggest it to Jack.

The evenings are shorter and cooler. I build a fire and enjoy a silly movie with my children. The cottage has been such a wonderful place for us to share as a family. I wonder what will happen to it if we cannot reconcile our marriage.

Our children know we have been having some serious issues and it has been a stressful summer. I have lost twenty pounds and people tell me I look great. I know my marriage is an important part of my life, but it is not my whole life. I am thankful I have so many friends and acquaintances, so many professional connections and so much positive in my life, as I struggle with this personal hell.

I awake in a panic. I just dreamed that I was driving into Gravenhurst, moving very quickly. I raced through the town. I was being chased but I couldn't tell by whom. I felt I would be safe if I could only get to the cottage. I pushed the accelerator to go faster. I saw the warning lights of the railway crossing at Torrance ahead. A speeding train was approaching. I pushed the gas pedal even further. The blaring whistle was deafening and as I shot over the tracks the train just barely missed me. I still feel the fear from the dream as if part of me is still in it. There are no train crossings between Gravenhurst and the cottage. *Where was I going?* Sometimes I feel as if everything is moving too fast and I cannot slow down even though I am risking my life. *Is my life in danger?*

I lay awake, alone in the still darkness. My fear subsides. I hear a rustling in the leaves, then silence. *Is someone walking about out there?* I stiffen in apprehension. I listen intently. It is probably a raccoon or a skunk searching for food. I hope Pickles doesn't hear it. His little body is curled by my leg. He would bark if there was danger. At least I hope he would.

The sun is up and I can hear my children in the kitchen. Jack said he'd be driving up early today as he had just one appointment. Last night's fear has evaporated. In order to work on a loving relationship, I must not let my fears control my behaviour.

Normal fear keeps us from danger. Irrational fear makes us crazy.

We feel fear when what we experience does not give us the same message as what we are being told. Something says to us: This isn't making sense. We work to try to get the facts to fit what we feel is real. The inner conflict that occurs as a result of mixed messages creates stress. Doubt and concern cause us to feel irritated, watchful, distrustful and insecure.

When someone tells us that what they tried to make us believe was a lie, and admits to the deception, replacing it with truth, we can then make sense of the conflicting messages, trust our inner voices and intuition and feel more at peace. Even when the news is sad or creates feelings of distress, knowing the truth leads to healing.

We can confront our fears by risking. We risk having our fears come true but we also open the door to the possibility that something else might happen, something unexpected, that leads to our own growth and change. Confronting our fears can lead to a new exciting way to live and love.

Avoiding our feelings leads to indifference. The more we feel our emotions, the greater the depth of our emotional life. While some people fear they will be engulfed by their emotions, learning emotional control is part of being fully alive.

CHAPTER SEVEN

LEARNING TO RECONNECT

There is So Much to be Lost

The summer has slid past and I continue to try to convince Jack we need professional help. I hope he will listen to someone other than me about the disaster he is about to create. I want him to understand running away from our marriage will not solve all his problems. He repeatedly refuses, saying we can do this on our own.

I confide in several friends and colleagues and get some support to stand firm and not just turn away from the relationship Jack is having. Some say ignore it. My gut says I must continue to get things out in the open and deal with the issues. I have tried to reason with him and explore the effects of a divorce on us and our children. He listens and seems to agree we should work on our marriage, but soon changes his mind and comes back with fresh complaints and more avoidance.

I can hear excuses and reasons that do not sound like my husband. I believe someone is feeding him lines and pressuring him to see the worst of our marriage. I do not want to let it go on any longer. I ask questions and hear details that upset me, but at least the pieces are falling into a place where more and more of it makes sense. Beth's husband and I have kept in touch. Sharing our stories puts greater clarity on the situation. We agree to both give our partners an ultimatum on Friday of the final long weekend of summer holidays.

"Move out now, before the children are back in school or stop seeing her."

In early September, I meet Vivian for lunch at The Cheese Board and we laugh about things we remember from our spring trip. I explain that I made some mistakes in the way I approached the trip. I would probably have been happier if I had chosen a room mate, rather than shared with the only other single traveller. I left too much to chance. That way, we could have shared our experiences from a common viewpoint as we were already friends. My other option was to pay the single supplement. I could also have negotiated a better understanding with the woman with whom I shared. Perhaps turn about being the first to choose the bed. My conflict avoidance left me feeling like I lost every time.

I tell her I am trying to work on the book I planned while we were away, but my marital issues have been too distracting since I returned. As a marriage and family therapist herself, she is supportive and gives me insight into a few things I have been missing. After I confide more of the details of my struggles with Jack, she has a better perspective on why someone might have a stake in discrediting our trip. She has heard rumours that were attributed to me that I spoke out against the group members. I admit I spoke about my experiences, but I will not accept that I told confidences of group members. I spoke about my dissatisfaction with some of the planning, the crowded van and some of the accommodations, but I did not say the things she says she heard. From the details she tells me, I know where the stories come from. *This is worse than I thought! I am being lied about so I look like there is something wrong with me. This will be a slam on my reputation. It is a slam on the reputation of other therapists on the trip. Has it all gone too far to save?*

I share my concern with Jack that lies are being spread about me and my version of the trip. He says my suspicions are silly and I am imagining this. I say that some of the stories can be traced directly to his other woman and she is slandering me. He is no support. He defends her saying she would have no motive to discredit me. *Is he blind?*

I know I cannot be married by myself. It takes two people who want to be together with common goals and values to create a functioning marriage. Jack has to want to work on our marriage and stop all contact with that woman. I confront Jack regularly with my ultimatum. He stalls. I do not want a raging scene. I want him to make a choice as a responsible adult.

With our children back at school and routines re-established, I have some staff problems at work and cannot understand the tension in the office. Jack says he doesn't notice it and that I am just too sensitive. I know I am distant and aware some of the staff probably knows of his affair. I do not accept his assessment that it is all me. I look elsewhere for feedback.

Jack tells me he will stop seeing Beth and wants to put some real effort into our marriage. Her husband tells me they are going to work on their relationship too. Both claim it was a summer thing. We both very much want to believe them. We know it has been brewing for years, but hopefully they have seen that a relationship together is a fantasy and will destroy everything that has been built. There are so many people involved. There is so much potential for pain and disruption to so many lives.

I am cautious but enjoy the wonderful fall weekends at the cottage and assure Judy we are working through our marital issues. The fall colouring of leaves is more brilliant than I ever remember. Jack is inquisitive about who knows what and who gave me support through what he agrees was a horrid time. As far as I know, my sister and my husband do not talk about her disclosures. I tell Judy that Jack knows she and I discussed his relationship.

Our children are relieved and very happy to have the tension lessened and to feel like our "real" family again.

As my professional life continues to improve, I know the efforts I have made to develop a private practice in Oakville have been successful. I am a member of the Board of Directors for the local chapter of the Canadian Mental Health Association. I am excited by some of the professional opportunities opening up for me. I am a guest expert on a national television talk show, speak at a conference of school principals, to a prestigious women's service club and to students at the University of Toronto. I receive frequent requests for paid speaking engagements and to run workshops through my affiliation with a speakers' bureau. I enjoy my clients and the therapy work I do. The financial rewards of all the hard work allow me to clear the extra expenses from my spring Quest quickly, and to invest in more professional development.

One night, I have a dream that someone very angry comes up behind me and thrusts a knife deep in my back. I awake with an acute pain in my right shoulder blade. *I must watch my back.*

In October, Jack accompanies me to a conference of the American Association for Marriage and Family Therapy in Orlando, Florida. He spends time relaxing and reading while I attend workshops. He accompanies me to the president's dinner and dance and we share an enjoyable evening. He comments repeatedly at the difference between being a conference attendee and a spouse. He enjoys not having to think about work.

"I know why you like to come on my conferences" he teases.

We visit Disney World on an evening pass, fondly recalling our trips here with our children. We have had some wonderful holidays that have created a close bond as a family. It is nice to have those memories and another type of enjoyment to have time as a couple.

Following the conference, we have decided to take a week together wandering. Jack collects travel literature and charts a route. We head south west on the throughway toward Tampa I suggest heading down the west coast to our familiar territory around Fort Myers. Recalling our very first trip to Florida, when our children were very small, I ask if he wants to return to Treasure Island. He has a route planned through central Florida and wants to explore new territory. I am ready for an adventure after several days of intense learning. I accept his role as our official travel guide.

We cut off route four to head south on highway 27. This takes us through vast orchards of orange, grapefruit and lime trees. Large trucks filled with oranges are feeding the factories that will supply our juice. I am sure I will remember this when I pour myself a glass on a snowy winter morning.

Travel is a great way to understand the sources of different foods and to understand that certain foods need specific climates to thrive. We have chosen the slower route, rather than the Florida Turnpike that would have taken about four hours to get to the Miami area, as we want to get a different view of the state than we have had before. We are also going to drive back up the coast. Rather than retrace our steps and see the same area twice, this route gives us the most variety.

There are many lakes with cottages that have the feel of our cottage country. While the boats at home are stored for the winter, it is full summer style activity here. *How fortunate we are to have so many experiences in life! I am glad I live with a man who shares my love of travel.*

Driving into Lake Placid we remark at the number of places that have the same name as other places throughout the United States and the world. Settlers often named new settlements after places they immigrated from, so we have New York, New Hamburg and many others. I read in a pamphlet that Lake Placid was named to attract winter visitors from Lake Placid, New York. This is also an area where many people were defrauded out of money in real estate scams. As I read the literature and we chat about our reactions and memories, new understandings of historical lessons and our reading surface. It is totally understandable why a train down this way would be called the Orange Blossom Special.

The land rises and our route takes us past pine forests, rolling hills covered in scrub bushes, cattle ranches and quaint small villages.

We stop for lunch in Clewiston, a pretty town on the southwest shore of Lake Okeechobee, the second largest fresh water lake in the United States. We wander about small shops to stretch our muscles, and watch pleasure boats in the cross-state Okeechobee Waterway, which offers direct access across the middle of Florida. There are marinas with docking space and watching the activities again remind me of summer in our cottage country. So much the same yet so very different.

I assume the driving for the next while. We are heading to the south end of Miami for the night. Jack has a spot in mind, so we resist stopping in the interesting shops we pass in the quaint small villages of Lake Harbour and South Bay. There is a lot of highway yet to drive through the Everglades, where there is little in the way of places to stop.

Our time in Orlando was busy. I take this chance of uninterrupted time alone together, to explore some of the ideas put forth by Betty Friedan at the Presidential Banquet. Betty is a pioneer in the women's movement and a very strong voice for women's rights. I question Jack on his beliefs about women's roles and responsibil-

ities as compared to men's. He tries to change the subject and objects to my desire to have a probing conversation.

"Can't we just relax and enjoy our holiday?"

Vacation time is a perfect time to explore ideas, get in touch with our partners in a deep and meaningful way, and to work on creating our life goals. It is hard to do this when we are busy with daily demands and responsibilities. I want to use this week to build the bonds between us, explore our differences, find new ways to agree on issues and agree to disagree if necessary, and to mend the hurts from the past.

I love to discuss ideas and challenge him by asking:

"Are you sorry I turned out to be intelligent?"

I had met Jack at high school when I was fifteen, repeating grade nine. I thought I was dumb. I wasn't dumb, I just didn't know how to read and had been pushed through junior school with the others of my age. Once I was able to read, at about age twelve, I read regularly. During my teacher training, and through teaching children, I finally developed the core skills in language and mathematics.

In my years as a homemaker, I read extensively. I went for career testing and counselling in my mid thirties, to see if I would be capable of achieving an undergraduate degree. I needed a degree to return to my teaching career, something I had planned to do when our children were in school full time. When I was told I could achieve at a post graduate level, I set my sights higher. Achieving my master's degree was a very proud event. My only regret was that neither of my parents lived to see my success.

Many men think women should be seen and not heard, like children. Perhaps, in the beginning, Jack thought I'd stay dependent on him for my thinking and rely on him for decision making. I certainly did in many areas as I always thought he was so much smarter than I am. I changed from being an insecure follower of the ideas of others, to a critical thinker with the confidence to think my own thoughts and express my own opinions.

"Do you really think that running a home, raising children and supporting your career would give me enough personal fulfillment?"

"Why isn't that enough for you Marilyn?"

I explain that I want more intellectual stimulation and interpersonal involvement. I also explain that by society expecting women to get their sense of success through the achievements of others— their husband's and children's success—it denies women their own power and sense of achievement. If a husband is lazy and lacks motivation, and if the children fail to apply themselves to their education, then the wife who is powerless to make them change, is seen as a loser.

"It always comes back to power with you Marilyn."

"Yes, personal power and accountability. Each person must accept the responsibility to create their own success and achieve according to their ability in the areas where they have skills. Many men have better nurturing skills than the women to whom they are married and the women have better earning potential. Why can this not be seen as normal and that each using their best skills, be seen as acceptable?"

I use the example of several couples we know.

"Many men are better cooks than their wives and enjoy it more, and many women are more mechanical than their husbands. Why should they not enjoy their abilities and work as a partnership?"

I feel as if Jack is only half heartedly listening. *Is he just humouring me with his replies? Is he afraid of stepping out of the traditional male role?* He is an excellent cook, great with our children and can manage a home when he sets his mind to it. *Enough for now. Enjoy the drive Marilyn.*

Vast expanses of sugar cane wave in the breeze. Groups of men with machetes are clearing the land. Signs warn us that prison gangs are at work. Smoke plumes rise from piles of discarded burning brush and the drifting haze makes visibility difficult in places. They warn us not to pick up hitchhikers. I have no desire to stop or to pick up anyone. I imagine the snakes and spiders whose habitats are being disrupted. I wonder about alligators. Chills shiver up my spine.

Highway 27 crosses Alligator Alley and we discuss which route we want to take from here. We decide to stay as far away from the metropolitan area as possible, as we still have a good amount of daylight left.

I am pleased to have a swim and leisurely dinner then a chance to walk in the warm fall evening. Our plan for tomorrow is to drive out the long mangrove string of islands to Key West. How long we will stay there hasn't been decided but it is a place we have often said we wanted to go.

Starting out early, we are looking for an adventure. Our gas tank is full and we have drinks and snacks handy. After just over an hour, Key Largo tempts us with some interesting opportunities for sight seeing but we limit ourselves to a toilet break and resist spending further time, as we want to be in Key West for lunch. It is about two hours straight along the Overseas Highway, route one. The road was originally cut in the early nineteen hundreds, by the Florida East Coast Railroad. The railroad carried passengers throughout the Keys until a 1935 hurricane damaged it beyond use. The highway uses many of the original railroad bridges, and was completed in 1938.

The Atlantic Ocean is on our left and Florida Bay and the Gulf of Mexico on our right. I am reminded of the causeway from Fort Myers to Sanibel. Some of the islands have palm trees and small settlements, but mostly is mangroves and sand. It is one hundred and thirteen miles of roadway that includes 43 bridges. One of the bridges is seven miles long and rises over the water in a series of giant arches of concrete and steel. This is not a trip for someone who needs to stop frequently or who dislikes bridges. We are thrilled with the sense of driving practically on the water and delighted to see many shore birds. *I wonder if we will see an alligator.*

As the miles slide by, we share many long periods of comfortable silence. There is also time of shared conversation speculating on shipwrecks and snorkelling, the proximity to Cuba and how lovely our life is together.

I have brought my notes from the conference into the car, planning to share some of the learning I have just experienced. I talk with joy at having met Carl Whitiker again. His book, The Family Crucible, had inspired me to specialize in family therapy. I remind Jack that it was Carl with whom I had the week long training session in the Berkshires in 1985. He and our children had come along and spent the week touring and relaxing, while I worked. We had visited the Tanglewood presentation of the Boston

Symphony, with a dinner picnic packed by our hotel. We sat on a car blanket but some people had folding tables, white linen and silver candle sticks and cutlery for their picnic. Having taken our children to the Toronto Symphony for years, they had a good appreciation of the music and many of the pieces were familiar. It was one of those wonderful shared family experiences. Thankfully, we were blessed with perfect weather.

Recalling that happy time, and being here together now, I appreciate that I am blessed to have such a wonderful life. I find it hard to imagine Jack would risk it all by having an affair. I want to press the point that he risked so much with his romancing of Beth, yet do not want to mention her name. Rather than follow further down the family therapy thoughts, talking about how important an intact family is to personal well being and children's development, I switch to a safer topic.

I chat about new ideas of ways to market a private practice from the ideas presented in another workshop. Some of the suggestions would apply to his law practice and some to my therapy practice. Discussing changes we can make in office procedures starts to feel too much like work and we agree to drop that topic.

Key West is both bizarre and busy. It is the city that is furthest south in the United States and the buildings reflect both the old fort and fishing port and vividly painted and decorated clap board buildings.

We stop at the tourist office and gather literature about the attractions, accommodations and places to eat. It is soon evident that Key West is a haven for gays and lesbians. It was apparently rather run down and the creativity, for which homosexuals are known, started a regeneration of the city with renovations to the old homes. Many were turned into small inns and bed and breakfast spots, trendy restaurants and artistic shops, where the lifestyle they desire could be lived with acceptance and freedom.

Lush gardens, swaying palms and a perfect day are not enough to overcome our first surprise to this revelation. As we drive through the streets, there are also many heterosexual couples walking hand in hand, sitting eating at sidewalk cafes and in general just being tourists. Jack is nervous. I know this is not what he expected.

I suggest we find a place for lunch. Jack wants to see the light-house and the furthest tip of land.

"I do not want to stay here."

I am surprised by his comment and question why. He tells me he finds it unsettling. I am somewhat surprised, as he has had considerable associations with homosexuals as friends. The man he chose to be our best man is gay and they often went to gay bars. This man has a part to him that is deep and secret. Just when I think I know him well, something happens that shatters my confidence.

I suggest lunch in one of the hotel restaurants on the beach. He agrees. We order wine and fresh oysters. Laughing at the memory of the first time we had them raw, in a tapas bar in Spain, in the early seventies, eases his tension. I reminisce how we got the giggles, as we hadn't expected them to be raw when we ordered fresh. We washed them down with a good amount of wine and laughed about the experience for years. We were so innocent then.

We linger over a fresh salad then seafood entrées. I feel relaxed and sleepy in the lovely garden setting. I try to convince Jack we should stay here, but he is determined to leave. I insist we phone to Key Largo for a reservation at the Sheraton, in case we get back and there are no more rooms. He agrees.

With our night's accommodation secured, I ask to take time to explore some of the little shops. We wander by the harbour, poke through galleries and finally set back along the highway. The sky turns pink and the sun dips low. We stop for some cold beer and wine, and to enjoy the sunset from a thin strip of beach. Dinner is late in the hotel dining room. We poke about the hotel to check on the amenities. During our stroll around the gardens, I take Jack's hand. It is a beautiful evening. I feel romantic and close, joyful in knowing we are working on making our relationship more focused on us as a couple.

> Travelling as a couple is good for the development of the rela-
> tionship. So often the responsibilities and demands of children, take
> so much time and energy that a couple becomes disconnected from
> each other. Both are living in quite loneliness, wishing their lover
> would return, and they could be the people they were when they
> fell in love. The sense of isolation cuts deep and sharp, because the
> body of the lover is close, but the emotional connection has been
> lost. The physical pleasures they once found in each other, have
> faded to routine encounters or an absence of sexual attraction. This
> may manifest in anger. Resentment builds as each expects the other
> one to make a doorway in the wall that they have built between
> them. It is easier to blame the other than to accept responsibility to
> take the first step toward rekindling the love and affection.

As we share our leisurely days together, following our whims, indulging our wants, we touch more frequently. Our laughter flows more naturally. Our eyes connect and hold. The guilty avoidance and imminent tears are gone. We take time savouring, just being together. Sometimes our sexual encounters are passionate and full of energy and other times we move slowly, with gentle caresses and soft words. I do not want to forget the joy in the quickie before dinner that leaves me glowing and the morning snuggles with no interruptions and time to chat and share that is a great start to our day. I feel so close to Jack, that at times, I have the sense our beings are one. We tease and joke like we haven't in a long time. *I do love this man*

Our time together brings the ways we relate into the forefront. I feel myself give in to his wants. Being happy diminishes my desire to have something happen the way I would plan it or want it. As long as we are together, I really do not have strong desires about what we do.

Feeling safe and confident with Jack, issues that have been avoided, tickle at my mind. I question myself. *Do I want to risk these delicious feelings by bringing up a problem? Can I address my concerns without loosing the connection with him?*

Being alone together is a time where because there is no distraction of responsibilities, we can focus on areas we want to improve. There are expanses of time to share experiences and be attentive to each other in ways not usually possible. We can focus on developing new ways to problem solve. Involving others in our relationship dynamics is less likely when we are surrounded by strangers. We can work through the situations that confront us, learn new ways to relate, and rebuild our trust in each other.

I have been making progress in listening, without trying to fix a situation. I feel myself holding back with a suggestion, and asking Jack what he wants to do. I know I have tended to organize events and he has gone along with my ideas. This was one of his complaints of me. By my listening more, I feel we are reconnecting on new levels. I feel sad at the fun I have missed. I have spent a lot of time being responsible for our children, home, shared offices, our cottage, our parents, my siblings, and my work. When Jack tells me I take life too seriously, I agree. I am now practicing how to be more playful and less responsible.

I have been sitting on the patio, in a state of relaxation. The waitress has cleared the table. I have no desire to move. Jack returns from the washroom and asks if I am ready to go.

"Can we sit here for a few more minutes please?"

I explain to him, how I have been enjoying just sitting here, altering my level of awareness from one of alert planning, to a drifting daydreaming state where time and place melt in to nothingness. I am just being me in the moment. We explore the concept of altered states of consciousness, sharing stories of times and places where we find peace. I share a technique I want to try, from one of my recent seminars on Erickson's methods of hypnosis. I love the learning and trying out new possibilities. Our conversation stimulates more ideas, as Jack asks questions and puts forth arguments and ideas. He is sceptical of some of mine and of our ability to change our lives with changed thoughts. He is an intelligent conversationalist and provokes me to think about what I am saying. I polish my ideas or alter my acceptance of them. Time slides by with careless abandon. It would be hard to have this kind of conversation at home with so many responsibilities and interruptions.

As we wander north along the eastern coast, we delve into some of the ways we learned to be married. We talk about my mother's unhappiness, and feelings of wanting more than being a housewife could offer. Since she shared a lot of her experiences with Jack, we are able to stimulate memories and recall stories we had both forgotten. This is a definite advantage to being in a relationship with someone with whom we have shared so many years together. We have a shared history. We do not have to explain who people are and what we were doing with our lives because we were both there. *Oh, how I want to grow old with this man.*

The mental state of a mother has a huge impact on the whole emotional state of a family. Stories of his mother, and how he hated her yelling, brought us to a chance to look at the impact our relationship has on our children. Our happiness and ability to share happy times, teaches our children that playfulness and responsibility can live in the same place. As we work through our differences, we teach our children that differences can be accommodated in a relationship between two adults when they are willing to work toward a shared solution. Sometimes, people can disagree and agree that they disagree, without it ruining their relationship. How we are as adults has a major effect on the generations that will come after us.

We laughed about some of the silly things our children have done and shared our fears and frustrations about events in our past. We cover a lot of topics. Many times we return what we want from our relationship. It is easy to talk about what we don't want, but not always as easy to talk about what we do want.

As I listen to Jack's complaints, I have to hold my silence and ask questions to hear more of what he has found so difficult that he would consider ending our marriage. *Is he running to something and someone new or running away from me.* There is a very big difference. *Is he bored with me?*

I hear that I am more fun away from my responsibilities. Romance and responsibility are opposites. Romance is fun and fanciful. Taking care of the responsibilities isn't. I ask if he would rather be with someone who was not responsible, who didn't keep their word, who didn't carry their part of the marriage deal. He assures me he wants someone responsible. Keeping a balance between being responsible and being fun is the skill.

> Interesting people explore many subjects and find significance in many things. They are curious, questioning and want to know how things work, what is happening in the world and about the lives of people. They are not bored or boring.

> People who get bored tend to expect others to entertain them and create diversions for them. They tend not to like change, avoid thinking and making decisions and have few interesting stories to tell.

> It is possible to change from having a life filled with feelings of boredom. By chasing new interests, meeting new people and accepting responsibility for our own lives, we can make life an adventure of our own choosing.

Chapter Eight

NOT WITH MY COMPANY YOU DON'T!

Who Really Has Control?

I share my enthusiasm for our growth as a couple with friends and family. Everyone is pleased we have made it through a very difficult time. Family time is busy and social events are stimulating. Matt has been helping me with the computer and when I can pry him away from it, I know I am learning something that will have real value in my life. It will have many applications, both personally and professionally. Many of my friends vow they will never need a computer. I joke with them that someday they will find not only uses for a computer, but fun in the possibilities for learning and growth.

I am dismayed when Graeme, our accountant, requests a meeting with Jack and me on a Friday in late November. I know all the finances are in order. Jack is in court first thing, but assures me he will be back in time for the eleven o'clock meeting. He gives me no hint as to what the meeting is about, saying we need to go over some figures.

Graeme arrives before Jack returns. He suggests we start. It comes as a total shock when he tells me he is closing my company. I was incorporated in 1978, originally to do property and office management while I was working on my undergraduate degree. After I graduated with my master's degree, I have done my counselling practice and public speaking work through the incorporation. I am the only shareholder. I have complete control.

"What are you talking about?"

I am told Jack doesn't need my company any longer so they are going to fold it. He speaks in a way that sounds to me as if it is a completed deal.

"What are you talking about?"

After Dad died in 1978, and I inherited money, Jack wanted to leave the legal firm he was in and work independently. After much deliberation and consideration of my options for investing the funds, I bought a building in Georgetown and set up an office for him in what had been the living and dining room of an old well maintained house. Eighteen Church Street was one block from the main street. There were tenants in a second story apartment, so there was some income from them.

I hired a builder and did renovations to make it possible for Jack to have a self contained office on the front of the first floor. I decorated and furnished the living room for Jack's legal office. It was on the corner so there were large windows facing the street on two sides. The fireplace and a wall of bookshelves created a professional backdrop for an antique desk I had inherited. A pair of new wing backed chairs, as well as two tub chairs on wheels, gave him a grand place to work.

I put a secretarial desk in the dining room and furniture for waiting clients. With the large windows and French doors it too was impressive in a homey way. The kitchen and rear portion were closed off for a separate apartment. I bought office machines and leased them to Jack. I learned to do legal books. Linda had been his secretary for a number of years and she moved with him. This gave his work flow good continuity and the transition was easy.

I put a two piece bathroom in what had been the centre hall. I charged Jack rent and a fee for my management and bookkeeping services. This gave me an income from my investment of both money and time.

I leased the ground floor apartment to his parents for a nominal fee with an agreement they would do yard work and some office maintenance. After I graduated, I renovated the upstairs space for my practice and opened up access to the stairs so we shared the reception area. I also hired a bookkeeper for all the accounting and a part time secretary for myself. We kept this arrangement for over six years until we moved to Oakville.

Graeme explains that Jack wants to buy the furniture and office machinery from me at a depreciated cost, and that Jack is considering moving his office space as the lease is up at the end of January. He says Jack asked him to explain it to me so we could manage the details and terminate the contracts. He goes on to explain the way they reached the depreciated values of my equipment. His voice drones on. I can't hear what he is saying. My heart is pounding. My throat is very dry. *What is going on?*

"I will not shut down my company!" I am trying not to look crazy, not to act hysterical, not to scream and ask why Jack never spoke about this. I compose myself and ask; "Who thought up this idea?"

I try to focus on the figures and explain that I have leases on some of the equipment like with Zerox for their copier. They cannot be broken. This space is also too large for me alone, so I wouldn't want to renew the lease which is in my company's name. I explain that I will have to find alternate office space and change my letterhead and that this is not what I had planned. I feel as if I am babbling and suddenly stop talking. I cover my face with my hands and will myself not to cry. *Why just when I think everything is progressing well does something like this come as such a shock to me?*

It was only a few weeks ago that Jack had started talking about possibly moving the office. We had visited office locations as possible options. It had been my understanding that we were moving, not separating our practices. He did say that some of the locations fit him better than they fit me. *Have I really been listening?*

Dysfunctional families have denial as a major coping mechanism. This defensive adaptation helps us live as if our world is OK when it is everything but fine. *Have I been denying what Jack has been trying to tell me? Does Jack want us to sever our business relationship? This is what Graeme is telling me now.*

It doesn't make good economic sense to me. *Why have two offices? Why pay for two reception areas, two copiers, two ......?*

Jack arrives. I hear his voice speaking to the staff and my body goes rigid. I am afraid to look directly at Graeme. I feel his relief. His greeting to Jack is too jovial. I sit quietly as Graeme goes over the figures that he has just proposed to me, with Jack.

My mind is racing. In an attempt to still it, I focus on the bookshelf. One book on co-dependency seems larger than life. I stare at the spine, willing myself to relax. I breathe slowly and unclench my sweaty hands. I feel the sweat in my shoes. My feet always sweat when I am nervous. The men are watching me. I ignore them. I shift into focusing on the meaning of being co-dependent.

A co-dependent is someone who has been deprived of a good self image. They lack a sense of security and lack the ability to have fun. This person puts others wants, feelings and needs ahead of their own. Clinically, I know the signs. Now I see that I have been co-dependent and Jack is trying to break free.

I have believed that what is good for Jack, as the primary breadwinner, is good for us as a family. My fantasy was that he would look out for us and take care of us. When my desires are not taken into consideration, and as I stand up for my wants and my needs, and not worry just about his, it is as if I am alone. I must think of myself because Jack is certainly not taking my wants into account. I have the expectation that someday when Jack has been given enough, when I have been a good enough wife, it will be my turn to get the attention and support that I crave. I seem to get enough support to go a set distance. Then I must return to my responsibilities. He is off on some new idea that he has concocted. I am just beginning to really thrive. Now he wants to put on this burden of relocation.

Both men talk as if my objections carry no weight. This has obviously been well discussed before being presented to me. They assure me they will help me in any way they can. The bottom line is they are both telling me to close my practice and walk away from something I enjoy and that is vital in my life.

"What do you expect me to do instead?"

Jack patiently explains that he thinks I should return to teaching as it would give me a regular salary and a pension plan. He tells me I can make good money and have my summers off. *Is this really happening?*

"I do not want to return to teaching. I plan to gear up my work load as our children grow. Since I haven't been in Oakville for long, I think I am doing very well. Remember, I am the one who took time to set up the offices, help our children settle and ……" They are not paying any attention to me. I sound like a child justifying myself. I stop and focus inward. I am growing extremely angry. Anger comes when our expectations are not met and these two arrogant men are not meeting my expectations. Not by a very long shot!

I hold my voice very steady and speak slowly and in a paced low tone. I look directly at Graeme and say; "I am not closing my practice! I am not folding my corporation. I will not become a classroom teacher. I will think about my options and let you know my decision."

"Don't wait too long Marilyn." Graeme replies jabbering on about Jack's year end and tax consequences.

In a very determined tone I say: "I will be getting my own accountant as well. I do not believe you have my best interests at heart."

The tension in the room is acute. I turn my eyes to my husband.

Jack avoids me and suggests we all go to lunch. Exclaiming that he just needs to check his messages, he leaves the room. I am humiliated.

I follow him out the door, snatching my purse on the way. I grab my coat and tell our receptionist I will be back on Monday. Thankfully, I have no further clients booked.

"Tell Jack I can't make lunch!"

I do not give a damn what they think of me. I MUST think of Me!

The stories we tell about ourselves and others help us to understand our experience. There are lessons that can be handed down to our children about how we have learned and lived. *What are my children going to hear about this? Is this going to be another opportunity to tell stories about how I over react emotionally? How can I protect my children form this latest turn of events? I thought things were settling down nicely.*

How I tell this story will manifest my beliefs. My attitudes toward sexual power and equality will play a part in what I teach. *Do men have the right to control their wife's destiny? Can a marriage survive a major difference in opinion? Is this about who earns the most money? Is this about personal choice? Is working in any capacity just about earning money?*

CHAPTER NINE

AM I CRAZY?

Can I Hold on to Me When I Am With You?

December 1986

I am filled with hurt and anger but try to swallow it as I ride down the elevator to my car. I briefly wonder if Jack will try to follow me. *Will he try to persuade me to go to lunch and act as if I am not seething inside? Is this purposefully done so my reaction will be seen by the staff as emotionally out of control and unprofessional? Why was it done in the office in the middle of a business day? He could have told me this was why Graeme was coming to meet with me, when I asked why we were having this meeting.*

I feel like a child, running off alone to nurture myself and sort out the facts to try to make some sense of this. I have no one I feel I can trust with this terror that grips my chest. I do not want to go home. There are too many triggers there to thinking about my present problem. I must find a place to think.

The confidence that is usually in me has evaporated. My sense of wholeness and balance that I have when I am filled with a sense of my Self is gone. I have lost my Holy Grail. I am reacting to what has been said to me and by what they are trying to do. I must not let them control me. I must get back into my Self and take back my self control.

I drive past the turn to my home, and see the sign for Gairlock Gardens. I park my car and button my coat. There is a clear bright cloudless sky. Some warmth is still in the sun. I manoeuvre past the geese and their droppings and stride through the park toward the lake. The soft swells of waves gently lapping the retaining wall, and the swans gliding across the water, soothe my spirit as the tears start to slide down my face.

Who am I? What is happening to my life?

I feel out of control of what is going on around me. I feel abandoned and my only solace is what I can find inside myself. My mind turns to the people I have tried to count on over the years. The one person I was hoping would be my closest ally and most trusted companion is heading off on a path that does not make sense to me. I pace the stone path and pause to stare out across the lake. *Dear God, help me find my way.*

I wander through the deserted gardens, prepared for winter with straw over the flowerbeds and earth heaped on the roots of the roses. I remember their blooms from visits last summer. They will bloom again if the winter doesn't kill them. My mind races forward. I will need to find myself an office. I will have to move, absorb the cost of moving, new letterhead, business cards... I want to continue with my clients, my speaking, and writing my book. I do not want to return to teaching as Jack suggested. Jack's wants to rid himself of me as a professional partner. Just when I thought we were settling in financially and professionally, he wants to destroy the whole thing. My feet are cold and I am hungry. I return to my car and drive the short distance home.

This is the house I did not want to buy. Jack insisted I sell the Georgetown property and put my inherited money, plus the growth in value, into a matrimonial home. I wanted to keep the proceeds separate and designated an inheritance. I know the growth would be shared if we split, but the actual amount inherited would be separate from matrimonial assets. It would have been my safety net. Somewhere, I still have reservations about Jack making decisions about my best interest and not just his own. I didn't like the layout of this house. It is too open with no doors between the living room, dining room and family room. I have worked over the two years we have lived here to remove the wrought iron from the inside, decorate it so every room is not a different colour and carpet and to make it feel like our home.

Pickles is deeply asleep and doesn't run to meet me as I quietly enter the house. I poke in the kitchen but find nothing I want to eat. I climb the stairs and slide under the duvet, pull my knees to my chest and sob out of control, shaking with the intensity.

Matt wakens me when he comes home and I hear concern in his voice at finding me in bed. I truthfully tell him I am not feeling very well and offer to make him some hot chocolate. I sip a cup of tea and he tells me about a plan he has with one of his friends. I thank God for the joy of being a mother. The girls arrive home and notice nothing amiss. Before long the music is playing, the phone ringing and it feels almost normal.

Jack arrives and announces he isn't really very hungry for dinner. Apparently he and Graeme had a very long lunch. He asks in a casual way; "How come you didn't come to lunch?"

Breathe, count, one two three four five six seven, all good children go to heaven, if they swear they won't go there, so one two three four five six seven.

Mom taught us to say that to stay still if she put drops in our eyes or ears. I must stay still and not react. This is how he tries to get me to flare into an angry outburst and then say I am being unreasonable or hysterical. Perhaps I should have known this was coming and it is my denial that made it seem like a shock. He is acting as if everything is normal and I am taking this latest development all in stride.

I must stay in the present, focus on what is immediately happening right now, to protect myself from falling into this pattern.

If I allow my anger to take control, I will give him the opportunity to say I am unreasonable. He will calmly tell me we agreed on this plan. He will say in a patronizing voice that it is for the best. He will sound so logical. When he points out that I really am not making enough money from my therapy for the amount of education I have, and I am not building a pension like I could as a teacher, it will sound as if it is about money. He will deny that we agreed that private practice was the most responsible choice for me, since it gives me time flexibility to be the primary parent with three teenagers. He has little control of his time when he is on a big trial and since he is often in court out of town, one available parent is what I believe we chose as a parenting style.

Teenagers need available parents to avoid the pitfalls and problems of a turbulent time. While they will say they are alright on their own, and he will tell me he was on his own a lot and he turned out alright, we both have a lot of exposure to teenagers in deep troubles. We have both agreed that teenagers need supervision and parental guidance. Now he acts like this is not an agreement we have made and the argument will go round and round. His communication skills will wear me down, just as I know he does with witnesses in court. I am too emotionally exhausted to even start.

Have I pushed him into a life style and parenting style that I want and believe is best for our children that he does not really support? Why is he so supportive some of the time, and then as if from out of the blue, he totally shifts position?

It is as if I live with two men. One is controlling, demanding, stonewalls communication and withdraws from meaningful exchanges. The other is funny, loving, a responsible parent and my close friend. We share our hopes and dreams, our triumphs and our frustrations. In this mode we solve problems well, set and achieve goals and parent our children together. Never knowing which personality type will manifest is stressful.

I want an open trusting relationship where conflict is normal and problems get solved. Sometimes, I feel my opinions are respected, I am being told the truth and our relationship has integrity. I feel solid and safe. Then there are times I feel lied to, distrustful and purposefully confused by changed versions of stories and altered memories. Something as simple as saying one of our children has a commitment, and he tells me I never told him, then the child recounts that it was a discussion at the dinner table and he suddenly remembers it with clarity.

Intimacy is created with shared experiences when there is trust that the other will respond with empathy. Betrayal breaks intimacy. Jack is a master at building the trust in me, acting as if we are close with an attachment that has lasted for almost thirty years. He is attentive to me and I build my confidence that finally we are growing into an affinity with a reciprocal commitment. I start to believe our relationship will grow and change. Then the whole thing falls apart with a lie or insensitivity. Perhaps his tolerance for intimacy is limited. *Does being too close frighten him?*

Many people fear intimacy. They think they will be swallowed whole if they let someone too close. Their distrust is that the other person will stop them from what it is they really want to do, and they will lose control of their life. Parents who smother their children emotionally are trying to get their emotional needs met from the child. This happens when they cannot get emotional needs met in relationships with adults. This scares the child so later in life, closeness feels frightening. A child cannot take care of an adult emotionally. Feeling responsible for the adult evokes a sense of powerlessness. Jack cannot take care of me emotionally. I must find my own centre and learn to accept that I am responsible for my feelings. I can share them and experience them but no one can make me feel anything. I feel a feeling when certain things happen. At the moment I am feeling hungry.

"When's dinner?" Matt asks. I suggest he take orders from his sisters and he can call for the pizza. "Cash or charge Mom?" He likes the responsibility and a chance to be in control. I give him my topping preference, as does his father and he runs off with pencil and paper to find his sisters.

I feel settled by the familiar parts of my life. The evening was planned for us to watch a video with Matt. The girls are out at events with their friends. I put a fire in the fireplace while Jack gets the drinks and popcorn. We enjoy a family evening together.

Finally the house is quiet. I settle alone at the dining room table with my journal.

"Strong, in control, denying adults, do not want to feel their pain, be seen as losing control with their feelings or embarrass themselves." The words stab at my heart as I read them from a page of my journal. I was about to pour my thoughts onto a new page, but my book fell open here.

Is this a time when breaking that coping strategy is necessary? Is Jack staying in emotional control as if ending our working relationship is an easy thing to do? Can I use my feelings constructively to get what I want? What do I want at this stage? Do I want to try to change Jack's mind about separating our offices?

I do not want to return to teaching. It has been nearly twenty years since I was a classroom teacher. I must find myself a new office. I'd love to work from home but this house is not a good layout for a private office. Perhaps we should look for a new house where I could work from home. I'll have to think about that.

I can feel myself shifting from reminiscing to looking forward. It is like the shift I made in Ireland, when I decided to rent the car. Suddenly possibilities appear and hope in a new future eases the former hurt and fear. I can decorate my new office in a softer way than what suited a man's legal office. I can play soft music and have more plants. It must be a place with good light and a pleasant view. I'd like to stay downtown as the parking is good and my clients are used to this location. It is easy to tell people how to get here and lots for them to do if they arrive early or want a place to go after their appointment. Lots of couples go out to lunch or dinner after seeing me. They also remark that they like the fact it is private. They can appear to be going into the bank, to visit a stockbroker or one of the other corporate offices. Confidentiality is very important to the type of clients I see. *I wonder if there is a space in the present building. Could I afford it on my own?*

Over the next weeks, I evaluate my options. Jack is not going to budge on the separation of our space and the lease expires at the end of January. I ask him where he is going. He is evasive and cold. The accounting files are now locked. I have no way of checking his expenses or his phone calls. *Has he put a deposit on alternate space?* If so, I wonder if the staff knows. He is tight lipped and avoids me at work. It is as if, suddenly, we are strangers. Working in the same office is tense. *What happened to the man I was with in Florida? What happened to the man who said he wanted to work on our marriage?*

I try to speak with Jack about what is happening between us. He stonewalls and avoids. He seems to keep himself busy at another part of the house, have errands to run and in general avoid me. He works long hours, often returning to the office in the evenings. Other times, he lugs huge briefcases full of files home, and works at the dining room table.

Following leads for office rental space is time consuming. I have an offer to share space with two psychiatrists. We have several meetings and visit offices together. Our expectations and tastes are quite different. I know I like to be independent. I'd hate to get in with someone and have the same dynamics develop that occurred on the trip to England that was my first Quest. I was pushed out of the best space and I let it happen. They also seem to feel I will be their office manager. *It is time for me to have the office I really want.*

Staying in the same building is really my first choice. I go to the management office and meet a new woman behind the desk. Dee introduces herself and we get chatting. She asks me what I want. I decide to be honest and explain my situation.

"I have been all over town and there is nothing that suits me as well as this building. Is there any chance...?"

"When do you need it?"

"My lease is up and I believe Jack is leaving at the end of January. I guess then."

"No he isn't. He just renewed the lease in his name. Oops! Perhaps I shouldn't have told you."

I am stunned. Dee sees my upset and immediately apologises. I assure her I am very thankful for the information. I ask her to keep my request confidential and she asks me not to tell about her slip. We agree to hold each other's confidences.

"Leave it with me. I'll see what I can do and get back to you."

So Jack is planning on staying in the same space. *Why then must I move out?*

My mind runs back over all the hurts and disappointments that are triggered by the recognition that I cannot trust the man to whom I am married. Embarrassment at having a property management office secretary tell me something so vital surges through me. *Who else knows?*

A discreet call from Dee, several days later, informs me that there is a possibility of some space on the fourth floor, on the south facing end of the hall. I am shocked. When she shows it to me, I am delighted that it faces Lakeshore and with the leaves off the trees, I can see Lake Ontario. I will walk right past the present office every day. I love the bright sunshine that is so different than the north facing present space. It is everything I want and more. I can hardly believe my luck.

Some fights are worth fighting. I tell Jack that I know he is staying in the building. I watch his face as I tell him I am as well. At first he thinks I am refusing to move out of what is to be his space and starts to protest. I know he is shocked when I tell him I am having a new office constructed on the front side of the building. I ask if he will insist that I move out when my lease is up at the end of January. Begrudgingly, he says I may stay where I am until the office is constructed and even though I know this will be tense, I am pleased. He insists that the paperwork ending our business relationship be completed before the end of the calendar year. We return to the routines of seeing clients, running a home and raising our family. Inside, I am devastated.

I share some of my misery and doubts with my sister Judy and I know it puts a strain on our relationship. Cottage weekends are not as easy as they once were. As I watch the interaction, I see that my stress is being seen as the cause of the problems between us as a group. They laugh and joke with Jack as if there is no part being played by him to cause my insecurities and increasing my responsibilities.

I plan my office and supervise the construction of walls. Jack carries on with his work with barely an interruption. He is in great spirits as he leaves for a week of skiing in Whistler. While he is away, I have quiet evenings to consider my position. I love the anticipation of independence, yet a part of me feels very isolated and alone.

I decide I want to use a computer rather than buy a typewriter and know the staff Jack uses are shocked at my choice. I hire a secretary and disengage my operations from Jack's. I leased the large new photocopier less than a year ago and since it is far too big for my needs, Jack will continue to use it and I will charge him for copies. I still have some involvement in and profit from his practice, until that lease runs out. I buy an answering machine and several new phones. Jack helps me choose them and pays more attention to their features than I do. Moving day is April first, April Fool's Day. Am *I being a fool taking on this responsibility?*

I choose a power pink for my working office and a soft purple grey for the consulting room. I invite Jack to see the progress. He hates the pink and tells me to change it. I defiantly tell him I do not want to change it. I chose it. I love it. *It is my office. I'll have it my way.*

As I make decisions for my new letterhead, with my new phone and suite number, I am reminded of a time just after I moved to Oakville, when I met a woman at a networking function. She told me she had a public relations firm and promised me she would make my name known to the people who would most likely refer clients. I paid her company a substantial retainer to create a logo that would go on my business cards and letterhead. I was excited to feel I had someone on my side as a part of a team to get my practice established. She seemed competent and confident. I was elated.

The process involved an initial interview where I talked about my work, my goals and what I wanted people to know about me. The second stage was to choose a design for letterhead, business cards and promotional pieces as well as approve a press release written by the company and sent by them to the local press. The third was them creating camera ready art. I would choose my paper, colour of ink and quantity to be printed with their guidance.

When I met for the scheduled assessment interview, I was disappointed that the young woman who came to my office seemed to be a teenager. She worked for the company, but I was suspicious that she was a student doing a job placement. I asked if she was going to do the work on my file and she said yes. She assured me it was going to be supervised by the woman I had met. Not wanting to be difficult, I answered her questions and told her my dreams for my company.

After several weeks, I called asking for news on my work and a meeting was arranged. The shock of seeing the product left me speechless. There were several design and colour variations of the same sharp edged logos of my initials turned sideways. There was a three D effect and some differences in shading but none gave an indication of the need to be seen as understanding, empathetic and anything to do with marriage and family work. There was nothing that looked like growth, change, or a sense of spirit. The press release had spelling mistakes that I saw immediately. I am a poor speller. It had a glaring grammatical error and a quote attributed to me that is something I would never say. I was shocked. *If this gets out my business will be dead before I really get it started in Oakville!*

I had pointed out the problems with the same young woman who presented the material. I was not happy with her response. She suggested I think it over and take some time to look at the options she had presented.

The first chance I got, I asked Jack to take a look at the proposal. I was shocked that he didn't see much of a problem with the work. I pointed out the spelling and grammatical errors and he was disinterested. I asked him if he wanted me to succeed and he said it really wasn't a priority as he made good money and he didn't believe I would ever make enough as a marriage counsellor to support even myself. He bluntly asked me what I expected of him. I said I didn't know, but I did know. I wanted enthusiastic involvement like I had given him for years and years as he developed his law practice. *What is the point of asking for something I know I will be refused?*

I called the woman I had originally met. I felt more alone than before I hired her firm. After leaving several messages, I finally was able to talk to her and explain my dissatisfaction. I was not pleased with her attitude or lack of interest. She said I had been given what I asked for and all that was left was camera ready artwork on the proofs I had been shown. I just needed to tell them which one I wanted. I didn't want any of them and they were all pretty much the same. She said there would be an additional design fee if I wanted more choices.

As I stewed over my dissatisfaction, I questioned myself about what I wanted right now from Jack. *Do I want to be rescued? Do I want him to agree with me and be upset? Do I want sympathy? Do I want him to make it better for me?*

I approached Jack. I asked him to give me some ideas of what to do. I did not feel the work was worth the money I had paid. I did not trust the company to do good work for me. I wanted my money back. I had lost several weeks of promotion time and wanted to move on with getting my business established. His reaction was noncommittal and basically he told me it was my problem.

By this time, I was feeling angry. I decided to seek help through two women I trusted. One was a financial consultant and another was a lawyer. Both agreed the work was horrid and not worth the money charged. One of them knew of someone else who had been dissatisfied with the work of this company. Both women advised me to get my expectations clear and ask for what I wanted. It was wonderful to have their support. My uncertainty that I was asking too much for the money I had advanced, was soon dispelled. I shouldn't have jumped at the first person who offered this service. I should have looked at some of the work they had done for other clients and assessed if I liked their styles. I should have read other press releases written by them. I should have spoken to more companies and made an informed choice. I didn't get a quality press release and I didn't really get different choices of logo, just variations of one unacceptable style. I wanted my money back!

In that situation, I did get my money back. I also learned a lot. I must ask for what I want or I am not likely to get it. I must research businesses I want to spend my money with, to see if they are capable of delivering what I want. In that case I went on to work with another firm and got a lovely little bush with roots and leaves that gave a definite message of growth. It had a butterfly that represents transformation. I am very happy with it and have had a lot of positive comments on it. So out of my dissatisfaction, I learned some very useful lessons and went on to get something I really like. The same process seems to be working with my office space.

I use the same general layout for my printing with the phone number and suite number changed. I choose a recycled paper with a hint of green and at the suggestion of the woman in the print shop, have a few more leaves added to my bush. She thinks it looks a little sparse. I agree. I see the new logo as a sign that I have grown larger and more mature.

The way we present ourselves to the outer world is a reflection of our inner sense of Self. Our clothes, our cars, and the way we speak and act, all give outward views to our inner self. We are not consciously aware of this presentation but it is the first impression we give to others. Making a first impression that is intentional and planned in areas where we want to make a specific statement requires thoughtful consideration.

CHAPTER TEN

SEASONS CHANGE AND SUNSHINE FOLLOWS RAIN

One Part of Life is Not Our Whole Life

Semester turnaround at the beginning of February gives both of my daughters a few days off. With all the stress in the family, I feel I want to spend some "girl time" with them, doing something fun. I book the three of us into a resort on a Bahamian out island for four days. They are not too sure travelling with Mom will be fun, but the beach beacons them away from the cold winter weather. There had been some talk of a ski trip but I want a rest more than an adventure and activity-filled holiday.

The roads are unplowed when we leave home, just after four in the morning. I am concerned about being late and wonder if our flight will be delayed. When we reach the county line, suddenly the pavement is just wet and the ploughs and salt trucks have been out ahead of us. I am relieved as I do not want to miss our charter flight.

By noon we are on the beach. As the girls head for the water, I settle in a chaise lounge. It feels so good to have time with no phones and no set agenda. I am hoping this shared time with my daughters will give us a chance to talk and relax. Things have been so tense lately. I let my mind wander back to Oakville. *Why am I doing this? You can worry at home Marilyn. Go have some fun!*

I swim out to meet my daughters on a sand bar and laugh as the waves nearly knock me down. I love the buoyancy of salt water. I float on my back and watch the clouds slide across the sky. In order to float comfortably, I must relax my muscles or else I sink. I work through the areas of my body, willing myself to let go of the tension in each muscle group. As I do so, I feel a deep sense of sorrow mingled with a great joy. The sweeping emotions unbalance me. I feel a shudder of release and reach down with my foot to the ocean floor below. I cannot touch it. I search the waves for my daughters and they are on shore manoeuvring beach tricycles into the water. They see me watching and wave. As I swim closer to them, they suggest I try one too. From the trouble they are having I am not convinced I'd like to try.

Back in my room relaxed and glowing, I am slightly sunburned from the day on the beach. I run a comb through my shower wet hair and apply my lipstick. I am excited for no apparent reason. My daughters are discussing who will have the next shower. I have no schedule, no destination except dinner somewhere in the next two hours. It is the time of day that I enjoy a glass of wine, a chance to watch the world go by, and the sun set. I gather my camera and room key.

"See you down by the dining room in about an hour."

"OK Mom."

The hibiscus flowering profusely in every direction and the birds singing and calling contribute to my joy. I think of the snow and cold I left behind as I walk toward the harbour.

I love water. After a full day on the beach with the rolling waves, the calmness of the sheltered harbour in the dying light of day is soothing. I feel joyously excited yet peaceful. This is exactly how I want my escape to be.

I wander down by the harbour master's house where boats register when entering port. Exploring along the docks, I admire the luxury yachts. The sky is turning pinks and orange. A few wisps of cloud decorate the sky. It is such a beautiful evening.

The freeform swimming pool reflects turquoise beside the thatched roofed Tipsy Seagull Bar. People are gathering for pre dinner drinks. The atmosphere is friendly. I walk around the groups and find a single stool. As I sip my wine, I watch the people around the bar. It is built in a circle with the bartender in the middle. There are couples, singles and a few groups. People smile and exchange greetings.

A couple of young men in swim suits with gold chains around their necks are teasing and joking in loud voices with objectionable vocabulary. They appear to have had a considerable amount to drink. I watch the bartender to see his reaction. Occasionally, he gives them a look and they quiet a little. One young man sees me watching them and introduces himself as Dave and his companion as Al, then asks my name. Part of me wants to say "leave me alone." I wish they would go away. I am glad my daughters are not here. I tell them my first name then I swivel on my stool and turn my back to them to discourage further conversation. The first lights come on in the gardens. Oh the short days of winter.

I hear a deep male voice send the young men off to get ready for dinner. He apologises to the group in general for their behaviour, chats with several people he obviously knows, gives me a smile and says hello, then follows after the rowdy fellows.

Throughout dinner there is a running banter between our table and the ones nearby. Everyone is in a holiday mood and happy to share their afternoon adventures. I enjoy my meal. My daughters are chatting with a group of young people at an adjoining table. I am feeling out of place and want to move. I remind myself I would rather they had fun than be stuck with a group of people my age and find little interest in our conversations. I excuse myself and return to our room. I consider reading my book but decide I'd rather be out and about. I can't remember what activity is planned for tonight.

I hear drums in the distance and recall there is a steel drum parade and festival tonight. I wander toward the sound and join a growing group of onlookers. Christmas lights are glowing from strands hooked between palm trees and there are some open fire torches. Drums made with stretched skins are leaning against a tree with Sterno cans lit under them. I ask a man standing nearby "why the heat" and get a mini education in drum construction and care.

A group of musicians are playing calypso music and some people are dancing. I hear a deep voice at my right, "Hello again. I'm John, remember me?" I am caught off guard and start to chat about the drums and the information I just learned. He appears interested and slightly amused. I look for ridicule but find only interest. With the suddenness of a train flying over a crossroads, Dave and Al appear. They are friendly and full of energy. Dave asks me to dance. I decline. I am ignored. The two of them pull me out onto the grassy space where others are dancing.

Since fighting them seems a lost cause, I decide to dance with them and the three of us turn and laugh and dance until that music ends. One of them insists he get me a drink but I am breathless and decline repeatedly. A rum punch is thrust into my hand by their dad, who I now know as John. They tell me he is really nice and trustworthy. I laugh and ask why they are telling me this. They say they want to meet some friends on the beach but don't want to leave dad alone. If he is with me, they feel free to go. I ask if he needs a babysitter. They say no. John says: "Yes, if it is you".

I am being seduced. I look about for my daughters but there is no sign of them. I cannot see any of the familiar faces from our group through the crowd. John suggests we stand back a bit because we were directly in front of a speaker and the music is very loud. We move back and stand under a tall palm tree watching the activity, not talking much. I feel excited. I ask if he got the drink from the bar table set up by the music and if he saw it poured. He laughs and asks why I am concerned. I explain that accepting a drink from a stranger isn't the wisest thing for me to do, especially since it is an open drink and not in a can or bottle that I can see opened.

He assures me he knows a lot of people here, comes here regularly, and trusts the drink is safe. I cautiously sip at the drink and try to relax.

After awhile of watching others dance, John asks me to dance. The music is fast and the crowd large so I accept. I like being who and where I am. This is fun. At the end of the music John asks if I want to stay dancing. I say no.

As I walk away from him a voice inside tells me to keep walking. I stop and turn to look for my girls. They are not out dancing. I return to the dining room area and I can see them sitting in the lounge. They are having a good time and plan to go out to the festival momentarily. They ask if I am having fun. I assure them it is an interesting evening. I leave them with their new friends and return to the group outside. A man I'd spoken to on the beach when he was helping Julia with her sailboat says hello. We chat for a while and I realize I am in the middle of a group of others from our flight. Everyone is friendly and talkative. Several have seen me dancing and comment on my energy. I do love to dance.

I decide to get myself a drink and stand in the line to get a ticket. I know the person in front of me from dinner conversations so we chat as we wait. He turns around as it is his turn. I hear John's voice in my ear. I am thrown off by his presence, his nearness. I have not seen him for awhile. He offers to buy me a drink. We argue for a moment but it isn't the time or place to get into a power struggle. I request a rum punch. I rarely drink rum but I didn't want beer and there is no white wine. Better to stick with it now anyway. Changing drinks is not a good idea. He pays for the tickets and gets our drinks. We walk back under the tree where we stood previously. I am being pursued and I am flattered. Standing with him so close beside me, attentive and smiling, stirs something deep inside me that is a lot more than just the effects of rum punch.

John asks me to dance again and I decline. I am fearful to put my drink down in case someone puts something in it. I am aware of my emotional vulnerability and dancing exposes me further. I suggest I look for my daughters. His sons are nowhere to be seen. We find the girls where I last saw them and his sons in the bar. I am relieved they are not together.

I suggest we walk. The moon is reflecting brightly on the water and the air is soft and warm. I feel myself following an inner guide and just letting it all be. We chat about boats, the distance to Florida, raising teenagers and being middle aged. Our laughter comes easily. It is a very long time since I have been in a situation like this. He knows almost nothing about me. I am not a therapist, an expert, or any other role I play. I am Me. There is a wall with a concrete bench and blossoming bushes falling over it. I sit between the branches and John sits a near distance away.

Time is standing still. We sit in silence, exchange a few words, and then silence again. He stretches his arms along the back of the concrete behind us and rests his fingers lightly on my shoulder. "You mind?" he asks. I respond by slowly moving closer to him and saying "You mind?"

Some level within each of us is responding to the other like magnets. He asks if I am married, I say yes. He asks if I am happy in my marriage, I say yes. He asks if the sex is good and I again say yes. "Then why are you here with me now?" he asks and I am lost for words. I try to explain that I hadn't intended to be, that I brought my daughters away and I don't really understand myself. I like company and I like men. I just feel like I am where I want to be. It has been so long since I felt attractive and desired.

When I ask why he is here he says he doesn't know. I ask about his marriage. He tells me she is gone. She left him for someone else. I do not want to get into his marital issues or mine. *Is sorrow our joining force? Do we somehow sense someone else's loneliness?*

I suggest we each just get up and walk away. He challenges me, asking why. I respond that I will walk away when I am ready. I also tell him I am content sitting with him. With that he gets up, walks a few paces away, turns and says I am different or difficult. I am not sure which and it really doesn't matter. I agree. He walks away.

I sit in this idyllic setting with my stimulated emotions and a desire not to have the evening end. Several people walk past, including a security guard, and we exchange quiet greetings. "Lovely evening" I feel safe and happy.

John reappears. I look up at him as he approaches. He walks up to a spot directly in front of me, places his hands on either side of my head on the concrete ledge behind, and leans over me. He looks into my eyes. I look into his. I feel no fear, only connection. Nothing is said for what appears to be a very long time.

Finally he moves and sits beside me. He confidently encircles me with his arms. I feel so accepted and lean against his shoulder. It is as if some dam inside my soul breaks. I start to sob, tears running down my cheeks. He asks "What is this?"

"I feel like I carry the world on my shoulders. Being here, being away, having you want to be with me, you holding me, I do not feel so alone. I suddenly feel I can just let go. I am sorry."

"I don't believe you are happily married. I won't ask any questions but I believe you are fooling yourself."

He gently wipes the tears from my cheeks and kisses my forehead. I feel the gentle pressure of his hand on my chin. "I want to kiss you."

His face comes toward mine. I twist to get away. He is too quick for me. I tell him he tastes like cigarettes. My resistances are low and my desires high, but I manage to turn. As I withdraw, he asks "Why?"

I stand up and turn away. He says "Wait! Don't go."

I know this struggle will escalate and my defences deteriorate. I have allowed myself to be too vulnerable. I do not want to go where this is leading. I walk away hearing his demanding tone say "Get back here!" I do not like to be ordered about. I feel a slight sense of fear. *Be careful Marilyn!*

I walk to the Tipsy Seagull and look at the group gathered there. There is no one I know. I see John approach on the opposite side. I don't want another drink. I don't want to sit distant from him with part of me wanting him closer, wanting to be held.

Trying to look in control of myself, my heart pounding, I turn around to him and ask if he will walk a bit with me. He follows me a short distance. We are out of the area where others can hear our normal voices, yet close enough that I could yell if he tries to grab me and to be seen, if anyone is watching. I turn and look fully into his eyes and thank him for being in my evening. He asks me to stay, to return, to... but I cut him off with a gentle kiss on his cheek and turn and walk away with more determination than I feel. I do not look back to be tempted.

Returning to my empty room, I am glad to be alone. *Is this just sexual passion?* It didn't feel like just a sexual turn on. I feel like something deep inside me has been stirred. It hasn't been touched for a long time. I felt so connected to him. *Was it just a pick up opportunity for him?*

The morning is bright and beautiful. I see John after breakfast, walking with determination toward the marina. He told me he was going to another island for several days. We exchange a brief greeting, a lingering look and he disappears from my life.

This chance encounter has opened a place in me that I have forgotten existed. I was relaxed and happy, open and vulnerable.

Was he an angel to show me I can be loved? Was he just a lustful man who tried to seize an opportunity? I do not care what it was for him, I feel as if he touched my spirit.

I return to my room and change to a swim suit. The girls have left a note that they are off to breakfast. I find them eating, then head for the beach. I have my paper and pen and plan to reflect and enter journal notes.

Sitting under an umbrella I am happily working away when a woman approaches asking if I am a writer. I'd love to say yes as it is my lifelong goal. I had asked the girls not to tell that I am a marriage and family therapist because people will want to tell me about their problems and ask advice. I am on holiday. Given it isn't a total lie, I am working on my first book, I tell her yes I am.

"Let me tell you about my life, I am sure you will find it interesting."

I assure her I have more than enough material for my present book. Fortunately, she wanders away.

A little boy runs to the water's edge with a plastic boat clutched firmly in his hand. His mother calls him back, signals his limits, and then securely fastens a life jacket around his little body. He heads into the waves to armpit depth. She turns to settle in a beach lounge, lotions her body, turns into the sun, her child ostensibly forgotten behind her.

The boy is lost in a fantasy of diving submarines and power jumps. His imaginative play seduces him through the gentle waves. The boat gets away, floats to deeper water and the seemingly fearless child swims out. He casts a wary eye toward Mom to see if reprimands are forthcoming. No notice from her.

The child pays little attention to his position. He plays at a depth just a toe touch from too deep, moving further and further down the long stretch of sun drenched beach. I keep an eye on him. He isn't ever in any real danger. The sprinkling of people sunbathing provide a ready assist should it be needed.

I can see the eyes of adults, long past the age of parental responsibility; follow the child with private unspoken thoughts. Whatever their concerns or judgments may be, they are silent.

Parental interest roused, mother calls as she strolls her lean tanned body down the beach. With real interest and attention, she hears tales of sea adventures, battles and narrow escapes as she guides his return to a spot near where they started.

The pattern repeats. It is not my responsibility. Time for a swim.

Three days of good food, lots of sun and time in the water and I feel like a totally different woman. We have walked the beach, danced at a festival, watched dolphins, chatted with new people and slept well. The girls have gone off on scooters, sailed in little boats and wandered through the few shops, while I explored the resort, swam in the pool, read, wrote notes for an article and watched people at the marina.

I listen to the voices of people chatting and calling from boats. Two women laugh and hug, meeting each other unexpectedly, neither knowing the other was going to be here. One is touring on a boat and the other was on our charter. It turns out they are sisters. I am most likely to meet my sister Joan somewhere unexpectedly. She travels a lot with her husband's work and for fun with friends. I don't often know about it if it is a last minute opportunity. She is back before I even know she is gone. She never lets the grass grow under her feet. I am so fortunate to have such a lively sister.

Our final day is windy and cool. The weather forecast says it will be like this for several days. We take our time packing and sharing stories. I feel much closer to my girls. They have asked some hard questions about what has been going on. I have done my best to make sense of it to them. I know the situation at home has caused them to have difficulty focusing on their school work. I am pleased to have provided this chance for relaxed fun.

Marital conflict causes emotional insecurity and pain to children exposed to it but it can also cause developmental disruption. Children in homes with marital insecurity can internalize the problem and it results in low self esteem, sadness, depression and withdrawal from social interactions. They may also externalize the problems with aggressive and anti social behaviour. Some children look for affirmation elsewhere and try to form attachments to extended family members, their peer group, teachers and sports coaches. Sometimes, this leads to victimization of the child while the parents are too distracted to notice.

Depending on what the marital dynamics are, children who witness poor physical and/or emotional control in their parents can fail to develop the capacity to regulate their own impulse controls. They may also have difficulty separating their own emotional issues from those of their parents. If the parents cannot care for their children and are having trouble caring for themselves, the children feel lost and abandoned, even though the parents may be physically present.

Emotional control does not mean a suppression of all emotion. It means not being overwhelmed by emotion to the point that the shift from the emotional state into the thinking and acting mode is not made. The ability to feel our feelings and use them to direct our actions and decision making is part of being authentic and whole. We want to be fully alive emotionally, physically, intellectually and spiritually. The ability to balance in these areas leads to a state of connection with our wholeness.

We behave differently when we are feeling fear rather than joy, although both might result in a loud vocal expression. Feelings of fear can lead to an outward expression of anger which is the fight response or a feeling of sadness, hurt and terror which can lead to the flight response. Too much emotional expression can lead to exhaustion and the individual may shut down on all levels, leading to a state of depression.

I know I keep myself active and involved for my own self esteem. I am responsible to take care of my Self and I want my daughters to learn ways to do the same for themselves. Through my many involvements, I gain respect and appreciation and a sense of confidence and self worth. It helps me from becoming overwhelmed by too much of one challenge. Having many involvements and types of relationships allows me to express myself in different ways. When I am with my children, I can easily ignore demands from other responsibilities unless I am specifically distracted or choose to focus on something else. A phone call is an example of this. Shifting our focus and attention is part of having healthy personal boundaries and prevents emotional and intellectual overload.

I want my daughters to feel confident and valued. I want them to find their own Holy Grail. I see my job as a parent as being a combination of protector, teacher, guide and role model. As much as I want to have a friendly relationship with my children, I know I am not their friend. This trip has been a great bonding time for us to share fun times together. I have not felt I had to parent them as they are really very self reliant and responsible.

Travel with our children gives them a chance to see us functioning and relaxing in new situations. It also allows time for discussions and pleasant pastimes. Waiting at airports, travelling between places and idle time on a beach or ski lift can be times to interact casually. It also provides parents a chance to see how our children deal with change, stress, meeting new people, making new choices and life in general.

Shared experiences create shared memories that can build bonds that last a lifetime.

CHAPTER ELEVEN

CREATING ILLUSIONS

People Want to Believe the Privileged

I am excited and happy to be joining the board of the United Way. I feel it is a privilege and am feeling honoured that I have been accepted. Volunteering has been a rewarding part of my life. My mother's many years of volunteer work set the expectations that to be involved in giving to our communities is part of having healthy and safe neighbourhoods. It is a way to meet people and share skills, as well as learn new ones.

I invite Jack to the meeting where I am officially accepted onto the board. We agree to meet for dinner as my clients run until six and the meeting is at seven. It will be pizza night for our children. They are happy with that.

I walk the few blocks west along Lakeshore to the restaurant we often frequent for lunch. I expect Jack to be there, as he had said he would go ahead and order two glasses of white wine. I have less than an hour to eat but the meeting is just across Navy Street in the library, so I should be fine. There are a few others eating when I arrive but no sign of Jack. I tell the waitress I am being joined by my husband. Five minutes pass then ten and I ask to use the phone. He isn't answering his cell phone and our children haven't heard from him. Not wanting to be late for my meeting, I order my dinner and wonder what has happened. He could have at least called the restaurant when he knew he was going to be late.

My dinner is served and the waitress asks if I want a second glass of wine. I decline. It doesn't matter if Jack is late for the meeting, but I do not want to be. I drink the wine I had ordered for Jack and finish my dinner. I have been alone in the restaurant for over forty-five minutes and my anxiety level is high. *Where is Jack? Is something seriously wrong?*

I descend the long stairs and see people I know chatting. The meeting is obviously not yet convened. I wave and smile and turn to move into the meeting room. Like a punch in the face out of nowhere, Jacks laughing face shocks me. He is chatting with Terry O'Connor, a colleague who is coming off the United Way board. He looks as if there is nothing amiss. I feel my face flush and my body tighten. *Hold on Marilyn, smile and breath. Do not make a scene. One two three......*

The executive director approaches me and shakes my hand welcoming me to the meeting. I am asked to sit near the front and as people are taking their seats, I know it will be too obvious if I ignore Jack. That is exactly what I want to do. *Where was he?*

I put my purse on a chair and move across the room saying hello to people I know. As I approach him he looks nervous, and then in a daring voice, asks me where I have been. I say hello to Terry then turn to Jack and tell him I was waiting for him in Café Galleria as we had arranged. I ask where he has been. He names another restaurant that we have never frequented. I know it was not where we had agreed to go. I feel unsteady. I keep my voice as even as possible and ask what he had to eat. I know he is playing to his colleague and something is amiss. He responds to my questioning by asking me if I have been drinking again. I turn from his mocking expression and know somehow this is very wrong. He knows we agreed to meet and that the first one to arrive would order the wine. We do it frequently.

I have no responsibilities at this meeting. It is a formal annual meeting and at many such events they even serve wine and cheese.

Is he trying to imply I am drunk and that I messed up a dinner date because I am confused?

The meeting goes smoothly and I proudly accept my position on the board. I am sorry I invited him to join me. I must not give him opportunities to discredit me.

Passive aggression combines the worst aspects of aggression and passivity. It can be used in an attempt to retaliate for a perceived wrong. It appears agreeable but is really controlling of others. *Is he trying to get back at me for something? Is he angry?*

Passive aggression comes from a sense of personal powerlessness to directly confront problems. It keeps the passive aggressor powerless because it is usually ineffective. The desired outcome cannot be achieved. There is no honest expression of thoughts and feelings. There is no sense of relief as feelings have not been heard and acknowledged. It does not solve problems. He is being passively aggressive toward me and I don't know why.

I have used passive aggression when I would avoid talking and interacting with my husband hoping he would ask me what was wrong. I felt powerless to ask for what I wanted and hoped he'd care enough to ask. Instead he would appear to act as if I was just in a mood and would eventually come out of it. So now I have a choice to act passive, blow aggressively or act assertively.

Sometimes, when I am hurt or angry because my expectations are not met, he will listen carefully. He accepts some responsibility for not living up to what I thought was our bargain, and he admits he let me down. Other times he attacks me and says I hadn't explained myself clearly. He claims he had never agreed to that and I was mistaken. When I asked if he agreed with me sometimes just to get me to go away and stop being so demanding, he agreed that he did. I was left thinking we had made a deal and he was not even really paying attention.

Sometimes, when the problems were really large and unavoidable—like the times our children were hurt or a parent dying—we could get to a place where we both could admit we were scared, sad and fearful, and I felt I really had a partner. He was my best friend and support. We worked through some pretty trying times together.

While an aggressive blow-up can induce a sense of power at the time, because the feelings are expressed, if the other person does not acknowledge the message and denies it by saying things like: "You are just upset. I am not going to listen to you when you yell" it leaves the aggressor powerless.

Some people feel better after a blow-out. They feel strong, controlling and proud that they have been able to bend people to their will. They use blow-ups as a tool to get their wants and needs met. They think having power over others makes them powerful. They confuse fear with respect. Their anger is cleared and they are often unaware that the effect of their outburst lasts a long time in the heart and mind of the other.

People who are subject to regular rages learn to shut down and tune out the loud messages. This can infuriate the one trying to give the message and lead to another blow-out or withdrawal. It never leads to intimacy.

Some people use angry aggression to purposefully block intimacy. They fear of too much closeness.This prevents them from being open to others. This can be a fear of criticism. They may fear they are not really good enough so they hide their true Self .

So here I am, filled with fear and confusion. I mingle with the group and make my way to the door. Since we have two cars, I am not dependent on Jack to get home. Without further contact with him, I leave and walk out with a group of others. I presume most people there would not even know he was my husband. However, I do believe that if it was a choice between believing me or the two men who seemed to share some silly secret to discredit me, I believe most people would want to believe them. People tend to want to believe that politicians, lawyers and other people in positions of power and responsibility are honest and honourable.

As I walk back to my office, Jack passes me in his car. I have pulled deep inside myself. I must cut my emotional connection to this man. I must stop caring what he thinks of me. I must separate myself from him. He is my husband. I will not fight with him tonight. *How can I do this and stay married? Do I want to stay married to this man?*

I am often intuitive. I have a sense of something about to happen and feel things that turn out to be true. Being intuitive means we know things based on our intellectual capacity. We use logic, experience and learning to arrive at certain conclusions based on the facts we have before us. It happens automatically in our brain. When I am emotionally upset it is hard to be intuitive. My churning emotions distract from my sensitivity. I need to be sensitive to be good at my work, to bring out my creativity and to be intimate with others. I had no intuitive warning about tonight's charade. I must protect my Self. This is no way to live.

There are fights worth fighting and some that it is best to just let die. Knowing the difference is a skill worth acquiring. If the fight will lead to new understanding, a solution to a problem or the recognition that change is necessary, then the fight can be constructive. It must, however, stay focused on solving the problem. It must also be done when there is a clear idea of what the problem is and what outcome is desired.

If the fight is about attacking someone's character, proving who is right or to gain control over another, it is a fight that is best left alone. The need to be right, in control of another or seen as better than the other requires energy that would be better spent elsewhere than on fighting. Name calling never solves problems. Bullying can never lead to an open loving relationship.

Fights that are avoided can turn into grudges and in extreme cases into feuds that last for generations. People who carry grudges sometimes forget what started the differences in opinion. This can make it very difficult to resolve the issues as the source of the conflict can not be reconstructed. When people carry grudges and hold onto their anger it can cause them emotional and physical damage. It takes energy to hold the anger.

Some grudges and feuds become a central part of a person's or group's life. Giving up the time and energy to maintain a grudge causes fear about what will hold the group together if they are not united in anger. Some religions promote fear and hatred to maintain their control over people. When conflict is unresolved and more anger is created it can lead to violence and war.

Fear and love cannot live together. Fear closes us to other people and isolates us. Love opens us to others and to new experiences.

Peace is possible when we conquer our fears.

CHAPTER TWELVE

TENSIONS EXPLODE

When We Fail to Choose Life Gives Us a Push

As the days turn into weeks, I try to keep a positive outlook. My work is progressing well and my client load has increased. My office atmosphere is calm without the urgency of the law office. I love seeing the first ships on Lake Ontario and I enjoy watching people below on the sidewalk. I can make decisions about my work that do not need to take anyone else's needs into account. At times I feel selfish, but it is the delicious selfishness of taking care of my Self.

The leaves appear on the trees and I watch as the various blossoms come and go in the gardens below. It is harder to see the lake through the summer foliage but the sparkle of the morning sun or the glimpse of a sailboat between the trees reminds me I have a special spot for my office. I am so glad I did not move from the downtown as Oakville has so many lovely shops and restaurants. I enjoy walks at noon and eating a sandwich by the lake. Jack joins me when he can and we dream of a home right on the water. I know it would have to be in the future as I have just signed a three year lease. I'd love to work from home though.

I quietly slip from my warm covers, grab yesterday's clothes from the chair and creep out of the bedroom. The surface of the bay is calm. A clear reflection of the far shore sits motionless. The pines are a deep green and the maples have tinges of red and orange showing promise of greater splendour as summer slides into fall. I love cottage mornings.

I use the bathroom, change into my jeans and a sweatshirt, hang my PJ's on the hook on the bathroom door and head for the kitchen. As I quietly fill the coffee maker, the horrid memory of the vicious argument sweeps back into my mind. *Why were Jack and Judy so angry with me last night? Why do they think I want to sell this refuge? Why did my husband just sit there without saying a word? Why would he not defend me or at least try to calm my sister down? What was the point of saying I have no friends? Why did they keep saying they know I was planning to sell the cottage behind their back?* I do not want to sell. I love this place. It is even better with the new carpet that we just put in.

I can feel the tension all through my body. A part of me wants to run away. Stress is high and the flight response to danger acute. I feel afraid of what the day will bring.

Just as the delicious smell of fresh brewing coffee fills the air, my nephew quietly comes into the room and with tousled hair and a large yawn asks: "Are you really going to sell the cottage?"

"I am definitely not going to sell the cottage!" I tell him with shaky assurance. I explain that sometimes adults have differences of opinion just as kids do and that we will work it out. He says "Oh good. I'm going to tell Matt." and runs quietly back to his bedroom. I feel sad for what our children heard.

"We cannot stand the craziness with you!" *What did that mean? Why am I the one responsible?*

The words echo in my ears and I want to scream; "You have always treated me like I was dumb—like you were smarter and more capable. You talk down to me and try to insinuate I do not know what I am doing. You snicker and draw out your words with an emphasis that drives me to distraction. Can't you talk like an adult to an adult with me?"

There is this insidious polarization in my family of origin between the dumb ones and the smart ones. The smart ones fight with each other trying to prove who is smarter and the so called dumb ones get verbally abused, yet keep coming back for more abuse, in the hope that someday they can be peacemakers. The smart ones try to tell the dumb ones what they are thinking, how they are feeling and what they should do. Often it isn't even in the words, but in the tone of voice and insinuations.

As one of the dumb ones, I worked very hard to get my degrees. I hoped that someday I might be accepted by my family as intelligent. I loved the learning but somewhere I felt I needed more education to be taken seriously. I had always wanted my mother's love and approval for being smart. She was proud when I taught school but it wasn't like her praise of Bill. She was always so proud of my older brother's achievements. I was in the shadow academically. I got recognition from her by helping with domestic chores. I knitted, sewed, cooked and kept a clean and tidy house. She died before I could show her I was a university graduate of the very campus of the University of Toronto that she had worked so hard to have located in Mississauga.

My dad was dead before I graduated. He saw my education as a waste of time and money. I got approval from him by helping with lawn and garden chores, being his assistant in repairs, and by handing a hammer or running for something he needed from the basement or garage. I was like a son when my brother was busy with school work and reading. I learned a lot about fixing things. To this day, I love visiting hardware stores and knowing how things work. *What do I have to do to feel I am good enough? Why do I bother wanting their approval? If at this point Judy thinks I am the problem, there is nothing I can do to change her mind.*

As I sip my coffee, I feel scalding tears flowing down my cheeks. I do not want to fight and I do not want to sell the cottage. I recall the joys and fun we have shared here and feel like I am in the middle of a bad dream. *Who ever planted the idea that I wanted to sell? Why will they not listen to me and why do they keep telling me that I want something I do not want?*

I can hear the boys playing in their bedroom and know that the bond they have will be hard for them to break, if in fact this is the end. The girls must still be asleep. The door to their room is closed. Something deep inside me feels like lead. My heart is heavy with sadness. *How have we ever come to this?*

I quietly pull my jacket from the closet and head out the door. My family is busy with their own interests and I feel agitated and confined. I have cried and pleaded to find a way to change the course of events but my desires fall on deaf ears. I have tried to talk to my sister but she will not speak with me on the phone or meet with me. Jack acts as if the sale of the cottage is inevitable. He does not want to support buying it from Judy. I am confused and surprised. Our children are upset and miss their cousins on the weekends. What a mess!

Once I accept the sale is going to proceed in spite of my wants, I speak with my friends Steve and Wendy about getting a fair asking price. He is an appraiser and she is in real estate sales. They suggested Mark Gidley, a long time resident and agent in Bala. "It is best to get someone who knows the area well, someone local." If it has to sell I want the best price.

Walking out the drive, I am sad to see the For Sale sign on the large pine tree just over our name sign. I had told neighbours it was going up for sale so they wouldn't be surprised. I suggested they refer anyone who they think might be interested. Apparently, Judy had planned to buy me out of my share and had a real estate appraisal during the summer. They thought I knew and was part of the plan. I was shocked. Judy had seemed distant and angry. I never thought she would go behind my back. We used to be so close. I trusted her so very much. *Why has she betrayed me?*

I climb through the woods behind the cottage to a high promontory of granite from which I can see into the larger expanse of Lake Muskoka. Sitting on the hard rock, warmed by the morning sunshine, I watch a chipmunk scamper among the fallen leaves and mossy bedrock. The bright colours on the trees shine orange, yellow and red against the clear blue sky. I hear a blue jay call from across the bay and the words from a poem I had to memorize in high school run through my mind. I have grown to love these words and reciting them calms me.

INDIAN SUMMER

Along the line of smoky hills
The crimson forest stands,
And all the day the blue-jay calls
Throughout the autumn lands.

Now by the brook the maple leans
With all its glory spread,
And all the sumacs on the hill
Have turned their green to red.

Now by great marshes wrapt in mist
Or past some river's mouth,
Throughout the long, still autumn day
Wild birds are flying south.

William Wilfred Campbell (1858 - 1918)

CHAPTER THIRTEEN

A BIGGER PLAN IN THE SCOPE OF THE UNIVERSE

There Are Things We Do Not Know

Thanksgiving 1987

I am sitting on a folding chair, behind a card table, at a psychic fair. The woman is young, kind and glances repeatedly into my eyes as she shuffles the cards. I was going out to shop and run a few errands when I heard the notice of this event on the radio. I followed my instinct and here I am. *What drew me here?*

She asks me to cut the Tarot deck into three piles. She then picks them up and turns them over so they are face up. She then lays them methodically on the table. She pokes the record button on the tape player and starts to talk.

"You are grieving. It is very deep and strong. Who isn't coming to Thanksgiving dinner?" she asks with concern.

"I'm not coming to dinner."

I try to hold back the tears that have sprung to my eyes. I must hold my self control. Unnoticed in the crowded, noisy mass of people, I wonder if her question is just a lucky guess. It hit a sensitive spot. Physical pain shoots through my chest.

She very accurately describes that I have had a place of rejuvena tion; a place where I heal that is obviously the cottage. She says the energy is good there for me. *Oh how right she is!*

She warns me of lies and deceit. People I trust are plotting against me. Apparently they think they are winning, but in the end they will lose more than they gain.

"You will have another place that will become even more of a refuge and where you will heal great hurts that are yet to come." Her head shakes slowly back and forth and her eyes avert mine as she solemnly looks at the cards spread before her.

She tells me she sees many troubled people around me. I tell her I am a therapist. She ponders that and then tells me that it is good as there are so many.

"You remember things, conversations, places and events. You keep records and like to have things make sense. You appear hard and confident on the outside but you have some very soft and gentle spots. You must protect yourself!" Her words are firm and she looks right into my eyes. The words strike me as true. I feel vulnerable.

"You are a communicator. You put a lot of effort into trying to make other people understand what you are trying to convey. Because you see the potential in others you sometimes get into conflicts when they do not want to reach for the opportunities you see they are capable of achieving." I guess this could be what is meant when people tell me I am pushing them. I set high standards for myself and others.

"Your marital relationship has had some trauma for you. It may not be the relationship you think it is. Your vision of it may be better than the reality. You need to watch carefully. You like to do puzzles so gather your facts and put the pieces together. You want balance and fairness but you will have many more struggles before you get to the quality of life you seek."

Pondering her words, as I return to Oakville, I am struck by her ability to walk right in to my mind and open my thoughts. She asked very few questions but when she asked if I wanted to hear all that she saw, I told her I did. I believe knowledge is a powerful tool and I can choose if I want to believe her and choose what faith I put in her predictions.

She sees more struggles and challenges. She sees this cottage gone but another one, even better, in my future. I wonder if that will really happen. The proof will be in looking back later. I feel supported by her words. My intuitive sense that there is a plan here with someone plotting against me has been validated. *Did she get all this from reading my mind?*

Psychic ability is the ability to see from a different perspective than our normal viewpoint. There is a realm of knowing beyond our physical state. This unlimited universal energy can be tapped into by those who are born with the ability, or who make the effort to tune themselves to its subtle vibrations. It is a way to see the past and present and to anticipate and see the future. Psychics are able to be aware of things most people would not usually notice.

Clairvoyance is the gift of seeing visions, images, or pictures. Some psychics use Tarot cards, tea leaves, a crystal ball, photographs, personal objects, work with an Ouija Board, read palms, do automatic writing, or go into trance to get the vibrations of their subject. Sometimes, what the psychic sees doesn't make sense to them, but will to the subject of the reading. Some pictures are of the past and lead up to the present and into the future. Being open to ideas and discussing possible meanings can make a reading more accurate. Being closed and overly sceptical can block vibrations and the reading.

Clairaudience is the ability to hear messages. Sometimes it is a clear voice but when people turn toward the source of the voice they see nothing. It can also be thoughts that come into our head from a spirit guide, angel, or our deceased loved one. Mental telepathy is also a form of clairaudience.

Clairsentience is the psychic ability where a person gets their information through smells and feelings in their own bodies in areas where their clients have a physical ailment.

The Gift of Prophesy is referred to in The Bible, first Corinthians 12. Jesus and the other prophets received their visions and messages through clairvoyance and clairaudience. And Jesus told us that we have these abilities as well. "These gifts I give unto you and greater works shall you do."

CHAPTER FOURTEEN

A LOSS THAT FREEZES TEARS

Saying Goodbye and Passing the Key

T he cottage sold quickly. The results of Mark's price comparison to other properties with similar amenities put it out of Judy's financial reach. We all lost. Judy and I have lost our relationship, our children have lost the fun family times and opportunities to see each other as cousins and no amount of money can ever replace those good times.

The purchasers want a December closing so they can be there for winter sports. I travel north with Julia to give them a tour of the plumbing and electrical systems and to gather the last of our personal belongings. It is a bright cold December day. The cottage was sold furnished and our clothing and personal effects were removed on the last family visit. Judy removed what she and her family wanted. There was no discussion about who took what. There is now little left to decide. I wander from room to room, choosing a few last bits that I want to take. I choose a serving bowl that was my mother's, surprised it is still here. Everything has memories. I dread the task at hand. What a beautiful day. I'd rather be outside going for a walk.

I cast my gaze at the sofa. I bought it from my parent's friends when I was twenty and setting up my first apartment. I recall the decision to have it recovered, not once but twice, over the thirteen years of marriage. It was well made and very comfortable. It stays.

The video recorder that we brought in on a toboggan for weekend movies before we paid to have the road ploughed stays. The cute animal pictures I bought when I was on the board of the Canadian Mental Health Association that were sold as a fundraiser will be left. I turn to more and more memories. The comfy chair by the fire—so many books read there. The bed I shared with Jack. There were happy times. The picnic table on the deck and the barbecue stay. Each evokes times of laughter and fun. It must all be left behind.

There is a trailer in the garage with a few things we had excluded but have no place to store. We are looking for a new cottage. The purchasers said we could leave them there for the winter. *I wonder what will become of them. Are we really going to get another cottage?*

It is fun to see the excitement in the new owners. I show them how the pump switches work and explain what heat we leave on so we have the use of the bathroom all winter. I caution them about the possibility of mice and tell them to watch for the beaver in the spring. It will get the young trees. They appreciate our tour and all the information I am leaving in my notes.

Sadly, Julia and I go from room to room, saying thanks and goodbye, then turn the heat back and lock the doors. We walk to the deck, high over the black frigid water and stand in silent melancholy. A Blue Jay scolds from the oak tree but now the branches are bare. I wonder if the new owners will put out birdseed. There is snow gently falling and the early winter sunset streaks in a narrow band across the western sky. We will not see this sight or hear the sounds from this place ever again. We hug and cry softly. With heavy hearts we quietly turn to make the long trip home.

Grieving is a process that can be worked through by facing the loss and acknowledging the sadness. By walking through a home and seeing it for the last time, acknowledging we had good times there, saying thank you and goodbye, we accept the loss more easily than if we turn away without a last look.

CHAPTER FIFTEEN

MAKING DREAMS COME TRUE

Working Together

I didn't want the house we live in. When we decided to move from Georgetown, I wanted a house where someday I could see clients from home. I wanted to be able to work and keep an eye on my growing family. Teenagers need supervision. I really wanted to be home after school when they came in with their friends. I also wanted to have a family home that my children could return to with their children some day. I wanted stability and security.

I found a house that was perfect from my viewpoint. It was close to the schools so no bus rides were needed, had easy directions to get to it, a long drive with good parking, spacious bright bedrooms, a lovely kitchen and a wonderful sunroom. It also had a basement with windows above ground, with a side entrance to a room I'd love to work in. A two piece washroom was close by and our living areas were private. It was also considerably less expensive than this house.

Jack insisted on the more expensive home. I argued that the proceeds from the Church Street property I'd bought for his office in Georgetown should be considered my inheritance. I wanted to keep that money separate. He was determined to have all our money in one investment, our home. His arguments were persuasive and I gave in.

I wonder if Jack is threatened by money that I have that he cannot control. I try to make our relationship one where we share all that we have acquired as a couple. This is not just about money but about the use of vehicles, our home, and our relationships with friends and family. I also believe we both have equal rights to follow our dreams, develop our careers, and spend time with friends and family. I do not feel money from an inheritance falls into the same category.

He has always been open to discussing women's equality for opportunities. He appears sensitive to the limits put on women in many areas of society. Yet somehow, when an issue of women's rights is brought up with our friends, he acts more chauvinistic than I expect. The men joke and call me a libber, and insinuate I must be a challenge as a wife. Someone actually asked him once why he didn't put me in my place. I retorted by asking what he thought my place was. His reply was both insulting and sexually degrading. Some of the others laughed. It wasn't funny to me. Jack said it was just a joke. I wasn't laughing.

So many men see women only as mothers, sisters, wives, secretaries and in roles supportive to men. Conversations often turn to women in the workforce as stealing men's jobs, especially in the professions.

There is also the problem with women who do not see themselves as worthy of being treated with respect by men. They see themselves as only worthy of supporting men and not of being their colleagues. I have been asked if I hate men. I am not by nature a hateful woman and such a sweeping statement seems silly. I am accused of being against the family. I try to explain that to me feminism is really personism—where every person has the right to be taken seriously, to be respected, to be financially responsible, to make decisions about their own welfare and that of those for whom they are responsible and to set their own goals. A well functioning family is one where every member has a chance to reach their own potential and not live their life just to please others.

The feeling of being protected by being passive is a false sense of security. Only if the protector is kind and patient, responsible and caring, is that role safe. It may seem like a path to marital bliss, but too often it is a set up for abuse, manipulation, rejection, and living with a sense of powerlessness. If we all have power over ourselves, and are held accountable for our words and actions, like responsible adults, I believe there would be a lot more peace and happiness.

A well designed kitchen is a dream and a poorly designed kitchen is a constant source of frustration. A dishwasher should not open into the refrigerator. Because ours does, putting away leftovers is impossible while the dishwasher is open. I'd thought of moving the fridge over, but when I tried, I saw that the vinyl flooring was missing right under it. Since the sink and dishwasher are in an island, moving the dishwasher is not an easy task. Also, the right side of the sink has one inch of counter before the end of the island. I had made dinner preparation a family event with someone setting the table, while another makes a salad or mashes potatoes. The sink was across from the stove so two people could not move easily in the confined space. I also hated the pass through window from the kitchen to the family room. While it would have allowed me to watch our children more easily when they were little, it just meant the noise from each room carried into the other in a distracting way.

Jack asks me what feature of our house I think a purchaser would have the greatest objection to. He says he wants to get a good price, if we are selling. I am surprised by his question but have no hesitation in saying the kitchen is the worst part of the house. He suggests we look into renovating the kitchen. That will create a big mess!

Since we don't have cottage expenses, and I have the income from the mortgage on the old cottage, he says it will be a good investment. We hire Basil Markow Kitchen Designs and before I can really get myself adjusted to the idea, we are having a new kitchen personally designed to our wants.

I want a greenhouse window so I can put plants in it. Jack wants an indoor barbecue. We both want a larder with roll out shelves and lots of space for tins and boxes. We are faced with choices for so many things; I wonder how anyone builds a custom designed house. We are presented with several plans and we pour over options. We are excited when we are able to make one of the plans final. We each initial the large pages showing several viewpoints. The construction date is set. *This is so exciting! This is so expensive!*

We buy all new appliances at Tasco Appliances in Toronto. Basil sends us there to look. I have never seen so many elaborate and impressive stoves, fridges, barbecues and more. There is a whole new world of kitchen options. I didn't know things like this existed. A trip to Country Tiles on Davenport is at first overwhelming—so many choices. We soon agree on a mural of hanging grapes for over the barbecue and stove, an assortment of fruits and vegetables to be interspersed with white tiles for the backsplash, and a border to go along the section where the counter meets the wall. I am told the square edge is European style. *I love it.*

The old kitchen is removed with most of it installed in the basement play room. It gives us a wall of cupboards and a sink for school projects, crafts and extra storage. The fridge will go there too. This will make a great place for our children to entertain their friends and store their drinks and snacks. We eat out a lot and watch the design take shape. Decisions on many small details are still needed. I have no idea how people go away when renovations are done. I love to watch every step of the process.

Each evening we tour the work and marvel at the advancement. Our children have good suggestions as we pretend we are using it to prepare a meal. An extra plug is added and a light switch moved. Basil assures us it must be the way we want it so we are happy and not just the way the designer drew the plan.

One day Basil says he has an urgent need for a meeting. It turns out that the house was built with no support right under where we are planning to put a side by side fridge and freezer. He shows us how the floor is already sloping. He calls in Don Kerr, an architect. I know Don from speaking at one of his Rotary Club meetings. The verdict: We need to dig a four foot by four foot by four foot hole right through the basement floor. It will be the base for a steel support post. I am horrified. It must be done. It slows the upstairs work. I am afraid of the mess.

A good construction crew is a delight. It could have been so horrid. The dirt is carried out in buckets and the men clean up after themselves. I am amazed at their professional work.

Finally, the kitchen is complete and it is truly a dream. The two corner sinks allow for easy group participation. The washable flooring goes right to the entrance hall ceramics, so the worn carpet is gone. Pickles has trouble with the slippery surface but soon learns how to navigate on it. Everyone is delighted.

I am looking forward to some new dishes and kitchen linens to match the bright colours. We will also need a new round kitchen table as the rectangular one does not fit.

People say to be careful what we wish for because our dreams can come true. This is much better than any dream I ever had. I am so pleased it has come true.

There is a part of me that worries about so much money being put into this house. I have been reassured that a kitchen renovation is an investment that will pay off on sale. I have no desire to move now.

Jack has really settled down in the months since the office separation and I think in hindsight, separating our working space has been a positive experience for our relationship. He moved his desk into the larger office I had been in, and uses his old office as a research room. Breaking the co-dependency has really allowed each of us to have greater autonomy.

I was surprised when he hired a friend of my sister Judy's to consult on decorating and the purchase of some new pictures for his walls. It was completed before I knew it was happening. *Why was*

Judy involved? Why had he kept it a secret? It was a relief to me not to feel responsible for his space.

Our marital relationship had also improved. In spite of the upheaval of the renovations, my husband is being thoughtful, humorous and seems more involved in family activities. It is silly of me to worry over the colour of paint on the kitchen walls and the shape of the door handles. It is called compromise.

We sign the final papers on the kitchen and pay the last instalment. *I love it!*

A partnership marriage is one where both parties accept responsibilities in various areas of responsibility. If one person is responsible for the laundry, then they should have a louder voice in the equipment and supplies used to complete their task. When both people share responsibility for an area or task, they need to compromise on the organization of the equipment and supplies. Negotiating skills can be learned.

CHAPTER SIXTEEN

OUT OF CONTROL

A Time to Wait – A Time to Act

June 1988

It is a lovely spring Friday evening. My thoughts turn to Muskoka. I'd love to be going north to continue our search for a new cottage. I do hope we can get one we can use this year. Mark, our real estate agent has said there is nothing new on the market to show us so there is no reason to make a trip north. We have been looking at cottages, cottage lots and been considering building our own new cottage. We have spoken with builders and visited some of the cottages they are building. We have talked about ideal size, location, frontage and distance from home.

We saw a beautiful wooded lot on Lake Rosseau but the frontage was very steep. The granite of the Canadian Shield dropped off to very deep water and would be a real danger to small children. We will have grandchildren one day, I hope.

Another place with low frontage and easy water access was for sale with the cottage built to the stage of the electrician and plumber being next. It will be ready for this summer. It faced north and would not get much lakefront sun. There was a long dock out to a deck and the shallow water was weedy. It was the last on the list Mark had to show us. We had stayed and sat in the April afternoon sun, exploring our options from the properties we have seen. Jack is very particular about which direction we face and I am determined not to have a long cottage road that would prohibit winter access. I love all the seasons in Muskoka. I also do not want a long twisty road after a long highway drive. I like to be at the cottage alone and I want to feel comfortable that it is not too isolated.

I comfort myself with the thought of missing the mosquitoes and black flies that are sure to be swarming. They love me and I always get well bitten in the spring. Instinctively, I scratch behind my ear in memory of the many bites I've had. Funny how a memory—just a thought running through the mind—can bring a physical response. I think of something happy and I smile, or the thought of the pain of a loss can evoke tears, or perhaps the thought of food gets my mouth watering. *What's planned for dinner?*

I poke through the fridge and freezer and assemble a meal in my mind. Our children all have plans to be out, so I relax as there is no rush. I expect Jack soon and consider perhaps a bike ride or a walk. We sometimes go out for ice cream after dinner. I smile as I contemplate a relaxing evening. It has been a busy week with clients, presentations and meetings. Jack arrives as I am changing out of my business clothes into casual clothes. When I descend he is pouring two glasses of chilled white wine.

I detect nervousness in his manner. He avoids a hug and eye contact. *What now?* I hope he isn't going to start something that ruins the evening.

"Where do you want to sit?" he asks as he offers me a glass.

As we settle into the living room, I feel a tension I do not like. I sip my wine and wait. He is sitting forward in his chair not looking at all relaxed.

"I need some space."

"What kind of space?"

"This is difficult for me, but it is something I must do if I am to retain my sanity. I cannot live like this any longer."

"Live like what? What is wrong with the way you live?"

"I am not going to get into a long discussion about this, Marilyn. Do not try to start something. I have put an offer in on a town house. I will know by eleven o'clock tomorrow morning if they accept my offer, but I am pretty certain they will." He drains his glass and asks if I want more but I have only just started mine. I sit in stunned silence.

I hear him refilling his glass in the kitchen. He returns looking frightened. *Remain calm, breath and count.* I focus on the liquid in my glass. I feel the rough points of crystal of the stem between my fingers.

"How long have you been looking?"

"Not long. I found what I wanted very quickly."

"What did you find?"

Jack describes a four level townhouse in a small wooded area just north of the Queen Elizabeth Highway off Trafalgar Road. I am not familiar with the spot. He seems like an excited child as he tells me it even has a roof deck with a hot tub. *This is bizarre!*

"And what are you doing for money?"

As he explains his plan, I realize that part of the money that I thought was going to go toward the new cottage I believed we were buying has been allocated by him to this new place. There will be no cottage. He thinks our children will stay with him every other weekend. He is ending our marriage. Tears flow down my cheeks and suddenly I have no energy. It is as if somehow all my hopes and all my dreams of our future are melting. I am melting. In my minds eye, I can see just a big wet spot on the couch and part of the carpet where a human woman once existed. It will dry. I will be forgotten, unless, of course, I leave a water mark that someone notices once in awhile and asks: "What is that?" *Will anyone even remember the story of my life? Will anyone care?*

After a silence that seems like it lasts eternities, I hear his soft voice as if coming through a fog. "I thought you would scream and yell and try to make me change my mind. Say something Marilyn."

"I cannot change your mind. Only you can change your mind. I cannot control you and I cannot make you love me or want to live with me and share a life ... we ... have created ... together..." The sobs start from somewhere very deep. I gasp for breath. My body shudders and Jack gently takes the wine glass from my hands.

"Please Marilyn, don't do this. This is very hard for me. Please stop crying." He hands me tissues from a box he gets from the kitchen. Gradually I exhaust myself. Thank God my children are not here. *Did he plan that?*

I retrieve my eye glasses from my lap, wipe them and put them back on my face. I look directly at my husband and sit quietly until he returns my gaze.

"If this is so hard for you, why are you doing it?"

"I care about you Marilyn, whether you believe me or not. I am just not in love with you. I want a new chance at life."

The clichés come streaming from his mouth sounding like some script that every cheating client I have ever had got from the same book. Or is it the endless movies about liars and adulterers that feed these lines.

"Please give me the respect to tell me the truth. Are you seeing Beth?"

"This isn't about Beth or any one else, it is about how I feel in this marriage. I want out. I cannot stand to live like this any more."

"What is wrong with the way we live?"

"It isn't fun, I work too hard and there are always hassles and conflicts."

"What do you expect in a home with three teenagers and two careers?"

"I want peace and stability. I want to know what's going on in my life, not all this coming and going, never knowing who is here and who is out and when they will be back. I never know when you are out at a meeting or off to a conference. I want to be with someone who stays home in the evenings and I can count on to be with me or I'd rather be on my own."

"You could get a personal calendar or look at the one in the kitchen to know the girls work shifts. I agree they do change rather erratically. You could get some outside interests...." I can tell by the look on his face I am taking the wrong approach. I am trying to convince him that if only he would change and fit into the changing pattern of our family life, he wouldn't feel so abandoned when the rest of us are involved elsewhere. We have discussed his feelings of having missed so much of our children's earlier years with long hours of work. Now that he has the freedom to take more time to be home, they are not little children anymore. The years of us needing him home on a consistent basis are over. We are all independent individuals with busy lives.

I can feel the changes I have made. As my children became more independent so did I. I remember pleading with him to spend

137

more time with our family and let the political work and some of the more time consuming cases wait until my children were older. My requests had fallen on deaf ears. My determination to spend my time productively outside of home responsibilities with getting my education, doing volunteer work and with my profession has resulted in us being on different wave lengths. I will not give up my full active life because he wants constant company.

Many women devote their lives to their families and make being a homemaker a full time occupation. They make sure their children and husbands are well fed, well dressed and their belongings are well cared for. The job of homemaker is demanding and is often unappreciated. For women who relish this role it allows them the time and freedom to create a wonderful environment for themselves and others. They have the flexibility and freedom to do the things they enjoy. Craft classes and tennis lessons are filled with homemakers.

I was taught both by example and in plain and simple directions that my life was to be about being a good homemaker and wife. That meant my job was to ease the path for my husband so he was able to work outside the home and his home was his sanctuary. He would want to come home if there was a warm welcome, a good meal on the table, a cheerful smile and no fighting children.

I learned that children must be well behaved and parenting was my responsibility. As a little girl, I would have to interrupt my play and change into a dress when my Daddy was expected home. I tried to have my children ready when their daddy came home. It was so annoying when he was late and didn't call and the children became bored or impatient waiting. Trying to amuse them and have a dinner ready often resulted in my being less than sweet and happy when he arrived. I am sure it would have been easier if he came home at the same time every evening or called before he left the office. Finally, I abandoned this concept, fought my inner guilt

and my mother's words, and relaxed. I know it was easier on me and our children. Jack seemed more relaxed too. His expectations had never been like mine in the first place.

Another part of the traditional belief is that if the children annoyed their daddy it was because they were misbehaving and never because he was tired and cranky. As a traditional wife I must allow him to talk about his day, his experiences and his challenges. I must always appear interested. If I have solutions about a problem he is having, I must know that if he uses my ideas he will claim them as his own. If my advice doesn't work out, it will always be my poor judgement. He must never hear about the broken washer, the lost school books or the challenges in my life. I must have no other interests but him and his interests. He must not hear a vacuum, see a mop or hear the noise of a housekeeping machine. Whatever he did that day was harder than whatever I did. Life in a rigid traditional marriage is about him.

I was taught to wait for my husband to invite me to dinner. It must not be my suggestion or I was not keeping up with my role. Being frugal was a virtue, as was not wasting his money, as of course it was his money – he earned it after all.

I also learned that divorce was unacceptable as an option for a Catholic. I am allowed one marriage and unless it is annulled it is my only chance to be married. Having teenage children takes the main reason for an annulment out of the realm of possibility. Failure to consummate the marriage is not our problem. *Why am I thinking this way? I am no longer a Catholic and I do not follow their rules. I can remarry if I want. Who would want me? Could I ever love another man?*

"Does this mean there will be no new cottage?"

As soon as the words are out of my mouth, I know they sound stupid. *Why was he going north with me over the past few months, acting as if we were getting a new cottage, when he was also looking at a place to move to on his own? Why was he leading me on?*

"We will sell this house and what you do with your share of the money will be your decision."

"What about the lovely new kitchen?"

"I asked you what you thought was the biggest drawback to getting a good price for the house and you told me it was the old kitchen so we redid it."

I am stunned. So he knew, as we planned and shopped and made decisions for the kitchen, that we were not going to live here to enjoy it. He had a plan but he failed to share it with me. Anger smoulders in my guts as I see how manipulative he has been.

In a hard cold voice I ask: "If I had stayed an uneducated housewife, not set out to have a career that will carry me through the years after our children are gone, would you have been happier?"

"I don't know. It is too hypothetical a question. I just know I am not happy now. I want out."

"Jack, I accept that there are things wrong between us. But everything is not wrong. We have many wonderful parts to our relationship and our lives. Please don't throw it all away!"

"It is too late for that now."

My thoughts race back to a beautiful summer day, when I sat by my backyard pool in Georgetown, as my children and the children from next door splashed and played. I heard the tires crunch on the neighbour's drive and after the sound of the car door closing, the clicking of heels on their walkway. It wasn't long before

Flo was at the fence, asking if her children were a bother. I assured her they were not and invited her to join me. She thanked me and declined saying she had some calls to make. "Just send them home when you want." She called over her shoulder as she retreated from my view.

It had hit like a kick in the chest. I felt as if the wind had been knocked out of me. I could sit like a life guard or babysitter but she had more important things to do. Humiliation surged from deep inside. *I want something important to do! I want to be a professional woman with intellectual challenges. I want to be respected and appreciated. I want....*

I believe being a mom and wife is important! For the first time, sitting watching the group of children happily playing, while I felt an empty place inside, I really asked myself: "Is this enough for me?"

There is a part of me that wishes being a mother, creating a beautiful home, nourishing meals and arranging a stimulating social life with time to leisurely go shopping, play bridge and golf, was my calling. The priests used to say God called us to do His work. I knew I wasn't called to be a nun. I was too energetic, too interested in the boys and not obedient enough. I wanted children, a family and all the joys that lifestyle could offer. I also have always had my fingers in several pies at once. When my children were small I volunteered for the Children's Aid as a driver and board member and I worked at the airport once a week at Traveller's Aid. I had asked myself: "What if I put all the energy I use in volunteer work into a career for me?"

Coming out of my thoughts, I look at my husband. I am not sure how much time has elapsed while my mind wandered back through my life. I look around our clean and tidy living room and know most of the rest of the house is the same. I do have a beautiful home—well, I have a cleaning woman and have had for years—it isn't up to the minute in decorating but.... *Oh stop this Marilyn!*

You have exactly the life you want; it just isn't the life Jack wants. Does he even know what it is he wants?

Many marriages end when the children are teenagers as the parents are not prepared for the demands and responsibilities of young adults. There is a longing to move forward to a time when the car is not borrowed, the food is not consumed so quickly and the parents make the choice of entertainment. Adolescence is a time of power struggles and a time when a feeling of being invaded is present for many parents.

Many marriages also end during the years when the chance to have small children in the home seems past. Older men will seek out younger women and have a second family to appear and feel more youthful. Some men feel they missed the years their first children were small and want to have a chance to enjoy the early years with their second family.

CHAPTER SEVENTEEN

A DEEP SENSE OF RESIGNATION

The Pieces Come Together Like a Good Stew

I hear the morning birdsong and see a clear blue sky as I slowly awaken to a quiet house. Jack is beside me in our bed, apparently still asleep. *Is my marriage really over? Is he ending everything we have built together? Is my life over if my marriage is over? Somehow I feel like I am close to death.*

I have worked so very hard to make my life just like this. I thought Jack wanted what we have. I couldn't eat last night and I should be hungry. I cannot imagine anything appealing. I swallow and my throat feels tight. My face feels raw from tears and my nose raw from blowing it.

We had talked for quite some time about what and how to tell our children, our neighbours, friends, employees, anyone who asks. This still does not seem real. I wish last night was all a bad dream. I know it was not. Someplace deep inside me has known things have not been right. I have denied so many signs and made excuses for so many things. I have rationalized the symptoms and simplified the explanations. It has been as if I lived two realities. One I kept close to my heart and shared with no one. My visit to the psychic predicted deep sorrow ahead. The prediction about the new cottage appears to have been wrong.

Jack will be waiting for the phone to ring and the next step in our lives to be set in motion. If his offer is not accepted he has told me he will pay more. He has found just what he wants. He is determined. *Has he really done this on his own?*

I do not want to see the joy on his face as he learns of his new purchase. I asked what closing he put on his offer to purchase and he said it was mid month as it is available for occupancy almost immediately. He says he is ready to move. He has been planning this and making decisions without my knowing. No wonder he has been distant with me. His avoidance makes sense now. We have shared so much for so many years, I wonder if he ever thought of discussing it with me.

Jack had seemed almost oblivious to me. He was so caught up in his plans and excitement. Funny, how many times I have listened to his hopes and dreams and supported them. I will not support this as I think it is irresponsible and he has not thought through the consequences. I do however, carry a deep sadness. It is not rage or a need to try to talk him out of his decision. What I feel is acceptance, resignation and an increasing understanding about some of the things that have happened over the last months. There is a lot I do not yet understand. I intend to make sense of what has felt like craziness.

I had asked Jack why we had gone looking for a cottage, as if we were buying a family place, if he was planning to leave. He told me he knew how much the children and I love Muskoka and thought perhaps we might find something we could share. I am astounded. *Is he crazy?* He says perhaps we could take turns being there with the children. He suggested he uses one month, and I have the other, like we shared with my sister and her family. He thought we might do the same with our place on Captiva in Florida.

"I hope we can still be friends when this is all settled."

I had heard his words and thought he must be in denial of the fall-out from his present actions. *Does he really think that we can change our relationship from being lovers and spouses to being emotionally disconnected? If this is the end of our marriage, does he really believe we will sit down and discuss the needed repairs, taxes, who uses March Break and such issues, like I did with my sister? When, over the years, we each have new lives and new partners, does he believe we can share common living spaces?*

I do not believe any new person in our lives could tolerate the sexual energy that is still very much alive between us. Perhaps that is the one hope I have that he will pull out of this wild and seemingly crazy idea. We are great lovers.

I toss under the covers. I will not be able to sleep again. I think of touching his body and know where that will lead. I dress in shorts and a Tee shirt and quietly carry my shoes down the stairs. As I pick up my keys, Jack asks quietly from the top of the stairs:

"Where are you going?"

"Out."

"When will you be back?"

"Later."

"Are you OK?"

"No."

I shut the door quietly behind me.

I sound like my children when they say these words. I do not know where I am going or when I will be back. I consider getting a take out coffee but do not want to face anyone. I drive down to a private little park on the lake behind some expensive homes. Thankfully I find it deserted. The water is calm and ducks and geese swim lazily by in the morning sun. Reflections sparkle off the gentle ripples of

their wake. I feel a sense of peace surround me. *Thank you to all the forces in the universe that brought me to live by the water!*

Sometimes, when I am very distraught, I have a sense of something around me that is spiritual. It shifts me from despair to a state of almost awe or wonderment. It is comforting and soothing. It is as if my guiding angel has folded me within her wings and whispered in my ear. I feel in a place of timelessness and total self acceptance, as if the world is unfolding not as I want it to but as it is predestined to do.

I must let go of the desire to fight Jack and try to make him behave differently. He challenged me that all I wanted to do was control him. I told him if that if I had that control over him, I would make him thankful for all the goodness and blessings in his life and lead him to happiness and ways to find peace and joy. I would make him laugh more and see the wonder in the constant maturing of our children, be thankful for so many good friends and relationships both personal and professional, and... but I do not control him. I do not want to control him. I have enough of a challenge to control myself.

I feel the desire to cry as tears well up, but I shift my focus to the laughter I hear from children in a nearby yard, the sound of a lawnmower, a far off boat cutting through the water. My mind flies to Muskoka. My power boat is in storage. I'd love to be slicing through the water off to explore a new part of the lake or shop in Port Carling. Longing pulls as I think of driving north to take the boat for a spin. I know I can do this if I want, but somehow, I do not want the long drive and the solitary thrill.

I think of people I could call. My dear friend Maureen who has struggles of her own. My mind slides through a multitude of friendly faces. I imagine my friends and relatives on this beautiful morning. I do not want to take my sorrow to them. There will be a time for that.

I walk the length of the park over and over, and then return to my bench. Some small children start toward the lake and then are called back by a vigilant parent.

I am at a time in my life where I can make decisions about how I want to live. I must go forward from here expecting to be treated differently than I have been treated by my husband. His treatment of me has not been respectful. He has had a plan to leave and he has pretended to take my feelings and wants into account, but I can now see he has manoeuvred things for his own game plan. He wanted to separate from me so he had to untie some of the knots in our lives, like the ties to my sister Judy with our money invested in the cottage. He knew she wanted the cottage for her family. He didn't support me in keeping the cottage for our family or in resolving the differences with her because he wanted it sold and the money available. He wanted the money from the Georgetown office in a matrimonial home so I had no exclusion on it as inheritance. He wanted our business ties severed. He wants the home I thought we were building sold. He didn't care about a new kitchen. This is about his escape and money.

I must get a clear focus on where I want to go from here and a clear plan. I know from my work he cannot immediately put me out of the matrimonial home and he cannot walk away from financial responsibility for our children. I intend to ask a lot of questions. I have the right to have some straight answers, to take time to think about my options and to set my own priorities. Some of what he wants he is not going to get. I have given in to him in too many ways over the years. I must fend for myself and for my children. I can feel an inner strength building. I have a strong support network and people with whom I have loving relationships. They will help me. I have faith in my own future as I know I am a capable woman. I may be emotionally knocked off balance but I have a strong spirit and I can be a powerful woman. Jack may be making a very big miscalculation of who he is dealing with here.

I know I have been away from home for several hours. The sun is now high. I feel thirsty. Responsibility nags at me. I take one last sweeping look over the lake and turn to face whatever needs attention at home. Somehow looking at the long view of things eases my pain.

Marriage is a partnership on many levels. Emotional ties must be severed. Physical belongings must be divided. Financial resources must be shared. Parental responsibilities must be renegotiated.

How a couple ends their relationship is indicative of how they feel about their part in forming the relationship and what the relationship meant to them.

CHAPTER EIGHTEEN

THE POWER OF MONEY

Money Gives Us the Freedom to Choose

We start in the bedroom, deciding what furniture will go and what furniture will stay. Of course he will take the Bang and Olefson stereo I gave him for his birthday, plus his tapes and records. He has already packed most of his toiletries from our ensuite bathroom. We decide not to break up the bedroom set, at least not for now. I offer him some towels but he tells me he has bought new ones. *Really? I wonder what else he has bought. He sure is organized for someone who hasn't usually bothered about such things.*

The children's rooms will remain intact, as their furniture is theirs. We move to the living room and the beige velvet wing chairs, bought originally for his Georgetown office, and decide they are his. An occasional table that he bought years ago for one of his earlier offices that we had refinished along with some books and memorabilia are also marked to go. In the dining room, the decision is again, not to break up the set. He says the house will sell faster with the expensive furniture we bought with care over the twenty four years of our marriage. *So he thinks the house will sell fast does he? I have the right to make some of the decisions about where we go from here. It is not all going to fall into place as easily as he seems to think.*

We move through the family room, kitchen, and lower level activity rooms making decisions. The pool room, with all the decorative accessories, pool cues and score board will stay, at least until the house sells. He thinks he will want it for his lower level. I have no interest in keeping it for wherever I might move. Personal belongings like suitcases, his trumpet and my sewing machine are obvious choices. The old tube radio from my parents that he wanted when we emptied Dad's house, is his and the art pieces I inherited are mine. I am firm about the art pieces I want to keep. I will not negotiate. No is my first and final response to his requests. He can take what I do not want, but he is not going to take the brass rubbings we did in Cambridge as they suit the dining room. The photo albums, slides, wedding gifts from my family and friends and any piece I want, are mine. He seems surprised at my assertive stance. I know he wants to avoid a conflict or emotional outburst so I feel I have some power. I feel deeply sad and yet strangely powerful.

We are walking through our history. There are times when we get caught in the memories and laugh or we wipe a tear from our eyes, but most of the belongings are either his or mine or something we will leave to decide when the house sells. It is too soon to know where I will go. Getting out of this house will in some ways be a relief. I am not going to move until I find somewhere that I like. I feel confident, thinking that my options for my future are rich and varied. I get to start fresh. I will keep my favourite things. Thinking like this, lifts my spirits. What will I be able to afford? This momentarily frightens the hell out of me. *One step at a time Marilyn, one step at a time.*

He tells me his place is not very large, and he is prepared to buy new things. I wonder why if there are new things to be bought; he will be the one who gets them. I decide to keep quiet on this point. I go through the motions. It is as if somehow, this is not really happening. It is a bad dream. *I wish I could wake up.*

My children have questions, but basically stay out of our way. I have assured them that they will not have to move immediately. I tell them I am sure their father will honour his promises to them. Kathy and Julia, both at university, have major immediate expenses associated with their education. Matt will have education expenses in a few years. Jack has always promised he will pay for their education as long as they are achieving. I tell them I love them and their father loves them. Jack assures them this is not about them and that he loves them very much and always will. There are tears and pleading; "Daddy don't move out. Why are you doing this?" I have heard sobs in the night and whispers behind closed doors. My own tears and lack of understanding, give me few answers to comfort my children. *I hate this!*

I call some of the lodges I know in Muskoka, and book myself in to Rocky Crest for three nights. My children want to come along rather than spend the weekend with their father. Jack appears relieved. He had said they could stay with him alternate weekends, but so far they have chosen to stay home. It will be good to get away as new places demand that we focus on new experiences. The holes where furniture use to be, and the emptiness of my evenings home alone, are crowding in on me.

Jack has been dropping in unexpectedly and being awfully nice. He wrote me a letter last week quoting Wordsworth's poetry and saying things like: "we each have the power to withstand the tragedy of our loss" and "we are calling on inner reserves my love, that through complacency towards each other we never needed." He signed it "your old pal."

Why if he is experiencing feelings that lie too deep for tears, is he ending our marriage? Why is he calling this a tragedy? Why is he calling me his love? Why is he seducing me when we meet to make plans for our children's summer? Why does he come to my office and invite me to lunch?

After several days of swimming, boating, eating and visiting old friends around the Muskoka lakes, I feel refreshed. Mark has had several cottages to show us, but since I am now looking at just investing the amount I got from the old cottage, the places are pretty rustic. I explain that I want to see cottages both on the three main Muskoka lakes as well as some smaller lakes close by. I will get a lot more value with a cottage on a smaller lake but will not have the access to so much boating. I do love my big boat.

My children want the big lake as they have friends they can boat to, better water sport opportunities and for the status. Some of the smaller lakes are too confined for our boat. I am concerned that the lower priced cottages will need septic systems, a new roof or dock and are not winterized. I have been spoiled with calling a lakefront Muskoka home a cottage. I want this to be a home for myself and my children given we will be losing our family home. I have a lot to consider. I must look at my total life style before making a decision. Since there is nothing that even tempts me, I do not need to make the decision now.

Jack has the trailer that was his father's and is packing it alone. My instinct is to help, as I have been supportive of him in so many of his other projects. I must learn not to try to rescue or interfere. He is making a very important decision. I do not agree with his way of handling his stress, but I have no power here.

I have considered begging him to stay, trying to seduce him, and blocking his attempts to take things. I will not beg. He knows I am against this as a problem solving technique, power play or manipulation to get my way. He knows I love him and want our family to be intact, but he also knows I will not sacrifice my Self and my happiness to be at his beck and call. I will not kill my Self to be with him. I do not want a physical confrontation. I have never felt he would physically assault me, but I want to avoid any likelihood that this could lead to that. I tried the seduction, had a great sexual encounter and he continued moving his belongings. At least I know how to get my sexual needs met, if not my needs for a family and a spouse. I have thought he might be using me but if he is, I am also using him. We are still husband and wife so we are not breaking any laws.

I wonder what the neighbours think and feel embarrassed. We have not become socially involved with any of them. Casual road-side chats and friendly waves are common. *What will I say to them?*

As I stand staring out the kitchen window, seeing nothing, absently drinking a cup of coffee, the door bell rings. It is a lovely Saturday morning and Jack is packing the trailer. *Why has Jack, who is in the garage, not dealt with whomever is calling.*

Still in my nightgown and housecoat, I open the front door to see Don, the father of one of Matt's friends. He had come for his son's forgotten watch. I invite him to step in while I go to ask Matt where the watch might be. Matt gives me the watch from his bedside table and rolls back over to return to sleep.

A few minutes turns into well over an hour. I explain Jack is leaving me, and that he has bought a townhouse. I am surprised I can say it without crying. It is a matter of fact.

Don is surprised Jack is doing the move on his own. He questions why a man in his position would choose to pack and unpack a trailer by himself rather than hire a mover or even call a friend. He offers to go and help. I suggest that might not be a good idea. Jack has made his choice and in spite of my suggestions, has chosen to do it this way. He asks why the children aren't helping. I explain that they are too upset and are all still in bed. He has been through a marital break-up and is supportive, understanding and shares stories of his own children's reactions to their mother's choice to leave. I am glad of his company. He distracts me from the reality of what is happening.

I see the back of the packed trailer leave the drive, and a while later the car and empty trailer return. Don and I keep chatting like old friends. I have hardly spent more then a few moments chatting with him in the past, but I find his compassion and understanding comforting. Matt comes down and joins us. Don has had Matt stay over at his house many times just as Andrew, Don's son, has stayed with us. The boys are like brothers, sharing adventures since they were ten.

Don tells me to call him if ever I want to talk or if I need a man around the house for anything. I thank him but know I will not call. The last thing I need right now is another man. After he leaves, Matt asks why I didn't invite him in for coffee. I explain that since I am not dressed and I really do not know him well, that might not have been a good idea.

"It might not look good to your father."

"Well Mom, if he is moving out, you can do what you want. You'll have to stop trying to please him and learn to do what you want."

I dress and keep myself busy. I rearrange the furniture to fill in the spaces left by what Jack took, and wander from room to room trying to accept my new reality. I try to comfort my heart broken children as they see the trailer drive away with the last load. They are quietly angry and will not speak to their father when he tries to say goodbye.

Over the years of our marriage Jack has threatened to leave over and over. It has become a pattern. The children are convinced that he will move back, just as he returned with a packed suitcase when his stress level got so high he resorted to the flight response. I am not so sure. A small part of me is relieved to know there will be some time without the arguments about trivial things and the picking at me as if everything wrong in our relationship is because I do not meet his expectations.

Anger comes when our expectations are not met. I never expected to be in this position. Yet I do not feel anger. The other manifestation of anger is disappointment, fear and sadness.

I feel a deep sadness and twinges of fear. *How will I manage this big house alone? How long will it take to sell? When will I have to move? Where will I go?* I must provide a home for my children. Even though they are teenagers, there are many years ahead when they will need a home, guidance and support. My job as a mother will continue even after they are parents themselves. *What kind of lifestyle will I be able to create until they are educated and self sufficient?*

A call from my uncle surprises me. He wants my opinion on a decision about my grandmother's estate. There is an offer on her farm. He is asking if I think we should accept it or wait for more money. It is in a prime location for development and sure to increase in value if we wait. He is taking a vote from each family. As executor of Dad's estate, I am the representative for my siblings. I suggest accepting the sale as my aunt and uncles are still young enough to enjoy whatever freedom the financial results will offer them. I am sorry Dad isn't alive to enjoy the choices it would have given him. There are some clauses and conditions to consider and after a discussion of options, I gently put the receiver back in the cradle. *This puts a new twist on things!*

One after the other, I call my sisters and brother to tell them the news. We all agree to keep this to ourselves. It isn't a done deal yet. They support my decision to vote to accept this offer. My conversation with Judy is short but my brother Bill has many questions and suggestions. I tell him to contact Joe directly and keep me posted of any new information he discovers. Joan and I share flights of fantasy of what this could mean for us and the opportunities it will open. Even though I discuss Jack's leaving, my heart feels lighter and my future less daunting. I am a financially responsible woman. I have managed our household money for years and we have established a very strong financial base. With some inherited money that is all mine, I now know I will be able to meet my financial obligations without fear of Jack manipulating me with money.

I have worked with so many couples where the man manipulates and terrorizes the wife by cutting off financial support. She is left begging for money, borrowing to buy food and pay the utilities, and having to deny the children basic things like keeping the family dog, going on a school trip or returning to camp. I cannot imagine Jack ever denying his children the financial support he has the ability to provide. He is a kind and generous man. Having some money of my own is a comfort though.

Filled with new hope, I plan an impromptu trip to Muskoka to just feel the escape and change of scenery. I invite Maureen to share my escape. We decide to retrieve my power boat from the marina at Campbell's Landing, where it was stored after the sale of the cottage. I'd hoped to enjoy it at a new cottage this summer but I will make the best of what I have and live in my consecutive nows, trusting my future will unfold on a schedule over which I have no control. There are things that I can control and things I cannot.

I am exhilarated to feel the wind in my hair and the sun on my face, as I push the throttle full forward and head north up Lake Muskoka for Port Carling. Maureen has taken the car and will meet me there. As the familiar sights of Beaumaris and One Tree

Island slide by, I feel reconnected with my spirit. I feel great to know Julia and a friend will be joining us at Shamrock Lodge.

Later, sitting by the lake, sipping a glass of wine with the sun setting and the scent of pine in the air, I feel relaxed and calm. I want to visit my sister Joan, who is staying with a friend at a nearby cottage.

I called Mark earlier to see if there is anything new on the market that he can show me. He said he has a couple of places. I look forward to seeing them. Eager anticipation jiggles in my breast.

After several hours driving the cottage roads, none of the new for-sale properties tickle my fantasy or evoke a sense that I want to spend time there. One is on a narrow channel and the boat traffic, noise and water erosion is not my idea of tranquility. Another is lovely, with huge windows facing west. The sunsets would be beautiful from here. The boat house is in poor repair and the drive is shared by many cottages so the back of it is like a parking lot. Too close to others for my comfort. I want more trees between me and my neighbours.

Back on the water again, I stop by my uncle's cottage. He insists we return for dinner. Since I need to be back in Oakville tomorrow to see clients and have other people depending on me for a ride, I decline. He generously offers to let me leave the boat at his place. This saves me both the boat trip down the lakes and the cost of storage. He has a large property with enough boat and docking space to store my boat inside one of his boat houses. I gratefully accept. Life is falling nicely into place for me.

Family time and Muskoka fun revive me. It is hard to believe how liberated I feel. I also feel joyful, as if my Holy Grail, the vessel that is my Self, has been refilled.

Having a place where we can let our spirit soar, a place we can go when we need to connect with our Self, where we feel the love and acceptance of significant others, helps us make it through the saddest days and darkest nights.

CHAPTER NINETEEN

ACCEPTANCE OF THE INEVITABLE

Finally I Get the Picture

August 1988

T he counselling appointment with Cathy and Paul is not at all what I thought it would be like. We aren't working on our communication. Jack is telling me, in front of our minister and his wife, that he is in love with Beth and our marriage is over. There is no second chance, no listening to my wants, just a clear message that he has made the appointment to have witnesses to see how logical a decision he is making. I feel he wants witnesses to see how out of control and unreasonable I am. He now tells me he has booked this appointment to get support for me in dealing with this new reality.

I do not know myself. I scream uncontrollably.

"After all I have done with you, all I have done for you and your career, how can you...just...abandon....me?"

My thoughts flash to our recent sexual encounters at his townhouse and suddenly I feel cheap, stupid and used. In a nasty tone I question:

"You knew you were planning to be with Beth and we were not working on our relationship when you were screwing me during these past months, didn't you!"

"We can still be friends." He meekly replies. He hates it when I yell. He says it reminds him of being yelled at as a kid.

159

"Are you so stupid as to believe I want to be your friend when you have treated me so badly? I don't have friends who treat me like you treat me."

I am now not in denial of my deep hurts. The physical pain is intense. My head throbs and my heart races. My feet are sweating. I gasp for breath.

I grew up too fast and learned not to act like "a baby". I am now feeling wounded and battered and enraged. Somewhere in my adult body there is also a very little crying child, wanting to run somewhere and have someone tell me everything will be alright. I want to be held and stroked and spoken to softly, soothed and comforted. If anyone were to try and touch me I think I might hit them yet I long to be comforted. This cannot be real. He has denied his involvement with Beth over and over. I wanted to believe him. My closest friends have told me they have spoken with him and he as told them he is not involved with her. They were told that I was ill, crazy and impossible to live with and he could not take the strain any longer. Now he is sitting here with witnesses telling me he is planning a life with her. This is crazy making for sure.

My hands clasp and unclasp. I want to slap him in the face for his lies. My crying eyes glare at him. I ask him to repeat what he just said. His words about his long time relationship with Beth as his friend and wanting to fan the flames of their love hit me with a wry humour. I snort instead of laugh. I want to run. I want to run away from the outrageous situation I am in. I have just admitted being sexual with this man within the last week and not seeing what has obviously been right before my eyes. I am so stupid. He is such a good liar.

There is nowhere for me to go. I look from face to face and see grave concerned expressions. It is as if they are willing me to accept what I do not want to hear. There is no one I trust enough to turn to and to share my anguish. Obviously my friends have been told I am crazy. I sure feel like I look crazy now. All my life I have been told to grow up and act strong, like a big girl, like the mature adult that I am supposed to be. Instead, I feel like the villain, the hysterical wench, the frantic dumped wife. Tears streaming down my face, a wad of wet tissues balled in my hand. I feel hopeless, powerless and utterly alone.

I remember crying as they carried my mother's coffin around the corner of the house to the waiting hearse. It had been in the sun-room for several days and visitors came and went sharing memories and offering sympathy. Knowing Mom was leaving her home for the last time I sobbed and sniffled, gasping for air, while standing on the front steps with my father and siblings. Dad said "Think of something else Marilyn and stop crying. People are looking at you."

I didn't want to think of something else. I wanted to feel the pain of the moment knowing it was a breaking of my anger at her death. *This is so senseless. It is such a waste! She was such a great woman! Why could no one save her? I never got enough from her. I want more! I want my mother!*

I learned that healing blocked feelings and repressed emotions is about thawing out the hurt child at whatever age and stage it is, and re-parenting it to live in union and harmony with the adult Self. That means I must learn to ask for help and change my myths about how to deal with pain. I must learn how to heal my inner child. I must find a way to do this while helping my children through this quagmire of throbbing pain. I know also that I only hurt as deeply as I care. I care so deeply for this man. I care about our family and our future. I must find a way to stop caring without ceasing to be a caring person.

I went directly from being a child to feeling responsible as a "parental figure" in my family of origin. I learned the child and parent roles, but developed the adult role in my forties. Under intense pressure I revert to the child/parent behaviours. On the one hand, I cry and have a temper tantrum, screaming and yelling like a child, trying to get my needs met. On the other hand, I want to parentally pressure Jack into doing what I want him to do. I want him to get into the role of caring husband and responsible father.

What about the promise he made at our marriage? What about him loving me eternally? What about the promises he made in 1986 when he told me he was over her?

I want Jack to feel sympathy for me. I want him to put aside what he wants and put the well being of the family ahead of this plan. I want him to think rationally and make the decision I want him to make. I see him with head bowed, wiping tears from his own eyes. I know I cannot make him think or feel anything. His feelings and reactions come from inside him and his experiences. They are an outward manifestation of his beliefs. I feel so powerless and confused. My tears come easily and my anger explodes. *Damn Beth! Why didn't she work on her own marriage and leave my husband alone? I cannot do this. I cannot face this. I cannot accept this.*

As a care giver I often give away what I want from others. It is a reflection of my needs and wants to be taken care of and be near others who are caring. Sometimes, when others try to take care of me, I see it as controlling and a sign they think I am weak. I now allow myself the comfort of supportive hands as Cathy and Paul each reach out to pat my back. My inner turmoil causes the conflict between feeling that I should get a grip and knowing I must not try to deny this pain.

I slump into Cathy's embrace and let the sobs rack my body. Over and over and over until I just want to crawl in a hole and pull it in after me. The act of being touched and touching someone else settles me and calms my fears. I wonder if I am capable of pulling myself together to drive home. I raise my head and look at the concerned faces. I look at Jack. He is looking directly into my puffy eyes. I feel my jaw stiffen and my backbone go rigid. Defiance swells into my breast and inwardly I silently declare:

Even if you do not love me and want me, I am capable and loveable! I am valuable. I will recover!

Defiance replaces surrender. I set my jaw firmly into a grim scowl. I will use every ounce of energy I can muster to get away from here. I straighten my back and square my shoulders. I stare at Jack's forehead so the emotion revealed in his eyes does not touch me. *I'll show you! Just you wait!* My silent vow is repeated silently over and over as I stand and gather my composure as best I can.

What I tell myself inside my own head, gives me strength and courage. It is meek at first but it grows in intensity as I block the concerned conversation about me. They are wondering if I am alright to drive.

I learned to seek approval from adults who didn't notice my needs or hushed me, telling me my needs were not real. I learned to get attention by taking care of adults. I also learned to tell myself all

the soothing and supportive things I wanted to hear to gain inner strength. From this role reversal position, I am able to hide until I get back into the mental attitude that keeps me going. I can rewrite the words that run around in my head to positive affirmations. I will be loving and supportive to me! I will go forward from here, knowing I did the very best I could to be this man's wife short of killing off who I really am capable of being. I must now ignore everyone's needs but mine. I am not good for my children if I am not good as me.

In families when one child takes on the over responsible role, there is usually a child who is carefree, in denial of the families' problems, under responsible for practical chores and the feelings of others. This child is often overindulged and learns to feel entitled to the best of everything for themselves without a thought for what others might be going through. Their world is about themselves and others are there to serve them. Over responsible people often team up with under responsible people to keep the familiarity of the roles intact. It may be painful but it is a familiar pain.

Some families have a scapegoat who is blamed for all the problems of the others. The belief is that if only this person were to disappear the family would be fine. This role is filled with guilt and shame and there is a fear of looking inward. This family member is usually isolated in their pain and it is easier for the others to believe the scapegoat is the problem than to look at the family dynamics. The eldest child is often the scapegoat as they are the first to break out of the parents' control. It could also be a child who has a different energy level than the others or a disability. Sadly these children sometimes commit suicide and leave a legacy of guilt and sadness.

These roles smother the natural enthusiasm and joy of being alive. Once we can choose to change, adjustments are needed to not only survive, but to thrive. Moving beyond the grieving process of not having the family we wanted—one like the television shows portray—involves acceptance that we cannot go back and redo our childhood, but we can identify what we didn't get and then find ways to fulfill those needs. This takes a mature outlook and self responsibility for our wants and needs. I am not the problem. Lies and deceit, infidelity and betrayal are. I must regain the trust from all the people who have been told lies about me. At least now I know that I have been lied about, I know what needs to be done.

I turn to Cathy and know I do not want to confide in her any further. I apologize for my outburst. I see relief on her face. Her husband looks sceptical as I reach for my purse.

"I'll be fine. Thank you."

My words are shaky. I turn to face Jack and with determination to not cry, firmly say;

"Goodbye."

For me there is finality in my words. I want to say: "No more friendly visits, shared meals and no more sex." I am not sure I can hold my voice for that much and I fear it will just dilute the finality of my intention that this is GOODBYE.

Cathy follows me out of the room and just before I get into my car she embraces me in a supportive hug. I will myself not to cry. Enough tears in front of these people. I shut my car door with firm resolution not to look back. I turn in the opposite direction from home and search to find a place to stop. I find a parking space in a small park. After ensuring my doors are locked, I let my emotions flow.

After a good cry I feel spent and hungry. I head for home.

This emotional work will be hard as my norm is to appear strong and capable, not needy and lost. I need to find a place where I can safely shout, cry and hit something to get the energy of anger out of my system, without abuse to myself or others. I need a place where I can feel acceptance, trust that the place is safe and the support is non judgmental. I need to find someone who is prepared to help me handle my emotion and be honest with me. I need someone who is capable of experiencing their own pain and who understands that sunshine follows rain. I will not stay stuck in this quagmire forever. I do need help.

Group therapy could provide me with a new pseudo family. I have many years of experience doing therapy with groups and they can be a powerful force for change. The patterns from my family will surface within the group and provide tangible opportunities for me to deal in new ways within the old patterns. I will see the others as a mirror of my family and respond accordingly. It is important that I am aware how I will work in a group to recreate my life script. It will be natural if I fall back into my roles. I fought those roles on my Quest to England and Ireland. Control issues, my reaction to criticism, my desire to be pleasing, and accepting responsibility for others are but a few of the issues that will arise for me. Confidentiality, trust and intimacy issues will also occur. I am afraid. I am afraid for myself and for my professional reputation. I might have trouble opening up in a group. I do not feel as strong as I did in the past. I want to be nurtured, supported, listened to and acknowledged. *Listen to your wants Marilyn!*

I ponder my options. Perhaps individual therapy will be better. *What is it that I want help to accomplish?* I will have a better chance of choosing the right kind of help for me if I know my goals. Choosing a therapist is a very important decision. *What if I get a therapist who left their marriage and sympathises with Jack? What if they decide I really am crazy?*

There are times in life where everything we thought we knew and could trust melts away like an iceberg in hot water. We cannot rely on what we thought was true. The people and things we believed would always be present for us are gone and we are left without the structures that created our sense of security. In these times of change we flounder, thrashing about, trying to find some way to make sense of what we see as our reality. It is not like clinical insanity. It does not require drug therapy. It is not a time for hospitalization. We are not sick – we are temporarily unbalanced.

It happens when we have intense loss and all our usual rational thoughts escape us. It is like the non swimmer who jumps into the water to save their child, the person who returns to a burning building to save their pet or the victim of a robbery asking what seems like a totally stupid question. It is a beginning part of the grief process.

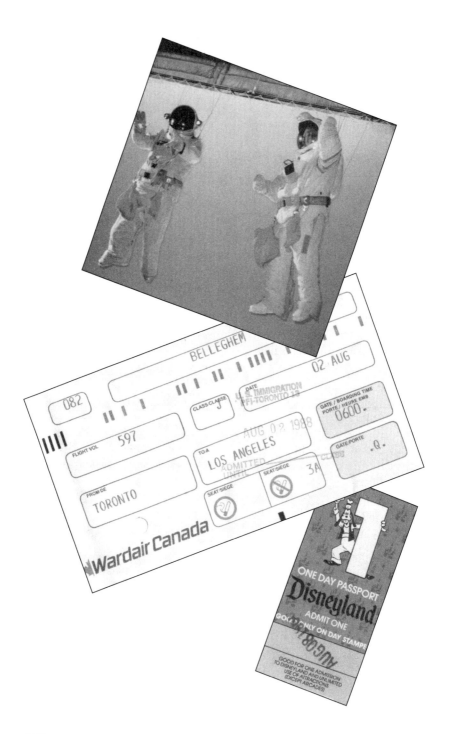

CHAPTER TWENTY

LET'S GO TO CALIFORNIA

Teenagers Need Special Attention

T his is a time when breaking the rules is necessary. My life is falling apart. I am falling apart. I need to stop worrying about image. I need to worry about what is "real." So much makes more sense now. Jack and Beth didn't stop their relationship, they put it on hold while he cleaned up some issues that kept us connected financially. He lied to me. I can see why he wanted me out of shared office space. Oh my God, I can see why he wanted me out of the cottage with Judy. That is why he didn't try to stop the sale of the cottage or offer for us to buy it. He has had this in the back of his mind for the last two years. He came back to dismantle our interconnectedness. The pieces now fit so clearly.

I need to find a source of hope, a new vision of my reality, a new direction for my life and a new idea of normal. I cannot make my focus just the future of my children. I must come face to face with my life. I must return to the idea of being the hero in my own life story. I need to rewrite my script. In spite of all my efforts to hold on to my marriage, I am going to be a single woman. I am only forty-five. I have many years ahead of me and a lot of life yet to be lived. I am beyond the life stage when my primary role is being a mother. While my children still need me, especially Matt, I have to be good as my Self to be good for them.

I must have the ability to face adversity without denial. There is a life for me without Jack. I survived my mother's death and then my father's death. I survived selling my childhood home. I survived moving to London, then Etobicoke, and then Georgetown, each time leaving friends and familiar places behind. I have built a home and left it, then built again. I know the processes of change.

Inner change is possible. It may take time. I have been changing my attitudes toward what I want my marriage to be for a long time. This is the shattering of the illusion that the differences between Jack and I can be stretched indefinitely. We have pulled too far from each other and the connection has been torn apart.

Ultimately, we are powerless to change anyone but ourselves. *Can I accept this is a necessary time of change in my life? Can I forgive Jack for forcing me to grow? Can I accept that I am growing beyond a point where I ever imagined I could go?* The road of life is not smooth. It is a long and continuous process. It is the process of living. I must direct my life and form a plan of how I want to live.

His leaving frees me to dance my own dance, sing my own song, and create my own life. I want to do it with playfulness and spontaneity. I want to live my life with purpose.

What do you really want Marilyn?

I want to run away! I want to go somewhere fun and ......

I call Karen at Uniglobe. I ask her where I can go that's far away, leaving as soon as possible, that is safe for a woman either alone or with up to three teenagers. She asks some very specific questions about my intentions and says she will check flight availability. She has known me for years through the Chamber of Commerce. It must be somewhere that English is spoken. I do not need the challenge of another language right now. She says she will put something together and get back to me.

Karen soon calls back and tells me there is an airline seat sale to England with a car but if the children go, we will need to upgrade the car to fit us all. There is also a charter flight with Wardair to California with a car. She explains that if we are all going, the larger American car would be a better plan. She tells me she will keep looking and may find something else.

At dinner, I ask my children, "Do you want to go away on a holiday with me leaving as soon as I can get a flight and arrangements done?"

"I'll go if it is to California but not to England" Matt says.

"What happens if we don't go?"

"You can stay with your dad."

"Let's go to California!"

The excitement is high and my fears flirt at the side roads of my thoughts. *Can I handle this trip with the dynamics that are going on between me and my children? I must get away! I must get my kids away!*

Once the flight is booked and Karen assures me our seats are reserved together, I write Fly to California in the kitchen appointment book for August second. I flip it back so the current week shows. Everyone in the family has access to this book, and it is their responsibility to enter their events. We use it for doctor and dentist appointments, birthdays, concerts, sports events, meetings, report card dates and everything other family members might want to know for scheduling. This gives ample notice of upcoming events and teaches my children planning and time management. When school notices come home at the first of the year or I know a board meeting is the first Monday of the month, I fill it in for the whole year.

Turning the page to the first week of August, I read Matt's words for the day after we arrive in California. "Rest arms from flight."

I chuckle, and then start to laugh, tears flood my eyes as I hug the book. Thank God he can make a joke of all this.

I have been so worried about how my children have been coping with the separation. There have been angry outbursts and tears, long silences and intense discussions. They have been to their father's place for dinners but tell me it seems weird. They have come home upset and asked me questions I cannot answer.

"How can Dad say he was never happy living with us?"

"Why did we go looking at cottages if we were not going to buy one?"

"What will happen to our boat?"

"Why can't you make him come back?"

My children tell me they are embarrassed that we are separated. They freely talk about how difficult it was when they had to listen to the conflicts between us, but say it was because they thought they were stupid fights about things we should have been able to settle easily. They hated being in the middle if the conflict was about something to do with them. They hated the calm after a conflict, as they never knew when the next eruption would occur. They tell me of times they started an argument with each other or with me just to get the strain to lessen. I assure them the separation is not about them and that a couple who have a good marriage cannot be split apart by problems with children.

I am sorry my children have had to live with so much turmoil. They are not problem children even though they do have their challenges. I am sure they would have many fewer struggles if our marriage had been smoother. I wish Jack had had a greater commitment to working on our issues and supporting our kids. *Why has he always run away? Is he running away from me or to something new and different?*

Julia asks if I want her to speak to her dad about coming back. I explain that it is not her responsibility. As the eldest, with the most memories, she wants to make her family whole again. She gathers pictures of happy times and is adamant that her dad was happy on many occasions. I assure her that he has not left because of anything she has done. He has left because he is someone who runs from the problems we are having and has done so for years. She remembers him packing his bag and leaving in an angry outburst when they were all small. She remembers crying and trying to comfort Matt and Kathy who were all upset. This type of situation creates distrust of both parents. *How can they trust me to create a safe emotional space for them?*

"It is my job as the parent to support and protect you. I am sorry I have not been able to protect you from so much sadness and fear of abandonment. I have not been able to protect you from the emotional abuse created by my marital situation. I will never leave you. I will be your mother even after I am in spirit form. I love you all so very much."

My children know I believe in spirit guides and protectors. I have many experiences of knowing my spirit guides are close. They do not believe this is weird or crazy. They find comfort in it and know that many people believe in guardian angels and a loving protective God. They trust they too have guardian angels and have told stories of times they have felt supported.

It is important that children address their own issues with the parents' separation and not parrot the parent's issues. My children have real issues of their own. Sometimes they want to tell me about things their father says or does. They want to understand what is happening. Usually I suggest they ask their father the questions, but sometimes they want my impression.

I have given my opinion on many issues over their lives then let them form their own conclusions. I have taught them to analyse a situation, a friendship, a TV program, movie or commercial. Teaching children to think for themselves is an important part of parenting. Critical thinking skills will help us to make decisions that are right for us and also make us less likely to follow the crowd. Sometimes our intuition helps us recognize the best course of action to take, while at other times we need to look more closely at our options, weigh the possible consequences, and then choose. The more important the decision, the more thought we need to put into it before we ask "What feels right for me?"

It is hard for me to decide what and when to tell my children about Jack's disclosure that he is again involved with Beth. I do not know what they know. I do not want them to feel it is a secret they must keep, if they are in fact aware of the relationship. *Dear God help me to do what is in the best interest of my children.*

> When children know about a secret infidelity, they carry a heavy burden. They are in loyalty conflict about disclosure. To whom should they be loyal?
>
> This is too much adult responsibility to put on any child at any age. Even when the child is an adult, knowing a secret of one parent that would seriously affect the other if it was told is an unfair burden. The child has no power to alter the situation. They doubt their own perceptions. They feel powerless, confused and frustrated. They may lash out at the parent who has betrayed the family. Many children lash out at the parent who they trust the most, almost daring that parent to abandon and betray them. They need to know they are secure and their trust is not falsely placed. They want their parents to see their needs and fears.
>
> When parents tell their children too much about the adult situation and it is not age appropriate, children feel bewildered and burdened. It can also be one-sided information that confuses the child about what is really going on in their family.

CHAPTER TWENTY-ONE

CALIFORNIA

Running Away

A rriving in Los Angeles, it is immediately apparent that the assigned rental car will not accommodate the amount of luggage we have brought. The girls seem to have packed everything they own. They knew their bag and weight limit. I told them to leave room for new things too. They had such fun deciding what to take to look like California girls. I wasn't about to argue with them. I want this to be fun. I had decided that if we need a roof rack or a van, I'll do what it takes.

The rental car company efficiently upgrades me to a Buick Park Avenue. Thank heaven for trolleys and good strong children. After loading the trunk and consulting the map, we follow the directions from the car rental agent and joyfully head south on the San Diego Freeway, destination unknown. We are in California and we want to find a beach. I feel free and happy and recall a similar feeling in Ireland. *I am so glad my children are sharing this adventure!*

We have maps and guide books and have decided to cut off the throughway south of the city. Long Beach is our first stop. It doesn't feel like our fantasy, so we move along Ocean Boulevard and then follow the Pacific Coast Road, Route One.

We are delighted to find a gem of a place. It's funny how intuition can lead us right where we want to go. Laguna Beach is quaint and beautiful with sweeping hills dipping down to coves with picturesque beaches. There are mansions perched on cliffs with splendid landscaping and then quaint little cottages with English style gardens.

As we drive through the main part of the town we see inviting shops and restaurants. I inquire at a gas station, explaining my wants for accommodation and get directions to Hotel San Maarten. It is a two story stucco structure with a terra cotta tile roof. It is rather plain looking from the street with no windows offering ocean views or balconies. I ask my children to wait in the car so I can decide if I think it is suitable. There is no point in taking our entire luggage in and then discovering they do not have room or I am not satisfied with the amenities.

I can also make the decision without their opinions. Choosing a hotel is my responsibility. Once inside I am delighted to see a fabulous courtyard garden filled with palm trees, greenery and flowers. A swimming pool is in the centre and the rooms open into the inner tropical paradise. The hotel dining room is set amid the plantings and fountain. This is perfect. I eagerly book two adjacent pool side rooms for three nights. One has a king bed and the other has two queen sized beds. It is decided Julia and I will share and Matt will share with Kathy. The two neat ones are sleeping together in one room and the two messy ones in the other.

We decide to start with a swim, then explore the hotel and head off to investigate the downtown on foot. Our internal clocks are still on Eastern Time so we eat dinner early. I am tired but want to adjust to Pacific Time. We walk and talk, explore the beach and pick up pamphlets at the tourist information centre. The girls buy postcards and we all choose snacks for the room.

Floating in the hotel pool, flat on my back, looking up at the evening sky framed by palm trees, I thank God for this chance to heal.

The air is sweet and warm. I sip a glass of white house wine I had ordered from the bar and recline in a chaise, watching my children swim. There are only a few other guests. I'm glad I have several

credit cards with either no limit, like my American Express, or high limits. I do not intend to be frugal.

I awake very early and dress quietly. I leave a note saying I have gone for a walk. The desk clerk assures me the area is safe. I head for the beach. There are a few joggers and dog walkers about. It is peaceful. The gentle sound of the rolling surf soothes my churning mind. Jack was startled at my news of the trip, yet I also sensed relief. I try not to think of him being sexual with another woman. I know that coming away was a smart decision. Being at home in familiar places filled with memories hurts too much. The clients I postponed were accepting of changed appointments. I told them I had a chance of a two week vacation in California with my children. Without understanding my real reason for a quick decision for a getaway, they encouraged me to enjoy myself.

> Changing from familiar surroundings to places that demand our attention and stimulates new thoughts helps the grieving process. Because we are having new experiences in new places, where memories are not lurking at every turn, we can replace the sadness with interest, the sense of loss with a sense of adventure, and keep from falling into a pattern of gloom and despair. While there will be things that stimulate memories, we can choose to replay the past or seek out new experiences. Gradually, the grief is replaced with new ways to be in the world and we heal. This is personal growth through travel.

This beach is not like the groomed one where we have our time-share condo on Captiva Florida. There are clumps of seaweed and bits of debris. I inspect it all with interest. I remove my shoes. At first the water feels quite cold to my feet then gradually I become accustomed to it. I leave footprints in the sand and recall a Pat Boon song, Love Letters in the Sand. My heart lurches momentarily. As the past tries to intrude, I push it away with thoughts of the new adventures we will have so far from home.

I hear the cry of a gull. I look up to see it gliding high above me in the early morning sunlight. I decide not to let myself be pulled back into sad memories. I think of Tintagel, the coastal path to Mousehole, and the gulls that followed the ferry to Ireland. I am sorry I have not found or made the time to work on the book about that tour. Life just seems to keep getting in the way.

I return to the hotel ready for breakfast. I make myself a cup of coffee in the room and urge my family to get moving. Sitting in the courtyard, waiting for my children, I savour my fresh coffee. The birds are twittering in the palms and gardens and the fountain is tinkling softly. I close my eyes and let the warm sunshine kiss my face. Matt wants a swim. The girls will take awhile. I am relaxed and feeling peaceful. The sense of anxiety that has been my constant companion drains from me. Matt wants to show me some antic and I laugh with delight.

As I sit with my mind wandering, I notice a painter working in the far side of the courtyard. He is painting hotel room doors a beautiful colour of deep green. I am sure that is the colour I wanted for my kitchen. Jack had chosen a pale green that I think looks institutional. The painter had followed his instructions and ignored mine, even though I had shown him the colour on the ceramic tile border. I suddenly decide that I will have the kitchen repainted.

I leisurely walk over and ask if the paint has a number and what brand it is. I wonder if it is available in Canada. The painter says that it is premixed for him in large pails and he puts it into smaller pails and there is no colour number. I ask if I could have a sample of the paint. Without hesitation, he takes a fresh mixing stick and paints the lower end for me. He tells me this is the first time anyone has ever requested a sample of his paint. I thank him. He smiles, telling me to stand it up with the wet side up, in a glass for a few hours to dry and returns to his work.

The day is filled with swims and shopping, eating and exploring. I look at planning our time and the places we want to visit. Everyone has a preference. We chat by the pool with maps and brochures spread about. Other guests offer advice and tell tales of what they found fun and interesting and what they recommend we not waste time and money seeing. I eagerly make notes. There is so much to see and do! The feeling of anticipation stimulates positive responses. I feel myself relaxing and healing.

Driving away from the hotel, leaving my children sleeping, I have a momentary pang of fear. *What if something happens to them? What if something happens to me?* I distract myself from these thoughts by turning on the radio. I'd offered to make this a group trip but there was no interest. As I drive south on my solitary morning visit to the mission at Capistrano, I recall Jack telling me about the swallows that return here every year on March nineteenth. One swallow always arrives a few days ahead of the flock, like it is checking that it is safe and still secure. Then as if on some invisible schedule, the little birds arrive. They build mud nests on the walls of the old mission. It is considered a miracle. He would often remind me when it happened or we would hear it on the radio and say: "spring really is coming."

The words from the love song slide into my mind. *When the swallows come back to Capistrano, that's the day you promised to come back to me.... Am I like the scout swallow, coming ahead of the flock? Will he ever want to come back to me as he has done over and over since we were teenagers?*

I turn off the Ortega Highway and wonder why I am here. *Is this like poking a bruise to see if it hurts?*

The mission was founded in 1776 by Fray Junipero Serra. I pay my admission and walk through the entrance to a garden enclosure. It is as if I have stepped into another time. The tinkle of falling water in the fountain masks the noises of the outside world. My pamphlet tells me that the stone church started in 1797 took nine years to complete. It was left in ruins by an earthquake soon after. Now it is without a roof and I can see the swallows nests and hear them twittering.

I think of the years of my life and how few they are compared to this place. How devastating to spend all that time building something just to have it crumble in ruins. Tears threaten to fall as I think of the hard work put into building my marriage and family just to have it fall apart in ruins.

I move through the adobe buildings and along the path to examine an olive press used for making cooking and lamp oil. The way of life of much simpler times is portrayed in the smelter, workshop and kitchen. Areas for school groups and tours are evident as well as modern toilets. Birdsong fills the soft warm air. The red tile roofs silhouetted against the blue sky remind me of Spain. Profusions of bougainvillea, roses, geraniums and flowers I can't identify, beautify the gardens along the worn walkways. There are few others about. I wander and explore in silence.

When the swallows come back to Capistrano, that's the day I pray that you'll come back to me. The words again sing in my head. *Do I want him back?* The swallows leave here on October twenty-third. Our seasonal timing is off. If he is gone for five months—like the swallows until March—I am sure I will have changed and become accustomed to a single life by then. It is much more peaceful without him. I am rather surprised by my thinking. But yes, it is much more peaceful without the silly conflicts that seem to have been created to put up walls between us. It is nice not to try to anticipate his criticisms.

I look up at the bells and wonder how they sound. *All the mission bells will ring, the chapel choir will sing, the happiness you'll bring.......* This is so peaceful. I say prayers of gratitude. My problems seem so insignificant given the age of this place and all the people who have passed through these sweeping arches over the centuries. They would have come here to pray for solutions and guidance for many problems I cannot even imagine. The bells toll as if in response to my silent request. They ring even if no one is here to listen.

I linger leisurely, enjoying my musings. The old Spanish alter, wooden statues and other artefacts rescued from the original church are carefully displayed. I read the plaques and examine the simple structures as the sun rises further into the California sky. *I wonder if my children are up and about.*

Laguna Beach is populated with many artists and after a swim, then brunch, we head out Canyon Road to find the Art-A-Fair. The wonderful collection of creations artistically presented give us several hours of enjoyment. I purchase a silver and lapis ring and replace my wedding band with it. We all have sparkles painted on our cheeks. We leisurely enjoy a delicious early evening meal.

My trip to Capistrano and the day with my children have revived my soul. A calm peace has settled over me and I am so glad to be away from the familiar stimuli of my life in Oakville. This is such an enjoyable place. After consultation with my children, we agree to stay a few more days. Fortunately there is room availability and we do not even have to change rooms.

We plan a day trip over the border into Mexico. My usual anxiety with border crossings is stimulated. The warnings about not taking a rental car across into Mexico further tweaks my sense of alertness. Thankfully, there are a good number of tourists going across just for a few hours. There are lots of tips on travelling safely and we agree we will make every effort to stay close together. With no drinking restrictions for age evident and willing waiters, I sit drinking Corona beer with my children in a street side café in Tijuana. I am sure Jack would be convinced I am corrupting them. Matt is just fourteen. We laugh as the conversation turns to: "What would Dad think if he could see us now?"

We wander through the market and joke with each other about buying huge Mexican sombreros. Laughter is good for the soul and we are all healing.

I sigh with relief as we return across the American border safe and sound.

We spend a day wandering south along the coast, enjoying beach walks, sea food feasts and whatever takes our interest. My credit cards get well used.

My children are sleeping late and I book a massage. My therapist's name is also Marilyn and we are close to the same age. As we chat, we share information on our relationships. I listen with interest as I hear what I choose to tell about my marriage. "He says I am not the girl he married." We laugh at the notion that we could go through so many life experiences and men expect us to stay innocent girls. She mocks a man's voice and says; "I'm looking for someone without baggage." It is such a common line. *Do men really think they come to a relationship without their history? Do they think the patterns of their past do not repeat in present relationships? I guess some men really want a dumb woman who will not compete with them or argue with their ideas.*

Thinking about Jack has become habitual. I must retrain my mind to stop. I believe we can change our thinking patterns but it does take some concentration and work. As I continue to listen to the words I choose, I am struck by the fact that the man I now know is not the man I think and talk about. I am remembering the best of times, not the reality of the cold man I now see. I grieve for the life I believe we could have had. I am sad that the plans I thought we were making as a couple will never be fulfilled.

On our final night in Laguna, we agree to eat at the hotel and pack up for an early morning start. The food is good and I enjoy wine with dinner. We are seated on the terrace with a terra cotta clay angel in a garden beside us. I notice she has just one wing. She is my friend, an outward manifestation of my Self. Years ago when a song called "You Are My Special Angel" was popular, and Jack and I were still in our teens, we danced to it. He used to tell me I was his special angel, but that I had a broken wing so I couldn't fly away from him. As I ponder this, I can see how it fits with the  pattern of keeping me thinking I am not acceptable, lovable, or as good as others, so I will feel unworthy and not stray. I know I am a special angel, a unique woman, with gifts to offer. Someday I want to meet a man who can see me as whole, not broken, and he will be happy to see me fulfill my potential. I do not have to be broken to compensate for his insecurities.

In controlling relationships the controller must always appear smarter and stronger than the one they want to control. In the beginning of my marriage I was in awe of Jack's intellectual abilities. I felt dumb, broken and thankful he paid attention to me. I am no longer broken. I no longer see him as superior in intellect to me. We are both clever people in our own way and those ways are not the same. I thought we complimented each other. I was happy with him so many times. I didn't know he was so unhappy with me.

I know infidelity occurs when one or both of the partners have low self esteem. If I had felt more lovable, more capable and put myself in a more valuable light, I would not have tolerated his flirtatious ways for so long. I come from a family history of men leaving women. Neither of my grandmothers nor my mother could role model for me, the way to be an empowered woman, confident of challenging men's ways and holding them accountable for the families they created.

While my paternal grandmother was able to carry on after her marriage ended, she had a lot of support from her children. I remember Dad going to his mother's every weekend to do chores. As teens we drove her to do her banking, get her groceries and other errands. A woman with children, making her way in the world, without the presence of a strong support system, is facing a formidable challenge. It is something I could do, but I have chosen not to do. My fear of being a single parent has led me to accept behaviour that is unacceptable.

My lack of higher expectations of a man led me to accept a relationship where I was capable and responsible, yet was repeatedly treated as if I was broken. He has not appreciated me as intelligent and capable. I have used denial to avoid conflict and made excuses for lies and betrayal. My insecurity has been manifest in my choice of a man. My fear of conflict has kept me from demanding better behaviour from him. I have forgiven too soon and moved forward without accountability. I must learn from my past or I am doomed to repeat it.

The view I had of marriage was an immature concept. It was more like each would parent the other and meet the unmet needs of the other. The man of course was to be the boss. Once married, it was a tragedy to divorce. As a Catholic woman I was taught I could never marry again. I should have left the relationship when I was a young teacher with income and professional security. I should not have tolerated his attention to other women then. I would not have sought attention from other men if I had felt securely loved in my marriage. I should have been more confident. I should have trusted myself more. I was afraid. I was afraid I could not cope alone. The social pressures to be married were great. I will never put myself in the position of such dependence on a man again.

Vows we make to ourselves and others, about what we will do if ever something specific happens, cannot be taken seriously, as we do not know how we will react until all the issues are available for consideration. Saying, "I would disown my child if they ever….." or "I would leave my spouse if they ever….." or "I will quit my job if…." are easy to say but hard to actually do if the situation happens.

There are many situations that arise in life that leave us confused and challenged to make decisions that will have very long lasting effects. Perhaps saying; "If ….. ever happens to me I do not know what I would do." or "I cannot imagine that ever happening to me." These responses would be more accurate and authentic. Sometimes our reactions surprise us.

Mission San Juan Capistrano

MAP and GUIDE

CHAPTER TWENTY-TWO

SILLINESS IS GOOD FOR US

Play as Stress Relief

T he Laguna Canyon Road is our most direct way to Anaheim. It takes us past hillside homes perched among brown dried grasses. While being surrounded with gardens and greenery, the potential for fire sweeping across the countryside seems great. This brings memories of my father's tales of the dangers of brush fires. He was raised on the prairies and on Ontario farms so knew first hand of their threat. I recount some of his stories about farm fires to my children.

I choose a basic hotel. I want to leave the bags in the room rather than the car as I feel less susceptible to theft. We check in and then head right out again. Fortunately, a room was available for early check in. My children were eager to get to the park. I recall our neighbour's story of checking out of their hotel and visiting Boston Zoo, leaving all their best clothes and new suitcases in the trunk of the rental car. When they returned, all of their belongings were gone and the car had been vandalized. Even the wheels were taken. While insurance covered the expense, it was a horrible invasion and inconvenience. This is not a story about "someone" but about a family we see every day.

Tinkerbell flies through the sky as I stand in awe. It is my twenty-fourth wedding anniversary and we have had a full day at Dis-ney-land. I remember saying years ago at Disney World, that if I was ever really sad or sick, to take me to Disneyland or Disney World. It is a hard place to be sad in, especially with three teenagers who are determined to have fun. I feel hopeful, happy and childish.

187

We arrive back at our room just in time to fall into bed. Leaving before breakfast, our exit is done efficiently. It makes it so much easier to travel as a group if expectations are clearly spelled out. Issues children can choose for themselves are left to them and issues they cannot have the power to decide are decided by the parent and then shared with them. I set the ground rules within the scope of their expectations. Our level of co-operation is high. I am sure the many years of packing up to go to the cottage and all the family trips we have taken have contributed to this. It sure makes it easy for me as we are all working together. Matt is great at packing the trunk and Julia is the final room checker to make sure no belongings have been left behind. Kathy is in charge of the food, making sure we have things on our list when the drinks, chips or cookies run low. I am, of course, responsible for the driving, the payment of expenses and making the ultimate decision of where we go and stay. Aside from entrance fees, each of my children has their own money for souvenirs, post cards and extras.

In answer to my question of their wants, it was unanimous that we go to Disneyland. Then they wanted Mexico, Venice Beach, Universal Studios and some open beach and pool time. The girls want to sun and to go shopping. Matt wants to windsurf.

Breakfast is fast food that we eat in the car. I marvel at the extent of the highways as we head north watching the names we have only heard about pass on the road signs. Everyone has a map and an opinion of which way to go. I tell my children to decide among themselves and then one person can relay the decision to me. We decide to miss the downtown as it is hot and not the type of day to be enduring traffic. A visit to the houses of stars and ultra expensive shops are not as appealing to my children as Venice Beach. I am happy to head to the beach too.

Our visit to Venice Beach, with the parade of remarkable people, stirs my anxiety. Vendors with unfamiliar products, attempting to

seduce my beautiful children into irrational purchases, rattle my courage. Before long, I see that they had agreed to lead me on and tease me.

"It's all right Mom. We won't get tattoos today."

We stand and watch a movie shoot, hoping to see a big star. We soon hear that it is for a commercial. No known star and not even a big name product.

"Wouldn't it be cool to see a real movie star."

Standing in the warm California sunshine, I watch as my family soak up the varied characters and feel the ambience of a place often seen on the TV screen. I am suddenly struck by the fact that I am a single mom and we are a family of four. I know for sure that it is far more normal to be a single mom here than at home on Carey Road. I am surprised that I do not miss home and even delight in being far away from it. *Perhaps we could just keep travelling.*

Universal Studio thrills us. Julia gets chosen from the audience to wear a space suit and soar above the set as if on a space walk. Matt takes part in an optical illusion display and it is fun to figure out how it was done. Kathy chooses not to get on stage when she is offered the chance. The action adventure show is thrilling and the back lot tour with Jaws lunging at our trolley adds to the excitement and enjoyment.

Tired and happy we decide not to head further north, but to find something on the beach. I love to be near water and prefer the ocean route to explore rather than the mountains. I book us into the Miramar Sheraton in Santa Monica. The impressive wrought iron gates, palm lined drive and lovely gardens seem imposing. It is centrally located to shopping and the famous Santa Monica

Pier. Our rooms are lovely and the hotel restaurant has something to please each of us for dinner. This really feels like California and we enjoy exploring and shopping. We want to experience the pier after dark but we are tired so our visit is limited to a walk to the end and back. None of us wants to go on the rides but an ice cream is nice. I enjoy people watching. No one here would guess my problems or even care. Travel helps us leave problems behind, to be dealt with on another day.

Exploring north through Malibu Beach, I am shocked to see how close to the surf some of the homes really are. There are also houses perched on the hills. They must have lovely views from up there. I wonder how deep the support posts must go to make the homes stable. I am sure the homes are very pricy even though some have small lots and are very close to the road. Privacy from the beach could also be an issue. I am sure the views would make up for the drawbacks.

We stop on a whim and marvel at still another perfect day. I want to be able to say I walked Malibu Beach, so we take some time to get our feet in the water. The waves curl in and we talk of surfing, swimming, beach volley ball and possibly seeing a movie star or two. We have seen lots of movies taken in this area. It has a familiarity yet we cannot really say we see something specifically familiar.

I turn off the Pacific Coastal Highway and drive up Malibu Canyon Road. We stop to look out over the coastline of Santa Monica Bay and I imagine some lovely sunsets from the decks of the mansions, hotels and guest houses behind closed gates. It is too early in the day for lunch, so we decide to head further up the coast.

As we drive, our conversation is about lifestyle options. We chat about what is real versus what is an illusion. We laugh more easily and chat more freely than we have for a very long time. We have finally arrived at a place where we can say; "I think Dad would like this" and no one even comes close to a tear in their eye. I gain confidence that there will be many more happy times in the future. In the grand scheme of things, we will get beyond our present sadness and insecurity. I am so very pleased that we all made the choices that we made to be together on this trip. We are growing as a family. We are learning new skills of co-operation and sharing that I know will serve us in the days, weeks and months to come.

The coast road leaves the water and we decide to head for Ventura for lunch. While eating fresh seafood and salads in a harbour side restaurant in the Harbour Village we have time to study the local guide books and make plans for our afternoon. We wander along the boardwalk enjoying the boats and consider a tour. There are so many options. I particularly enjoy the art galleries and shops while Matt looks at sports gear and the girls, of course, look at clothes, sunglasses and boys.

Again we decide to move on. The highway follows the coast and it is not long before we arrive in Santa Barbara. The Ocean Palms on Cabrillo is a lovely hotel across the road from the west beach, close to Stearns Wharf and shopping. It is an older hotel and we are able to get adjoining rooms. The pool and gardens are lush and tropical. A continental breakfast is included. This means I can eat when I want in the morning and the others can too. I tend to be up early and they all like to sleep late when they can.

> When we are hurting and healing, having someone take care of us gives us energy to restore our inner and outer balance. It is wonderful to have caring family and friends who take over responsibilities for awhile. When we have no place to go where we feel safe and cared for, paying for the services of others is money well invested.

> There is a difference between being taken care of and being cared about. I have many people who care about me and my children, but none who would take care of us. I want to be pampered and

feel taken care of and not by my children. I want them to be taken care of as well.

Our ground floor rooms open onto a garden courtyard. There are two queen sized beds in each room and sliding doors to little patios that are separated from each other with plantings. We immediately head for the pool for a swim before dinner. I have booked us into the hotel for two nights. Floating on my back, I can see the first star in the cloudless sky. *Thank you God for so many gifts and joys!*

Stearns Wharf offers us interesting choices for dinner. I feel safe and happy wandering with my children. We find a perfect spot.

As the longest deep-water pier between Los Angeles and San Francisco it was completed in 1872. It is also the oldest working wharf in California. It is an amazing construction. Named for its builder, local lumberman John P. Stearns, it originally served as a passenger and freight shipping terminal. When the railroad came to Santa Barbara in 1877, a spur line to the wharf linked it to the lumberyard and the Southern Pacific Depot. It is amazing it could hold a loaded train considering it is constantly pounded by waves. The spur and the pier were damaged by severe storms in the early 1900's. A logging car on the spur is a legacy of those times. Standing looking down at the water below, I imagine trying to build this. I really admire the engineers who designed it and the men who built such a wonderful structure. *Could they have imagined it as it is today? Can any of us really appreciate the impact there will be on what we build? I am so glad I am here.*

Building and destruction, rebuilding .....hmmm seems like a theme for me.

It is our last full day to enjoy California. The girls are happy to sit by the pool. Matt wants to find a place to windsurf. Ledbetter Beach has rentals and he chooses a board he wants. He is experienced on the water from lessons at camp and we have a basic board at the cottage. Off he goes. I settle with my book. I glance up often and see him getting further out from shore. *Not too far Matt!*

Sailboats and swimmers, beach walkers and sunbathers enjoy the breeze on this hot humid day. There is a haze on the horizon, but I can see oil rigs in the distance. It is hard to tell which sail is Matt's as he is really far out. I scan the beach for a rescue boat but there is no boat or lifeguard. The distant mountains silhouette against a clear blue sky and the peaceful scene is no comfort to my niggling anxiety. I refocus on the lovely day and trust my son is young, strong and experienced. I return to my book but cannot follow the plot. My mind turns to my fear of coming to California because of the possibility of an earthquake. The Discover Magazine I bought had an article on them. If one were to happen now, Matt would probably drown. *Could he ride it out? How could I ever go on without my children? Fear grips me. STOP this Marilyn!*

I must move. I wander along the large curving beach and back. Matt has been out over an hour. I scan the ocean for his sail. Just as I see it, he goes down. He has on a new wetsuit, life vest and harness. Another wind surfer moves close to him. In a few moments he is up again. He is such a fine young man. I do love him so.

I settle myself down and turn to a fresh page in my journal. I write the words "I Want" at the top of the page. I know I must get focused on creating what I want in my life.

- order – get a schedule as almost all parental responsibility will be mine

- routine – get a schedule with Jack for his time with our children

- laughter – make a list of fun things to do and fun people to be with

- time with my children – do not lose the good we have created by being busy

- good adult companionship – male companionship?

- exercise – start walking Pickles regularly

- health – I must watch what I eat—don't gain back the weight

- money management – meet with Jack to discuss without a legal fight

- challenge – in my work and volunteer activities

- positive attitudes – stop listening to his criticism of me – it is just his opinion

- achievement – make some things my way, paint the kitchen – new green

- find a cottage?

I look up to see Matt much closer than the last look. Relief flows through me. He sails his board close and asks for a hand bringing it ashore. He is tired and happy. He admits he got a little further out than he intended. The other surfer offered a hand but he was OK. I think it was a comfort to have the man offer though. We are both thirsty and he is very hungry.

"Let's go find the girls and see if they've had a good afternoon!"

CHAPTER TWENTY-THREE

WHAT IS REALLY IMPORTANT TO ME?

Looking at Long Range Goals

Returning to Oakville is not an easy emotional journey for me. While I have a job that gives me satisfaction and challenge, as well as many opportunities to express my opinions freely and get support for them, I also have a lot of emotional work to do. I know I must face my personal responsibilities. I must consult a lawyer and start the process of drawing up a separation agreement with Jack. I must know where I stand financially.

The children are happy to see their father and eagerly tell him of our adventures. It is strange, sitting as a family, laughing and joking. It is so familiar. Pickles has spent the time with Jack and he eagerly moves from one person to another, licking and nipping.

Jack is driving Matt north to Rosseau to camp. They need to leave early in the morning. I have laundry to do, so leave my family on the patio to start the washer. A sweet sadness fills me. *Why, when we can get on so well, must he end this marriage?*

I am surprised to find a card from Jack after he leaves. Tears fill my eyes as I read; "I remember a lot of little things, and times we shared that made me happy. Thank you for the memories you gave me. Marilyn.... when we get through all this I sincerely hope we can be friends. Welcome back to Oakville from sunny California."

I am very surprised at this message *What does it mean? Does he really think that he and I and Beth can all get together and be friends? Does he have no concept of how hurtful it has been to me to know she betrayed me? She pretended to be my friend while*

becoming involved with my husband. Does he have no idea of how hurt I was by her lies? I lost a friend with whom I shared so many challenges of motherhood. Does he not understand the loss our children have had because of the relationship mess? They have been cut off from their Georgetown friends. They do not want to see their father with another woman. Does he really expect the skiing at Caledon, the barbecues, cottage visits and hiking will be able to continue as before?

I tuck the card into my underwear drawer. No point in letting my children see it.

I take time, when the house is quiet, to write Jack a long letter. It isn't a love letter. I ask him to consider his actions, and before it is too late, ask if he will consider reconciliation and counselling. We have so much to lose.

My week is demanding. I have a new secretary starting first thing Monday and have the morning to orient her. My clients start at one. By Wednesday, I am in full work mode. I miss Matt but know he loves camp. The girls are working overtime to make up for the time they were away. The house is quiet, too quiet. A card from Jack surprises me. "I wish you a rainbow." *What now?*

He apologizes, "….for all the pain my actions have caused you both now and in the past." He says: "I guess we had it better than we knew, didn't we?"

Is he starting to see that it wasn't so bad after all? The final part where he says: "Don't write me off as a friend. Who knows what the future holds?" touches me deeply. I know I have many reasons to be hopeful of a good life alone, but my first desire is to grow old with this man who is my first love. I know I will never love with the reckless abandon the way I have loved him. I know our relationship needs a lot of repair. I am willing to try if he will. I tuck the card in my underwear drawer.

Another day, another card. "Just a note to let you know I am thinking about you. I don't know if you got the card I sent yesterday so here is another one. Hope you are feeling better soon. That dinner invite is still open. Jack"

I have no desire to be his friend and meet for dinner as he plans his future with Beth. *Is he looking for sex?* I shove the card in my drawer.

By Thursday, when Karen calls, I speak briefly to her between clients. She asks how my trip went. I tell her we all had a wonderful time and thank her for her help.

"I want to get away again."

I do not want to face the weekend here alone. Julia is going away and Kathy will be out and about with her friends. I suggest a resort in Muskoka. I want to drive my boat! I want the feeling of freedom and control. I want to visit Matt at camp.

Karen reserves a single room at Windermere House and arranges for a salad plate for my dinner as I will be arriving after the dinner service. Kathy will be home enough to deal with the dog. I eagerly head north after my last Friday client.

After dropping my overnight bag in the pretty single room I have been given, I go to the dining room and request my dinner. With the efficient courtesy of a first class hotel, I am settled on the screened veranda with a lovely salad. There are crisp cherry tomatoes and thin slices of cucumber nestled in a bed of lettuce. Slices of cold chicken and ham accented by cheeses, olives and pickles,

fill the plate. A selection of fresh rolls and bread, with a small dish of butter, sit in a basket ready for my choosing. A cool glass of Chardonnay is set before me. I relax into the comfortable chair.

I lift my glass and silently toast the reflections on Lake Rosseau of lights from passing boats, cottages on the far shore and the dock lamps. The air smells sweet from the flowers on the other side of the screen. Crickets are chirping. *To Muskoka, a place for healing and dreams coming true!*

After my meal, I wander down the stone steps and out onto the dock. The water is quietly splashing as waves from a passing boat curl at the shore and flow against the boats that dance on their ropes. I am eager to be on the water again. I recognize the man pumping gas and chat with him for awhile. His wife comes down to join us. I hear the latest local news. I have been coming to this area for many years, and feel like it is one of my homes.

As I wander back up the hill, music from the bar mingles with laughter. I wander around to see what is happening and if perchance there is someone I know. I go in, as if looking for a friend. It is busy but not crowded. There are no familiar faces. Suddenly I feel very tired, out of place and ready to end the night.

Heading back outside, ready to head off to snuggle into my bed, I pause a moment to look up at the stars. Millions of lights flicker in the vast expanse of darkness. I pick out the few constellations I can identify. I am so small and insignificant in the grand scheme of the universe. My troubles are so small compared to what so many go through. My mind slides over the years of star gazing. I remember my dad showing me the big dipper. I recall showing it to my kids. I say a silent prayer of thanks for so many happy memories and loving people in my life and ask for strength and support to face whatever lies ahead.

I wait until just after nine to call Mark to ask if there is anything new on the market in my price range. Since my trip was such a last minute decision, I didn't get a chance to let him know I'd be up. He tells me there is a place that the present owners are using as a home, but he thinks it would be perfect for me. It has just come on the market. It meets the list of things Jack and I had been searching for but since I had told him Jack left me, my criteria was downgraded. It is also more than I want to spend. I decide to have a look anyway. I don't want to go that high on my own, but it sounds like the best opportunity available. Looking cannot hurt.

I then call Uncle Joe. I'm not sure if he rises early. I ask if it is convenient to pick up my boat just after lunch and explain I want to visit Matt. He says he'll probably be there so anytime is fine. He tells me he'll leave the keys in it, just in case he goes out. He invites me to dinner. I gratefully accept.

I agree to meet Mark at his office in Bala. He shows me several pictures and tells me about the place he wants to show me. It is on a short private road, off a paved all year maintained road, with garbage pick up and school bus service. This fits my criteria of being all year accessible and not isolated. It is on a small shallow bay. He assures me it is deep enough for my boat. There is a lawn. I am not too excited about this aspect, but I have cut a lot of grass in my life and certainly know how. The living/dining room is L shaped with a fireplace insert. There are three bedrooms and a bathroom as well as a utility room with washer and dryer. This is good. The kitchen has a dishwasher and stove and fridge included, but no microwave. That isn't a problem for me. There is a winterized sun porch, two car open garage and lots of trees. It comes unfurnished but the vendor has a few pieces they are willing to sell.

"Let's go see it!"

As Mark turns off the main highway, I am pleased to see we are in a wooded area. I do not want to be too crowded and I want the feeling of being north. Some cottages I have seen are very close together with little privacy. I want privacy. The paved road curves along following the shore and there is a series of hundred foot lots with small cottages. Too crowded for my liking. The description says two hundred feet of frontage.

We curve again and then immediately turn down a wooded dirt single lane road. The second drive on the right takes into a parking area with a clap board cottage. My first thought is a little house in a big woods. It feels right immediately.

I step from the air-conditioned car into the soft summer air and breathe deeply. I cannot see a cottage on either side, just trees. I head for the lake. A rickety dock cries for repair. The frontage is mostly natural bulrushes and cedars. There is no deep water and I can hear my children's complaints. I love it. Turning toward the cottage structure, I see a sunroom that looks new. I know I'll spend a lot of time there.

There is a sense of coming home. I walk through the rooms, knowing I do not want any of the furniture. These people are smokers and it will need a good airing. I see potential problems but none that are so big I cannot cope with them. I ask about the pump, the electrical service and the septic.

Mark asks: "Are you doing this on purpose?"

I do not know what he is talking about. He explains that most women care more about the appliances and decoration than the plumbing. I assure him I know where the expensive problems will arise. I grew up in the country and worked side by side with my father, like a son. I've owned houses and cottages, renovated old houses and upgraded new ones. I want to know what I will be getting into here.

Slicing through the hot August afternoon, all of the 185 horsepower OMC motor on my Silverline boat humming nicely, I rejoice in the forces of the universe that push, pull and manoeuvre me to a place that fills my dreams. I am heading for Muskoka Woods Sports Resort at Rosseau to visit Matt. I cannot wait to tell him about the cottage I just saw. Being in Muskoka again, feeling the warm sun on my back and the wind in my hair, is invigorating. The spirit resides within the body as part of the whole, but as long as there is life there is a spirit to fan into flame. My spirit is being fanned and the glow swells in my breast. I breathe the air deeply into my lungs and smile and wave at passing boats. I am me again! I feel hope and joy. My beliefs about myself, when I am away from the insecurities with my husband, allow me to constantly expand into new ways to experience adventures. I know I am a growing, evolving person and I do not want to withdraw from the adventure of my life.

My trip to California was a healing journey for me and my children. We laughed at silly things and retold stories of our adventures again and again. Memories can get the laughter going and being playful is good for our mental health. We cannot think when we really laugh and our whole body responds with jiggles that release tension.

Playing and feeling joyful shifts our perspective away from worries and fears, allowing us to look at things differently. Playfulness increases our desire to live and connects with our own vital energy. I have high energy and love to be challenged. Allowing myself the freedom to play is going to be an important part of my recovery. *I must take time to be childish and to have fun!*

The trip to California was also a spiritual journey. I found my silly self again. Finding our Selves keeps us sane and centred. If sanity is the ability to meet ones own needs for living, I feel very sane and balanced! The inability to administer one's own affairs in a responsible way is a possible definition of insanity. Repeating behaviours that take us back to our pain is also a definition of insanity. My search for my Holy Grail, for that which is attained when one lives their own life, has been rewarded. This place in which I find myself is so much more profound than my freedom in Ireland. I must search for even greater depth to continue my heroine's journey. The dragons I must slay are my own fears. I will invite the fears to challenge me because in facing them, I overcome their power.

Through powerlessness we come into a new power—the power to live in hope, trust and love. Contemplating a new cottage that I choose for myself fills me with hope for many more happy family times and offers an opportunity to create a healing place that is all mine. I am committed to finding joy in my Self.

All cultures have stories of heroes and heroines who are exceptional in some way. I must find my special gifts and capabilities and carry them forth like a torch.

I raise my arm high over the windshield and stand with my feet braced firmly on the floor of my boat. I imagine I am a torch bearer charging forward with the courage to live my own sense of aliveness. I am with my Self again and I feel wonderful!

The words from an Ann Mortifee song fill my head; "We were born to live, not just survive…"

CHAPTER TWENTY-FOUR

CHIPMUNK CHASE

A Place for Healing and Growth

Fall 1988

My offer to purchase the cottage is conditional on my ability to arrange financing. I need Jack's signature on the financial papers because we do not have a legal separation agreement. I must have his consent and know that he will not block my purchase. This may mean we sell the house sooner than I expected but given we are living separately, the agreement shouldn't take long. Canadian family law is pretty specific about what we each get and what he is responsible for as the primary breadwinner. My share of the matrimonial assets will be released enough to allow me to have something conservative in Oakville and I can make the new cottage our family home.

I know I will have the funds from my inheritance and I have my share of the money from the cottage with Judy. It is in a mortgage to the present owners. Their payment to me will be put toward the new cottage mortgage. It will take some time to get the money from the matrimonial home, but I know it must be sold. I also have income from my work. It will take some financial planning and time. Up until now, Jack has no idea I have inherited any money.

As I sit before my lawyer, I know I must disclose the full amounts. Jack arrives looking nervous. He sits in the adjoining chair and I can feel my palms and feet sweating. As he settles in, he asks to see the offer I have made on the new cottage. I watch his eyes stare and shift when he sees the price.

"Where do you think you will get enough money to buy a place like this?"

His mouth turns up slightly in a smug smirk. He sits further back in his chair, as if I have expected he will be paying for this and he is about to refuse. I have seen that expression many times when he thought he had all the power.

I look at my lawyer and ask if I have to tell the whole truth. I know I do, but I relish the suspense, knowing I am the one with the knowledge for just this brief moment.

"I have some inheritance from Grandma."

Jack is suddenly alert.

"How much?"

"A lot."

I know that inheritance is not a matrimonial asset by our law unless it is put into a matrimonial property. The money is all mine. The only problem is, I do not get it all for two years. I need the equity in the matrimonial home for the cottage mortgage and he has half rights to that equity. I need his signature.

"How will you pay the mortgage?"

"I have an income from the inheritance for two years plus the old cottage mortgage owed to me. That will be more than enough."

I can see his shock and know his calculating mind is working fast. He asks many more questions and finally signs the paperwork necessary for the deal to proceed. I am overjoyed but keep my bubbling feelings in as much check as possible. *Thank you so very very much my dear Grandmother and clever Uncle Joe for your perseverance and brilliance!* My heart is singing as I turn and wave a cheery goodbye to Jack who seems stunned, standing by the curb outside the law office.

The phone call from Jack wanting to have a meeting surprises me. His serious tone and insistence convince me to meet him. I pick a neutral spot.

The words I longed to hear, the apologies and the declarations of him having made an error in ever leaving me, sit softly on my ears and my heart swells. He wants to reconcile! I have been convinced it was over and started to plan my future without him. I have been making independent decisions. Now he says he wants to reconsider and work on our marriage if I am still willing. A voice screams silently in my head.

"You cannot possibly be serious Marilyn. What if he just wants the money?"

I tell the voice to keep quiet. Jack makes more in a year than the total of what I have inherited plus the mortgage from the old cottage. He is very successful with more business than he can handle. He can pick and choose the cases he does. His fees are high and he is very well respected.

The next weeks are filled with flirtatious phone calls, flower deliveries and delicious sex. I ask questions about their sexual relationship. I must protect myself. He assures me I am safe from the possibility of a sexually transmitted disease. I have my lover back and the promise of our life together again. I flip between being sceptical and nervous and very happy. *Is it just about the money?* I want an intact family so very badly. I am "in love" with my husband and the thought of going forward with our lives.

"In love" is like a psychotic episode where caution is flung to the wind. I tell my friends and family about the reconciliation but not the inheritance. They are pleased. Jack was always such a family man, involved with his wife and children, that he couldn't possibly throw it all away. I was told Jack had had a mid-life crisis. I should forgive and forget and focus on my good fortune. I would smile and agree with them as I pushed my doubts deeper and deeper. I want to reconcile but there must be a new deal. Good relationships are based on making agreements and honouring them.

My practical Self shadows me and I am determined to negotiate his return to the matrimonial home. He must sell the townhouse as a symbol of his commitment to reconciliation, not make this just an experiment at living together. He balks and wants to rent it out. He claims he has someone who wants to rent it, and tries to convince me it will be a good income property. I have been a landlord before and I do not want the hassle. I cannot see that he has the time or experience to manage it. The story doesn't fit together logically. I do not trust the fellow he wants to rent it to. I am firm in following my instinct. I stick to my condition of him selling it as part of moving back.

We talk about the importance of creating our relationship so we both have our wants and needs met. I work hard not to be "our" therapist but he refuses to go for couple counselling. He finally agrees to go for individual sessions to work on not running away when the going gets tough and to work on resolving issues.

Our children are overjoyed with the process and there is no problem with them being home for dinner when dad is there. We all laugh and joke about old times and build fantasies of the new cottage. Seeing them happy is so important to me. One of my biggest fears is that I will make a decision that in the long run will hurt my children.

Our sexual contact is passionate and frequent. Because we have been intimate for so many years, we know what pleasures each other. We joke about "What will the neighbours say?" with seeing both of our cars in the drive mid day. Hugs are frequent but also tears flow freely with our new understanding of our selves and a new appreciation of each other. I repeatedly ask for details of his summer and their relationship.

I share my worries and fears as well as my joys and triumphs. He seems genuinely amused when I tell him about Tinkerbell on our twenty-fourth wedding anniversary. He assures me we will do something really special next year for our twenty-fifth. I so want to believe he loves me. He is giving every indication that he does. Perhaps we needed to nearly lose what we had to come back with so much appreciation and enthusiasm.

I work hard with clients, getting my children settled in school, managing the home and planning for the new cottage. Jack and I help Julia wash walls and clean cupboards in the townhouse residence at University of Toronto, Mississauga, where she is registered. We cart boxes and computer parts into Kathy's dorm at York University in Toronto. We go shopping with Matt for school supplies. Throughout it all, there are jokes, winks, hugs and lots of meals eaten out.

I wonder how Jack will react when I surprise him with the new California colour in the kitchen. I think the colour is perfect. The painter, who at first was surprised to be repainting the room so soon, agreed it was a much better colour. Jack loves it.

I watch Jack interact with the children and their friends in various situations and see a new confidence. I do not know this man like I thought I did. I do want to get to know who he really is. I had taken him for granted. I do not want to repeat my mistakes.

Since all our friends and family know we have been separate there is no striving to maintain the image of a "perfect marriage". However, I feel as if I am on a swing. One side is relaxed and very happy and the other is wary and fearful that this is too good to

be true. My laughter comes more easily when we are together, but when I lie alone in the dark of the night, my fears crash in on me. I doubt my sanity. *Can I trust this man?*

We make choices based on the information we have at the time. Some choices are made and the consequences are as good as we hoped or better. Some results are far worse than we ever could have imagined. We must learn to live with the disappointment.

Choices can be made with the possible consequences for others being considered or by just looking at what we predict will happen to us. Selflessness means we do not consider our self in the decision and do what we think is best for others. Selfishness means we only consider ourselves.

Maturity is the ability to accept the consequences of our decisions and to make new choices if we want to make changes in our lives.

CHAPTER TWENTY-FIVE

I WANT MY FAMILY WHOLE

A Time to Reconstruct

It is one thing to learn about affairs from reading and training, but it is an entirely different experience to confront the lies and betrayals personally. The chaos I have lived through and the beginnings of personal growth and healing must not be lost in order to reconcile. As much as I want to put the past behind me, I know that if the issues that led to the affair are not addressed, we are destined to fall back into the same trap. I must explore the areas that held their secrets so I can discover why he felt he could not have the life he desires with me. While on the one hand, I want the pain to just go away, I must be prepared to change and grow, both as an individual and within the context of being a couple. This must not be a quick fix. This will take the courage to change.

It is so hard to believe the person I thought was my most trusted partner could betray me and lie straight to my face. *Can I believe him in what he tells me now?* I so very much want to. *Is this wishful thinking?*

I believe it would be easier if this was the type of affair where my husband went off on a business or a vacation and was smitten with another woman. I am sure a one night stand would be painful to hear about and deal with, but not as painful as discovering both my husband and my friend misrepresented themselves to me. This is a woman with whom I had shared so many confidences, who I had supported through her first husband leaving her and so many of her personal challenges and who I thought was my friend. She is now remarried and settled. She too has betrayed me. The power of the double loss must be faced.

All affairs are not about sex. Some are about emotional betrayal, financial deceit, broken promises around family relationships, gambling or an affair with drugs or alcohol. When some factor or influence that affects the marital contract is hidden and lied about, it breaks the possibility for intimacy and builds distrust.

I have worked with couples where the sexual relationship in the marriage has cooled or become nonexistent, and the more sexual partner has had an affair because they want a sexual relationship. Some people have a sexual encounter to satisfy curiosity. I have also worked with couples where the deceit involved a man's relationship with his mother, where he lies about how much he visits and tells his mother about his marriage. Couples where one has been stealing to posture a better paying job, secretly using drugs or hiding their drinking, all involve deceit that if the partner knew they would make different decisions. The partner most often feels something is wrong but cannot always discover what it is.

I question Jack if this was a sexual attraction. He persuades me it was more of a friendship that bloomed into love. He tells me they have many things in common. She is more understanding and much calmer than I am. She plays golf, enjoys long walks and they do not talk about responsibilities.

Jack tells me I am too intense and too involved with too many things. From what he tells me and writes to me, I believe he wishes I could be more relaxed. I believe he wants a wife who is more available to him, not so focused on the children, has fewer outside friends and interests and over whom he has more control. I sometimes wonder if he is projecting his ability to have a secret relationship with her onto me and fears I have someone else. If only he knew how much I want an intact family with him as my life partner. The good times are really wonderful. If only we could hold onto them. It is the times when he gets so moody and so critical about such insignificant things that make it so hard. I try to explain that the hardest times always seem to be just before another round of his involvement with her. He acknowledges that he has compared us in his mind.

The comments he makes to me that convince me his intentions are honourable and he truly wants to reconcile and work on changing our relationship are spoken and written. While I want to believe him I do not want him to move back into what has become my home. It is the matrimonial home but I have possession. I want to take time to renegotiate the conditions of the new deal between us.

The children want to have some of their questions answered. I hear them both wanting to protect them and me from more emotional turmoil. As I listen to some of the conversations, that at times are more like cross examinations, I am sure that one or more of them would make a good lawyer. I think Jack is surprised by the depth of both their desire to understand and their hurt.

I consider his comparison of Beth to me. We are different women from different backgrounds and different value systems. I would find that list interesting to see.

I have had many clients come to me after they are involved in an affair and they have drawn up lists of pros and cons for staying in and leaving their marriage. They compare the lifestyles, the personalities, the sex, the conversations and the goals.

I have changed so much from the fifteen year old girl Jack met and the twenty one year old school teacher he married. I have gained my two degrees, developed a satisfying career and learned so much about so many things. I love my computer and he refuses to use one. He says I am not the girl he married. He is right; I am a mature woman now. *Have I outgrown him?*

All women change when they become mothers. It not only changes our bodies but it changes the way we think and feel. How we adapt to the responsibilities associated with being a parent will determine the changes we make. Since many women focus a great deal of their attention on their children, they tend to learn new things as their children learn. They are forced to adapt to new experiences, discover new coping skills and meet new people.

The more fathers are involved with their children the more they both will learn and grow. Many men learn to play with toys and to read books that they never had as children. Others return to the sports they played as a child and share their skills and enthusiasm with their children. Men who leave the parenting to the mother, tend to be left out of many experiences their wives share with the children and feel alone in their own family. They focus on their careers and miss the different stages of child development. I have had male clients say they feel their children grew up too fast. They acknowledge that their primary relationships are at work and they feel their wife is a stranger. The wife has grown in different ways than the husband and they do not know each other as people. Affairs are common in this style of marriage. Each person is looking for someone with whom they can connect.

I vow to myself to try to be calmer. I find it hard to live in a cluttered house. It is more stress for me to sit in a cluttered room than to clear it up and then relax. I seem to always be sorting piles of things that grow on counter tops and chairs. I will try to stop grumbling about junk mail and just learn to deal with it. I will try to be calmer about getting the children to be more responsible with their belongings. I will not let down on my parental supervision. I cannot play when there are issues that I feel are my responsibility.

My life is not about fulfilling the role he wants me to play. My life is about fulfilling my responsibilities and keeping my promises and finding meaning and a purpose for living. I do not want to give up the growth I have achieved just to be married.

I ask Jack if he is willing to accept that I have changed. He tells me he is. I explain that I have many interests and a lot of energy and I do not want to sit in front of a television every night. I explain that I am still building my business and that I need to work at that. This includes evening meetings. I do not bill my time at the rate he does and I do not have the staff he does. He tells me to stop competing with him. I assure him I am not competing as I could never imagine earning what he does. He seems willing to accept this.

I want to have meaning and purpose in my life when the children are grown and gone. I explain that I was very frightened when he left so suddenly and realized that I must be prepared to support myself. He asked why I bought the cottage if I was worried about money. I explain that I didn't want to fritter my inheritance away. Putting it into a property gave it some sense of stability and could be a good investment in the long run. It also gave me a safe place to go and have privacy and family fun.

I remind him I lost a lot of support and gained a lot of expense when we split offices. I do my own bookkeeping now. A book-keeper had done both our books since I started my master's degree. He has had a consistent secretary for many years, an assistant secretary, a receptionist and a bookkeeper. With the support of all that I do to keep our lives running smoothly, he is able to have more time and money for optional things. He has also been in business a long time and been supported to build his professional reputation so he does not have to go looking for business, and work to maintain referral sources. He has more business than he wants coming in the door all the time.

I remind him of the years when I supported his business development and he went to evening meetings. I remind him of the family connections my family brought to support his professional reputation. I am not going to be taken for granted. I want him to see how much work I have done to support his success and how little he has done to promote my success.

Jack accepts he is in a position to promote business for me and accepts that he could be much more proactive in helping me. He tells me to relax. There are many more years for me to increase my work. My practice does not have to be about earning money He convinces me that he will never leave me again. He explains that we will have a comfortable retirement and be able to put our children through as much education as they are able to achieve. I am not sure he is really listening to my concerns, but he repeats what I have said when I question him. He knows what I said. *Does he understand it? Does he accept it?*

I enjoy my work more than I believe he does. I have a different mental approach. I look at the joy of learning new things and meeting new people. I am excited to have time to get more focused on writing my first book. I am delighted with the doors opening for me with my photography. I love my computer. It stretches my brain and is very important in my relationship with my children as we are often talking about a new program or game.

Jack assures me he has stopped the relationship with Beth. Ted has told me he and Beth are working on reconciling. Since Jack still lives in his townhouse, and for practical purposes lives there, I have no way of knowing if they are meeting. I have his words and his cards and the long letters full of musings and promises.

Lying alone in bed when the house is quiet, I flip between joyful exhilaration and terror. I am trying to rebuild my trust and find forgiveness. I must know more about how he has spent the months apart and his time with her. I must go slowly. *How much is there to know and how much to forgive?* I must also accept that I have played a part in letting my marriage be vulnerable to this. It is a difficult struggle. I wonder why I do not just walk away and forget about this relationship. Sometimes I stop and look at my mother's picture and ask "What should I do?"

I have invested so much time and energy to have a family and a marriage. I do not want it to end. I want it to change. On the eighth day of the eighth month in nineteen hundred and sixty-four, I made a vow to stay until death parts us. *Does the end of keeping our marriage vows count as death?* Since eight times eight is sixty-four, it seemed like we were entering into something destined for eternity. I have the word eternally engraved inside my wedding band. I thought that we would always be together. *Where did I put that ring?*

> I wonder if we have lived past lives together. I believe our souls live before and beyond the life of our bodies. I also believe we can choose to be reborn to earth. This belief is part of the ancient teachings in Buddhism and Hinduism. Reincarnation was a doctrine once held by many early Christians. It is mentioned in the Bible that Christ taught that death means we are changed and it is not our end. Jesus identified John the Baptist as the reincarnation of Elijah. My years of reading and exploring these ideas have given me a solid belief system. Whether I call it my destiny or fate dealing me this hand, I will not walk away from one more chance to find lasting love and live in love.

> I know I am not over my caring for this man. *Are we here now to do soul work and complete past karma?* Karma is the principle of cause and effect. The consequences of our actions not only affect this life but the future of our soul's life as well. It continues throughout eternity. We reap what we sow. I want to work as hard as I can to sow love, forgiveness and find peace. Above all else, I do love my husband. I cannot say I have always liked what he has said and done, but I have done things I am not proud of too.

I remember when I first discovered that I could break our wedding vows. It was part of me taking my power from the religious teachings that are so paternalistic. It wasn't that I wanted to end my marriage, but it was the recognition that I could. It happened as part of my education when I met more and more people who had left abusive relationships and were much happier. Some were even in new marriages and very happy. God forbid! The church didn't allow that. But I started to appreciate that I could really choose my life path. I didn't have to be married. I wanted to be married. I want to be married now. Wanting to be married to someone we love makes a marriage very special.

I know that I can refuse to reconcile with Jack. I do not have to open my heart to him. I can protect myself from the possibility of future pain. I am just starting to heal. I can shut myself off emotionally from him and recreate my life. Someday I may even find someone who could love me and I could trust enough to open my heart again. *I wonder.*

I will not be able to support my children to the style they have become accustomed if I quit now. I am not a quitter. I will not be able to have an intact family. A lot will change. Jack will be able to afford a better home and better holidays. *Would they choose to live with him? Would he fight me for custody? Would they resent me for not giving it one more try? Would they blame me for breaking up the family? If he is not with Beth why should we be apart?*

Children see things from a different viewpoint than adults and basically want the best for themselves. That is as it should be. Parents need to take care of children. Children should not be taking care of parents. My children need to heal from the separation.

They are embarrassed that we are separated. They didn't want to see themselves living in his townhouse. They wanted to stay in their home. They are already grieving the loss of the cottage and the fun they shared with their cousins and friends in Muskoka. The new cottage and return of their father holds promises that there will be fun filled times again. I see the hope in their eyes. We talk about our feelings and they share with me their fears for our future without their dad daily in their lives.

My economic dependence on Jack for the quality of my life and my children's lives has definitely been a factor in my decision to stay through previous difficult times. As a housewife in Georgetown, after I gave up my teaching career in Etobicoke, my options for earning money were much more limited. Now in Oakville, with my practice growing and huge potential for more growth, as I put more time and effort into my work, I know I can live well. I am also not as concerned about money now. I will soon have my inheritance from my grandmother's farm. But we have built a very solid financial foundation as a couple and divorce causes financial devastation. *Why build it up to just tear it down?*

Reconciliation will protect our long years of investing and secure our future. We do have three children to put through university. Jack has always promised he will financially support our children in their studies as long as they are achieving. They are all clever and capable. I am sure they will go far with their education and be responsible adult citizens.

If I refuse Jack's advances, I am also afraid he will try to turn my children against me. When I did my university degrees he used to tell them that I loved my work more than them. They were little at the time and asked me in fearful voices if I had stopped loving them. It broke my heart. To think he might be able to convince them that I don't love them frightens me. He can be so convincing.

I also fear the emotional damage to my children. I have read, attended workshops and worked with angry upset children of divorced parents. I have seen the devastation emotionally and the problems socially. I want the best for my children. I want them to have the best chance at developing their own lives. They need a good education and a secure base from which to launch. They have been through enough already. I have been through enough. I want to be emotionally available as well as physically present for my family. I do not want to relocate and rebuild.

I have not been in the workforce full time in many years. I have had a lot of freedom running my own practice. I have been able to have the best of a stay at home parent, as well as developing a career. I do not have a pension and I do not want to be a homeless woman. I know this is building fears where I do not need to build them. There are so many considerations to this decision. I know by choosing to let Jack romance me, I am really deciding to reconcile. I want to work on this relationship. Jack must agree to counselling.

I must not just look at what my children need but also what I need. I have worked very hard to create our home. I know it is "just stuff" but it is my stuff and much of it has happy memories. Some of it comes from my parent's home and even some from my grandparent's homes. I look at an old cookie jar that has always been on a shelf. My mother prized it. It came from her mother. *I want to be married and together as a family!*

I remember my mother's comment when I complained early in our marriage that Jack was gone a lot of the time with his studies and his friends. She had told me:

"You made your bed, now you lie in it."

I have worked so hard to adjust and accommodate. I do not want to throw it all away. I do not want Jack to throw it all away. I know he has trouble adjusting to our children's growth. Matt is so proficient with the computer and he has taught himself to play the piano beautifully. He has expanded this into keyboard playing. He is an excellent skier both winter downhill and water skiing in summer. He windsurfs and plays rugby and so very much wants to show his dad his achievements. He has grown tall and can look his father in the eye. I often see Jack look inept when Matt has tried to explain something to him. This is normal. Each generation learns things the parents will never master. The children grow up in a different time and have different opportunities. Many parents feel threatened by being less knowledgeable or proficient than their children. I must help Jack accept that his children are young adults and they need his guidance and support. The girls are at university so the phone should be quieter. The cars will have less demand on them. He might find that calmer.

Even if our children do some things better than we do, learn things we do not know and go places we have never been, they need to grow and change to become themselves. However, they still need and want their father in their lives. He must adjust to their changes. He must see how important he is to all of us.

There have been difficult times and there have been so many happy times too. Accepting Jack back is the wisest decision, all things considered. It gives me back my relationship with the one person who has been in my life through so many experiences. I consider him my friend. I pause as I think this. *What does this really mean?* I thought he was my friend. Some of my friends haven't been treating me so well lately.

Reconciliation protects me from economic adjustment, the stigma of being a single mother and answering people's questions about what is wrong with me that I would lose a perfectly good husband. People do not see his manipulations. Of course, because he is so high profile and successful, so charming and witty, he is seen as perfect and good.

When I am with him I feel loving and close. He is being so attentive and thoughtful. I hope he is not just pretending. He appears so genuine. His letters and cards are so convincing. He really can be a good husband. I am not perfect. I am sure I am hard to live with. I have had so few men interested in me throughout my life that perhaps I would have a difficult time finding someone else. I do not want to live my life alone. Stepping into a new life without the man who has been a part of my life since I was fifteen seems very strange. Jack is giving me another chance.

When I look at my whole life, this is a really good time. I have many more good parts of my life than bad. The bad parts are really rather predictable. I have coped with the roller coaster emotional ride so long that it has some familiarity. I must relax and enjoy his decision to return. *Stop thinking so much Marilyn!*

The reconciliation time takes us to new levels of intimacy. The hope that this is the last time we will go around this cycle is exhilarating. I am going to do whatever it takes to help Jack accept that what we have is worth protecting. If I can get him to work on our relationship, I know we can have something very worthwhile for ourselves, our children and eventually our grandchildren. There is a big picture. Our behaviour affects many people.

A friend is someone we choose to have in our lives. Our neighbours, co-workers, and people in authority over us are not our friends because we do not choose them. We can however, have a friendly relationship with them.

We can also choose not to have people in our lives. We can end our relationship with people who belittle, bully, and abuse and disregard us. Ending a relationship is wise when there is no advantage to us in keeping the other person in our lives. Many people may want to be our friend for their gain. If it is not a relationship where both people give and get, it is not a friendship.

There are many kinds of intimacy other than sexual intimacy. Intimacy involves being in the same place physically, emotionally and/or intellectually. When we attain all three together, we can have a spiritual connection and awakening.

Some people with an intellectual intimacy start a relationship. Just as a physical attraction or emotional connection can be the trigger to developing greater closeness. I have had clients where a shared work project, a shared grief or feelings of lust start relationships that have no connection in the other essential areas. They soon find their partner lacking in emotional connection, sexual interest or intellectual compatibility.

When one area of connection is not in a relationship, people often seek out the area they feel is missing. They soon find that the connection they took for granted is now missing in the new relationship. This contributes to a great many relationships that start as affairs loosing their intensity.

CHAPTER TWENTY-SIX

BUILDING FROM THE PAST

Something New – Something Old

I am excited about the new cottage. I am getting it unfurnished. I have been planning what furniture I will take from home and what I will buy new. Now there is also the furniture Jack bought to take into consideration. I arrange one of my two pre-closing visits when we can all go to see it.

Everyone is excited and we are blessed with a lovely day. Jack noted the poor condition of the dock and his concern at tying the boat to it. He looks at the basic cottage construction and is pleased to see the building is a firmly built cement block structure, placed right on granite. The crawl space underneath, where the furnace and pump are located, slopes high at one end but is useful for storage and accessible through a small door on the end of the cottage. The electric heat in the winterized sunroom could be costly. With three sides of windows and a double pane glass entry door if would only need to be heated if we were using it in winter. The master bedroom is composed of two small bedrooms that have had the wall between removed to make one larger room. Unfortunately, there is a window from the sunroom into the master bedroom. Not the best for privacy.

Our children are disappointed it isn't on deep water. Matt is happy with having his own bedroom even though it is small and the girls like the large bedroom and closet they will get in the roadside addition. There are lots of questions and comments. We measure rooms and discuss furniture. It is a fun day.

Jack and I again go north for a weekend for the final inspection prior to closing. I have brought furniture measurements and I want to re-measure rooms and make a list of what will fit. After visiting the cottage and doing all the measuring we want, we go to Knapp's Furniture in Gravenhurst. We buy beds, dressers, lamps and a sofa and arrange for delivery next Saturday. They have good quality in cottage style furnishings and we feel they are reasonably priced. There is no point in buying things from several places then worrying about moving them. There is enough furniture moving to be done. We look through Canadian Tire and Steadman's and make notes on our lists. We can return to get the items once we can take them straight to the cottage. This will save time next weekend. We are like children spending gift money.

We arrive at the Muskoka Sands Resort and check in. I am so happy to be doing this together. I shudder at the daunting task of doing it alone but know I would have managed. After a lovely dinner, we return to our room. Jack has brought a bottle of wine chilling on ice in a cooler. We sit on the little deck off our room in the warm evening air. Finally the mosquitoes are driving me crazy. I plead the need to retreat. I hate to stop the intimacy of sitting in the darkness together, but I am being chewed to bits.

Laying in bed in the darkness the drone of the bugs continues. Finally, I decide the only thing to do is sleep with the sheet over my head.

I awake to near silence. I smile at the reality of the manly body beside me. I love open windows. The gentle lapping of the waves on the shore just below our room is delightful. Oh, I have missed Muskoka. As I open my eyes, I stare at the ceiling in horror. I reach for my glasses, and then start to laugh. A fit of giggles overtakes me. Jack awakens and sleepily asks what is so funny. I point to the ceiling. No wonder I was being eaten alive. The ceiling is thickly coated with mosquitoes, millions of them.

We start our day with laughter over a shared experience. It appears the bugs are not hungry and they do not bother us again.

We check out and go boat hunting. We have our big boat and my red canoe. Jack had bought it last May for the children to give to me for Mother's Day. I had been surprised as it was totally unexpected. It had only had one paddle. Jack had joked that it was time I learned to paddle my own canoe. I had thought this odd at the time. I had written it in my journal and felt a wave of fear at the possible implication. It is a large canoe, too large and heavy for me to put on and off the car alone. My car has a T roof and couldn't carry a canoe. It is too large for anyone but a strong competent canoeist to manage alone unless the water is very calm. It is also larger than my blue canoe that I left at the last cottage. I was sad to leave it behind but the purchasers had included it in their offer. No point spoiling a deal for the sake of a canoe. I was sad to lose it but felt confident I could choose a new one once we bought another cottage.

I had then been furious when Jack moved out and left me with the canoe in the back yard. He knew he was leaving when he bought it. He knew he had no intention of buying a cottage with me. I must find some time to ask about his reasons for buying it. I am reminded of the music tape I took on my trip to England and Ireland. *Was it a set up? Was the canoe another time when my concerns and objections would be turned into him calling me ungrateful and bitchy?*

I pay for all the purchases from my inheritance account, including a new Boston Whaler. Walker's Point Marina is the local dealer. We decide to get a fourteen foot with a forty horsepower motor, as it is more versatile and safer than an aluminium boat. I like the flotation features and the steering wheel, rather than the driver having to sit back holding a handle on the motor. I know our children will be the ones using it the most. They will be able to water ski behind it. I want them to be safe.

On our way out of Gravenhurst we stop at Home Hardware. I want a lawn tractor. Jack is surprised when I suggest it but the grass will need cutting before this year is out. I know I do not want to spend hours pushing a mower. I do not want lawn service as some of my cottage neighbours have. I know this is really a Muskoka home and not many people's definition of a cottage, but driving a lawn tractor seems like fun. The bright new tractor and trailer will be delivered next Saturday. We get the trailer for moving things about, like garbage to the road and lawn furniture in the spring and fall.

I sit quietly thinking about the changes in my life as the miles slide past. Jack is content to drive and we sit in comfortable silence. Our children are expecting us for dinner. It is as if we are on a honeymoon. I think of the pattern of leaving and returning that has occurred over the thirty years of knowing this man. After the devastation of a break-up, he returns all promises and apologies. He assures me I am his one true love. I have many cards and letters that I have kept over the years, even when he insisted I throw them out.

I am reminded of the physical abuse pattern, where after an assault, the abuser is calm, often gentle, and loving and makes promises never to hit again. Many abuse victims describe their partners as pleasant and affectionate when they are not angry and mistreating them. Just as the victim may be convinced that this abusive incident will be the last, I convince myself this leaving will be the last. I believe that things can change for the better, if only he will work at it. He promises he will.

The real estate deal closes. I have insisted it be listed only in my name. I make a determined effort to both share my joy and be very clear to Jack that if he ever leaves again this is my cottage and not a matrimonial asset. He agrees and says I can pay for the things we get and they can be mine. I suggest we get a reconciliation agreement. Jack refuses. *I hate feeling so fearful. I hate feeling so powerless.*

Cranberry Festival is mid October and the weather is superb. The girls head off to meet friends from our old cottage. Matt, Jack and I go in to Bala in the Whaler. We visit the vendors and eat junk foods. I sense Jack feels awkward when he meets Mark, but both are professionals and greet each other warmly. Jack assures Mark he is pleased he helped me find the cottage and it is a good one for us. A flight in a small plane over the fabulous fall foliage, with two passes over our bay, gives me lots of chances for photographs. I feel as if God is smiling on us.

In late October, I am off to New Orleans to present with two colleagues at the American Association for Marriage and Family Therapy conference. I fly alone. After checking into the Marriot, I attend the opening addresses by Evan Imber-Black on Rituals of Healing and Celebration, Michael White on Externalizing The Problem and Lynn Hoffman on My Life as a Family Therapist. I feel that at several points they are speaking directly to me.

At the welcome reception following, I meet a number of people I know. Some of them have met Jack at previous conferences. I am asked why he isn't with me. I do not want to explain. Groups are going off to dinner but I am not in a mood for sharing or partying. I am exhausted and want time to think. I also want to review my notes for tomorrow. I want a quick spot to have dinner. The hotel concierge makes several suggestions and gives me directions.

Travelling alone, I keep a keen eye out to be aware of my surroundings. I have my passport and credit cards in a pouch strapped to my body. My purse has a few dollars and some tissues, a comb and city map. I will let it go if I am approached. It would be stupid to struggle. An assailant wants my money not me. I try to look confident and not lost or confused. I avoid eye contact and look over people's shoulders when the street gets crowded. I also stop to look in shop windows and look in the reflection to see if someone appears to be watching or following me. I do not want to be approached.

Finding one of the recommended restaurants, I sit with my back to a wall, so I can see about the room. I mistakenly order my peel and eat shrimp Louisiana style, not knowing it means they put Hot Sauce in the water. They are too spicy and burn my mouth. I eat as many as I can, then fill up on bread with lots of ice water.

I meet with my colleagues over breakfast and we review our presentation one more time. I feel honoured to be presenting with such capable people. We are presenting on the stages of marriage at approximately the ten, twenty and thirty year level. How is marriage different when there are young children, from when the children are in their teens and then again, once the children have left home? How do societies' values for marriage and the state of our own marriages as therapists carry into the therapy room? I have struggled with my presentation. When I agreed to do this presentation, I had no idea Jack was leaving. Now he is moving back into our home while I am away.

My religious and cultural conditioning was to present myself as the expert, talk about issues from a third party perspective, not disclose personal information and maintain the façade of a good marriage, in the eyes of society and my professional peers.

I have decided that my best way to present is to be honest and face that we are among the statistics. Many marriages fall apart when the children are teens. I look at reasons and the chances of reconciliation. My research and preparation are very personal. I do not want to talk about trends. I want to share what it is really like, so other therapists can get a better sense of how to help clients at my stage of marriage. My presentation has statistical research, facts about clients and trends in the professional literature and personal disclosure.

I am nervous but confident that I have a valuable presentation. I am delighted with the reaction of the audience. I am also gratified by the support afterward. I am thanked for being honest. Several people tell me they hope I will present again, so they can hear how my story unfolds. I look forward to doing that as I get pleasure from public speaking.

I attend some interesting workshops. One is on getting a book published and I am eager to move forward with my writing project. I take a business card from a publisher's representative who asks me to send several chapters. She sounds interested in my subject.

I take a break and ride the trolley to the end of the line and back just for the experience. I shop in the mall and go out to dinner with colleagues. Wandering on Bourbon Street with a happy group in the evening is a wild and crazy experience. This is especially dramatic because people are dressed for Halloween. The following morning, I take an early stroll and start to adjust for my trip home.

I suggested Jack move in while I am away. I want him to be sure he wants to move back. I will not to interfere with his moving. Matt is eager to help and he and his dad will be spending the time I am away together. I do not want to be seen as in control of his actions as I am not able to control him. Jack has assured me he wants to be my husband and to commit to all that implies. *I hope I am not being too gullible.* He tells me he is really sorry for all the pain we have all experienced and that it won't happen again.

227

Marriage is an attachment system of care giving where each individual has their own story. They develop behaviours, skills, ways to express their feelings and their individuality. They also learn to play the role that keeps the marriage going.

We will never be the people we were before the separation. We are hopefully wiser and more aware of how fragile a marriage can be. We must be different together. While I was raised to believe that to have a good relationship with a man, the relationship is my responsibility, not his. I have grown beyond that and know that the marriage is something that both spouses must make a priority.

Marriages do not work. People work at being married. We must work at compromising, sharing, committing and being open to change. We must also work on true forgiveness.

MATT USING THE LAWN TRACTOR

CHAPTER TWENTY-SEVEN

I WANT TO SING

I Cannot Always Do What I Want

I am excited to be home. There is some unpacking to be done, but the furniture Jack has returned along with what he bought himself has filled up the spaces that have been vacant since last June. Some pieces will go to the cottage. We'll do that next weekend.

Long before I knew Jack was returning, I had booked a conference in Washington. He is staying home with our son. Even though I have only been back from New Orleans for just over a week, I am excited to be going to this event. It is entitled Releasing the Creative Spirit and I will be staying at the Hyatt Regency Hotel on Capitol Hill. I know no one personally who is attending. It was part of my plan to do new and exciting things. I am fascinated by the presenters and have read the books of some of them. I want to learn how to evoke my creativity for my work and in my personal life.

When I read the brochure and saw references to exploring the relationship between psychotherapy and the creative process to help therapists become more creative in their work and lives, it called to me. The thought of opening myself to the freshness of the moment through music, dance, poetry, writing, storytelling and more, fascinated me. I knew I would need to recreate my life, my goals, and my dreams and find a way to bring freshness to my work. I asked Jack if he wanted to come along. I could see if there was still space. He said he'd stay home with Matt.

The list of Jungian analysts, singers, healers, drummers, a choreographer, a film director, and a neurologist as well as authors and artists, made choosing workshops challenging. Titles of the workshops included Writing as a Psychological and Spiritual Resource, The Four Foundations of Creative Process, Dream Work as Therapy, Spiritual Discipline, and more.... Jack loves music and he writes poetry. I wish he'd said yes to coming. Matt could have stayed with one of his friends.

My room is spacious and comfortable. It overlooks trees and I feel safe and protected.   The hotel is friendly and the people on my conference are varied and filled with enthusiasm. This is unlike any conference I have been on before.

I focus on my creative process. In the workshops when the participants introduce themselves, I am asked what I do and what my dreams for myself involve. I share my desire to spend more time with my writing and the dream of working with clients in creative ways. I want to stimulate the creativity in my children who all have their own ways to express their individuality. I share that I hope to do more with photography and return to some of the creative artistic work I have done in the past. I have a specialist teaching certificate in art education and a course in music therapy. I find creative visualization a powerful tool both personally and professionally. I want to do more work with dreams and accessing the subconscious. I am filled with energy and dreams of possibilities of ways to expand and enrich my life.

I am thrilled to find myself dancing in a large group trailing silk scarves, drumming and singing, meditating and becoming lost in the stories and presentations. I sleep well and eat well and feel a healing energy pulsing through me. This is exactly what I needed to help me recover from the painful time I have been through.

Through the creative process we can uncover what is in our subconscious and discover hidden areas of our potential. Our individuality can be revealed. The journey of personal growth is to uncover meaning in life and acceptance of our Self. As we take this challenge and uncover the deeper issues that influence us just as a magnet influences metal, we can begin to ask questions such as:

What is the meaning of my life?

How can I accept and cope with despair?

What is my belief in God?

How can I accept my feminine nature?

How can I accept my masculinity?

What part do my emotions play in my life?

Can I trust my inner dialogue?

Do I like my Self?

Can I trust my own judgement?

Can I accept the parts of me that are unacceptable to me?

We need to learn to be able to grow and change. By challenging the things we have been taught, we can learn new ways to think and be in life. Letting my creativity flow opened many questions and brought to the surface many issues I had previously barely been aware were within me.

In one guided imagery session, I find myself imagining I am clinging to a slippery rock in the middle of a swiftly flowing river. I feel fear that I will be swept away. I think of letting go of the rock, my old ways of being, and allow myself to be carried with the current. I will be carried into my own future. But I will be alone. *Is there someone there to rescue me? How long is this river? How deep is this river? Will I be able to make it to shore?*

I cannot see the shore. Seeing the water come at me, I know that my present position is constantly changing. The water moves on and I stay clinging. My arms ache and I struggle to find the courage to let go. I desperately hold on. I struggle with knowing myself, my fears, and my knowledge that ultimately I must make the decision for myself. I am truly and utterly alone. A log slides past and I question reaching for it. *What if what I choose to hold onto is only an illusion of support? One, two, three ...I will let go. God be my guide!* I tumble and turn and gasp for air. I relax and let go of my desperation. I float, then swim, then fly into the air and soar like a huge bird of prey. I know I am multi coloured, light and free.

The narrator's voice brings me back to the room and I am aware of the thin mat on the carpeted floor of a meeting room. I stretch and know something dramatic has moved in my psyche. It is too raw and I choose not to share it with others.

As I snuggle in my bed and make notes on my imagery, I know it is a message to me from my subconscious. My childhood Catholic beliefs had me believe someone would rescue me. I thought there would always be safe shores and set boundaries. Clinging to my rock, I was not cared about, needed, or even in any relationship with anyone but my Self. If the rock was home it was not safe. It was hard work holding on. Yet I had no experience in the dream of a home. Home was within me.

My mind wanders off to many times in my life where I was totally on my own. I recall dreams of falling and of being lost. Yet in this experience, once I let go, I was able to swim and fly. I saw myself as beautiful and free. I had confidence and power. I trusted I could swim and I trusted I could fly.

A giggle starts very low in my gut. It swells upward and I feel a delicious sense of fun. I am suddenly aware that as the beautiful multicoloured bird, I did not sing. *I want to sing!*

The week after I return home we go to the symphony. Suddenly in the middle of a familiar piece, I remember the lovely bird and I want to sing. One firm rule of concert going is not to sing along unless it is the kind of concert that people are expected to sing along. The program states that the other patrons have not paid to hear me sing but to hear the people on stage. To be able to sing on stage and have people applaud must be one of the most exhilarating experiences possible!

Two days after the concert I have to have a root canal. The nitrous oxide that relaxes me also brings back my desire to sing. Holding on to my reserve, I alternate between breathing through my mouth and my nose so I do not get too intoxicated that I try to sing. The desire to sing stops abruptly once I am breathing room air. Heading home with my dear friend Maureen driving, I have no thoughts of flying or singing. I just want to sleep.

The following week I attend an all day seminar on marketing public speaking and do an evening presentation to the University Women's Club. Saturday I take the train to Kingston and present to colleagues on working with clients who are adult children of an alcoholic parent. This is not a time to sing.

I am enjoying my challenges but look eagerly at our coming holiday. Time to get away and share family time. Perhaps a chance to sing.....

CHAPTER TWENTY-EIGHT

A RETURN TO HAPPY TIMES

Time to Stop

For Christmas in nineteen eighty-eight we head to our condo on Captiva Island. This is a return to familiar family vacation time as we have been coming here for several years. I always find that living in the confined space of a two bedroom timeshare gives us many chances to be together. Since the girls have been at university our time as a whole family has been much less than is usual. There are lots of stories to share.

Jack and I drive down in his new Cadillac with Matt and his friend Andrew. The sound of their computer games gets annoying at times and we insist they switch to using the earphones and their tape players. Batteries are consumed at a great rate and frequent stops replenish the snacks and drinks.

The girls need to remain behind for university responsibilities but fly down in time for Christmas. It is hard to believe how responsible and competent they are. I worry about missed flights and lost luggage, the house being closed properly and other things that could go wrong. Thankfully they arrive with no delays or complications. They also assure me they completed everything at home so it will be safe on our return.

We eat out frequently. There are wonderful restaurants on Captiva. Shopping in Sanibel and Fort Myers also helps pass the cooler days. Rather than shop for gifts, we have given our children cash. Andrew's parents did the same. They are having a fine time making their choices.

December in Florida is not always warm and sunny. Our pool is kept nice and warm as our condo association believes in keeping it comfortable. Some days it is easier to get into the water than to get out. The cool air chills us quickly. We spend lots of time swimming and walking. Reading is another pastime. I find it a welcome change from a Canadian winter. Jack complains that he misses the snow and would prefer a ski holiday. He tries to entice the children with talk of fires in a fireplace, sleigh rides and snowball fights. They love to ski but are not swayed by his descriptions. They laugh and tell him they have never been on a sleigh ride. Christmas Day the local cable TV has a video loop of a log burning fire in a fireplace. It plays for awhile but soon everyone is off enjoying other pastimes.

Matt and Andrew love to jet ski. They look too difficult for me to try but I am tempted. The girls try but decide wave runners are much easier. I pay the rental fee and watch from shore. They try to keep up with Matt and Andrew who are very daring and love to jump waves. I love watching them all laugh. Their happiness is very important to me.

Waves are rolling on the sunlit shore. Soaring seagulls are calling; their cries mingling with the voices of Frisbee throwers, chatting beach walkers and the sound of the motor of a passing boat. My sun warmed skin is tickled by a gentle breeze sliding across my cheek. This is Captiva! I enjoy being able to just sit on the beach. This is a dream come true. A dream I hold in my heart on the cold days of winter that seem so very far away. I fondly remember the pong-a-pong of the tennis balls and the crackle of the palm leaves scratching each other in the breeze and smile. Now I am here. I feel in tune with this day. I am alone. Jack is having a nap. Our children are on their own adventures. My solitude has no regrets. I am happy with my choices. I am happy my husband is back. My children are happy we are all together.

January is busy for me professionally. I do a radio show interview for CFRB on the changes people make to their lives when they marry. I attend board meetings, present at a career night at the University of Toronto, deliver a corporate seminar, entertain at a business development luncheon to explore some new consulting work, see my clients and oversee my business responsibilities. I could never manage this schedule without a full time secretary. I have lunches with friends, family dinners out and an evening at the Opera with Jack. My life is rewarding and full.

Jack and I decided to visit Tybee Island, South Carolina. We need time as a couple, away from responsibilities to work on our relationship. We are using a free bonus week from RCI our timeshare company. We have packed books and warm clothes, knowing that even though we may walk the beach, it is not swimming weather. It will be a chance for us to be alone with no agenda.

When our flight lands in Charleston, we are shocked to feel the plane suddenly turn off the runway. We come to an unexpected stop and feel the plane tilt slightly. The engines are shut off and we wait in fearful anticipation. Our pilot turned too soon and the front wheel of the plane has sunk in the mud beside the runway. We are eventually bussed to the terminal, but not before some anxious moments.

Most of the touristy shops are closed. We find a great breakfast spot called The Breakfast Club and eat out every morning. Trips to Savannah and the surrounding area include lots of walking and quite a lot of driving. We poke through antique shops, book shops and old churches. We plan each day going just where we choose, with no set agenda. Some days we sit outside in a sheltered sunny spot away from the wind. It is restful and healing. We nap some afternoons, read books and newspapers in companionable silence, then debate philosophical issues from our reading. We walk the beach, commenting on the Christmas trees placed in rows next to snow fences. These will trap the sand and eventually make dunes. I carry my camera looking for interesting shots. Seagulls bathing in the tide pools, moss on the rocks waving with the tide and footprints in the sand are captured on film. I love the old mansions, the beach homes on stilts and the moss draped trees. It is quiet. It is intimate. It is perfect.

Our time in Tybee is balancing time. Relationships can be compared to a teeter-totter. At times they sit perfectly balanced, level, with neither side higher than the other. Each individual in a relationship is like one end of the teeter-totter. A well functioning relationship goes in and out of balance. At times it is quiet, still, equal, yet this can lead to boredom and a sense of being static. While many might think this kind of vacation would be monotonous, I found it restful. We have had too much teetering and tottering.

The more two individuals are different, the more difficult it is for them to find balance. A relationship where each is equal with the other allows the most freedom to either be in balance or to play with a shifting of balance, knowing that coming back to the balance state is possible and desired.

If one is always heavier, stronger, worthier, holier, etc., there is no contest, nor is there any interest. One will always be the one down, while the other will always be the one up. That type of relationship ends up being static and ultimately devoid of the potential for emotion or motion toward growth, just as much as one that never moves from the state of balance.

In any life, there is balance within the individual; the physical with the emotional, the intellectual and the spiritual, the sorrow with the joy, the pain with the pleasure, success with the failure. As each individual re-balances their own lives, it throws the relationship around them into a new balance. To go off balance, re-balance, again off balance, is part of relating and growing.

I can see how all the changes I have made in my life have unbalanced our marriage. Going from young lovers to responsible parents and professionals has required many times when we have needed to re-balance. We went too far off balance. A real separation occurred. The longer we were apart, the further away from each other we went. The more experiences we have that are not shared by the other, the harder it is to get back on the same track. I do so want to get on track and continue to rebuild our future together.

We have both worked hard to build our financial foundation. While Jack has been the primary bread winner, I made sure he had clean clothes, a clean home with the necessities like food in the fridge, toiletries, as well as planned family outings and social events. I believe the role of a homemaker is to make the home. The breadwinner gets the support and confidence of knowing domestic responsibilities are taken care of and the homemaker has the assurance the breadwinner is working and taking their share of the responsibilities they have agreed upon.

Good relationships are created when people make a deal and work to keep to their part of the deal. When one member of the couple breaks their part of the bargain, the relationship falters. I do not feel that I have let go of my part of the deal. I manage the cleaning help, organize the household and arrange for repairmen and maintenance when necessary. I supervise our children's activities, manage all the laundry, do grocery and clothing shopping and prepare many of the meals. Jack has increased his involvement in meal preparation and is an excellent cook. We support and relieve each other regularly as our schedules change.

We have reworked and adjusted our relationship deal when changes entered our lives. This included job changes, work hour changes, when the new babies arrived, house moves and when our children went off to school. Our deal has been changed many times. We started with me as the primary breadwinner and Jack was a law student. Now we both contribute to the finances in different ways, we both accept parenting responsibilities and plan social events. We spend considerable time talking about the changes we have been through and how we want to structure our deal now. I believe we need to heal the past to go forward. We need to learn from the past so we do not repeat our decisions that took us places we do not want to revisit. Jack assures me he is happy with our life together. I am happily relieved.

February is busy with more seminars, board meetings and I am delighted to be asked to chair the public relations committee for my professional association. I feel my energy is challenged and my efforts rewarded.

On March eighth, I recall that this is the thirty first anniversary of meeting my husband. We were at a high school band concert and my friend Sharon knew him from her church. She had pointed him out in the school band, so I had a chance to watch him, long before he knew I was alive. There was energy between us from the start. I was only fifteen. It wasn't my first crush on a boy. It was the most intense romantic interest I had ever felt someone had in me. It is also the fourth anniversary of my grandmother's death. She lived a long life and raised an interesting family. I missed the holiday celebrations at her farm. I missed the Ukrainian foods and the energy of being part of a large group of family. I wonder if I will live into my nineties as she did.

This also triggers my desire to have a special celebration for our twenty-fifth wedding anniversary in August. I ask Jack if he would like to have a party, either at home or at the cottage. He says he doesn't like big parties and would rather we celebrate just the two of us. I agree. We have never had gatherings for our other anniversaries. He suggests a trip somewhere. I ask if he wants to travel to New Zealand. Years ago he was active with his armature radio and had many people send him QRL cards from there with pictures of stunning scenery. QRL cards are a way to keep a record of people contacted over the radio. Their stamps were also lovely. We had often talked about travelling there "someday."

He says he is thinking of France. I am surprised and excited. I'd love to go to France. It is the ultimate romantic destination, a perfect place for lovers. He tells me he wants to plan the trip himself but will share his ideas with me before he confirms them. I am delighted as I am very busy with my responsibilities. Being taken on a magnificent trip to France by my husband is a dream come true.

My professional speakers' bureau has requested that for marketing to public speaking clients I should have a demonstration audio tape. I am working with a recording studio and using copies of tapes from some of my speeches to create one. This involves another professional photograph. I am told that in promoting myself, I should have a new one. The one I had done is from several years ago, and isn't suitable as it will make me appear dated. I find this process exciting. I am learning a lot about ways to market my speeches. Some of the advice I get is helpful and some is beyond where I want to go at the present time. I am not prepared to travel on a speaking tour as I want my counselling practice to be the focus of my income while my children are still home. I am also frequently asked if I have a book out. I have Questing Marilyn under development. I also want to get that done.

When I am offered an interview for the possibility of having my own radio show on CFRB, I am both surprised and excited. During the process of the interview, when the expectations of time and effort are clearly presented to me, I see that this is not a realistic goal for me at the present time. I decline pursuing the possibility further and know this is the right choice for me. When I meet my lifelong friends Roy and Yvonne for dinner and a production of Cats, I am resolved to letting that idea fade.

I am happy with the development of my career and share my excitement with my family. Jack is not very enthusiastic. I question him to see if we can solve whatever problems my work poses for him. He is vague and distracted. He complains a lot about his office location and feels overwhelmed with his workload. He has been approached by several other lawyers to either share his space or have him join a firm and move in with them. I wonder if either is really suitable for him as he is very self directed. I have repeatedly tried to convince him to get his office more computerized but he stubbornly refuses. Since our offices are now in separate spaces, I know little about what is happening in his practice. It really is not my problem, so I just listen. He must make the decisions to remedy his problems.

Spring comes later at the cottage than in Oakville and unlike our home where we have lawn maintenance people, all the work is ours to do. Walking around my property I find pussy willows and signs of a beaver. I have the trees wrapped in chicken wire to dissuade them from taking my trees, but the sticks stripped of their bark, with the large teeth marks at the ends, are unmistakable. The black flies and mosquitoes start biting and the robins search for dinner in the grass. Gradually, the wildflowers fill the lawn and reluctantly I get the lawn tractor going and mow them down. I do not like to keep long grass close to the cottage as it attracts snakes. It would also get too long for the lawn games. Getting the boats into the water and daring who will be the first one to swim have become cottage traditions.

Lyle McIntyre, a Muskoka portrait photographer, arrives in the early evening to take our family picture. Jack was given a sitting as a gift from a friend he had helped. Lyle chooses a position where we will have good lighting. In spite of the swarming mosquitoes, we gather under the birch trees. Lyle places each of us in a position that is artistically pleasing. We try to keep still. The buzzing bugs are hard to ignore. Pickles is on my lap and we are making progress, when suddenly a large raccoon and three small babies come out of the clump of trees just behind Lyle. Not wanting to get between a mother and her babies, Lyle shoes them back and hurries with the next few shots before the fading light is too dim. Fortunately, Pickles missed the raccoons as he was focused on our laughter. He would have been impossible to hold if he had seen them. The photo opportunity would have been lost.

Sending Lyle off with our thanks, I question Jack about his comments made at the last minute before picture taking started.

"Why did you suddenly suggest not being in the picture?"

His excuse about not liking to have his picture taken sounds like a weak excuse.

"It was a gift to you from friends who are glad we are a whole family again."

He brushes me off. I feel fear grip my heart. Every once in a while some seemingly little thing just doesn't sit quite right. Jack tells me the pictures are taken and to stop making something out of nothing.

I am surprised to have several therapists approach me to work with me. They want to rent my consulting office when I am not seeing clients as they build their own private practices. I research possibilities and rates. Providing office services complicates the issue. Building security during evenings and weekends is another obstacle.

I like my privacy and to book clients whenever I want. I decide not to have the added challenges and pass up the opportunity.

Several large employee assistance programs approach me to take on work. With both daughters in university, and Matt involved in a variety of activities, I have more freedom to work. I am enjoying my many involvements and responsibilities.

I accept a position on the board of the Canadian Institute for the Blind.

The Ontario Society for Training and Development conference provides new network opportunities for speaking engagements. I find the various involvements help me not burn out from some of the heavy emotional issues I work with in counselling sessions. I have a wide spectrum of professional associations and many new and interesting friends. *My life is very good!*

There are also financial rewards. While I lost income from my business association with Jack, it looks very promising that I will be able to earn that amount through different channels and perhaps even more. I have managed money all my life. I am confident with bankers, lawyers and accountants. Mom never had a sense of how much money there was in our family as dad kept that private. I remember vowing that I would always have a good idea what money we had available to us, and be a part of the decision making about how it would be spent. I want my children to be responsible with money. Jack and I differ on giving money to our children. He keeps giving them cash without accountability. I fear this will have a negative impact on them as money managers. It can lead to the expectation that there is always more money and that they will be rescued from being financially responsible. He claims I am just being controlling. We agree to disagree.

How a couple handles their money is indicative of the power in the relationship. Negotiating ways to handle decisions about money is a frequent topic of client couple sessions. Some people want to build security while others want to have a good time and let tomorrow take care of itself. Often the one who looks at the short term is also less concerned about the long term lessons they are teaching their children. They carry less responsibility for parenting and want their child to like them more than respect them. They can justify their actions by saying they never had things when they were growing up and they want their children to enjoy what they are able to provide. The one who wants to be responsible and who looks at the long term implications of what is being taught can be seen as the mean one. Since money is not a problem and we are able to provide very well for ourselves, I try to relax and enjoy what we have.

Travel styles and preferences are as varied as people are different. Having similar preferences and expectations makes the journey through life and on holidays easier. Some people like to have their itinerary planned weeks in advance and reservations made and pre-paid. The rigid expectations of the court system have conditioned Jack to follow a schedule and be where he is expected to be on a daily basis. He likes to know what to expect and not have too many surprises.

I suggest Jack contact Karen at Uniglobe. I know her from the Chamber of Commerce and was pleased with her help in the past. I like her direct approach. She gives him a wealth of material. As he progresses with the planning, I feel confined by the tight scheduling. I like time to do things on a whim and to alter plans depending on the weather. In some situations I like to be well planned and in others I like spontaneity.

Yvonne asks me how I am feeling about our upcoming trip. I share my feeling of being over planned and fears that I will be led about like I was on my tour to England and Ireland. I am concerned that I will miss things I might want to do and see.

"What if I want to seize the moment, follow a newly discovered possibility or take a day to walk a beach or take time to shop?'

She reminds me Jack and I have travelled many times and many places both as a couple and with our children. We have been across Canada, north to James Bay on the Polar Bear Express and South to the Caribbean islands of St. Lucia, Grand Cayman, Jamaica, and to the Bahamas. We have been to Bermuda, England, Ireland, Wales, Spain and Portugal. Some places we have been to more than once. We are experienced travellers.

I am not sure why this feels so different from other trips. Perhaps it is because we have been growing in different directions as people. Wherever we go we take who we are with us. Our relationship is different than it has ever been before. Our way of relating is new and our financial position is more solid and affluent than we have ever been before.

I hate wandering about looking for a place to stay every night, so mapping out a route and making hotel reservations is wise. It affords us the maximum time to see what we want to see. No chance of a night without accommodation. I try to relax and accept what Jack is planning. I trust Karen and she has been very helpful. I distract myself from my concerns by focusing on what I will take to wear. When we first travelled I took a minimum of clothing. By the time I returned I was so sick of those three outfits I never wanted to wear them again. I took too much luggage on my Quest to England. Too much to be wandering in a van with the luggage on the top. On this trip, we will have our own car. We will also be staying in some nice hotels. I must choose some light weight easy care dressy things. *Why am I fretting?* I have travelled a lot and know how to pack.

I am hoping that even though I am not being asked for my opinions, my wants are being considered. He should know the things that matter to me as I have told him often enough. Yet I fear he will twist what I have said and try to convince me that what he has planned is exactly what I wanted. This reminds me of situations in the past.

I consider my choices and know I will have many opportunities to make decisions for my time, my actions and how I react to whatever happens. I left a tour in my last Quest and I know I can leave this one too. Holding firmly to My Holy Grail and venture forth into what for me is the unknown. *Passport – check. Spare glasses – check. Credit cards – check.*

Knowing the difference between sharing a hug and chaining a soul is part of understanding life. Being alive isn't about dependence and control, fear and manipulation, security and keeping on a familiar path. It is learning from experience, accepting defeats, picking up the pieces and going forward. This must not be done with the mindset of a child but with the confidence of someone who can plan ahead, accept the consequences of decisions, endure the unexpected, and go forward knowing each day will bring a new adventure. It is about becoming not being.

We must learn to make our decisions based on what we know today, because we cannot know for certain what tomorrow will bring. Our future which lives in our hopes and dreams has a way of crumbling, being delayed or turning out different than we imagined. So we choose today with the certainty that the choice will have to be made again as circumstances change.

CHAPTER TWENTY-NINE

HAPPY TWENTY-FIFTH WEDDING ANNIVERSARY

A French Holiday in Style

August 11, 1989 Arriving in Paris

Our flight to Paris leaves at seven twenty this evening. I am filled with excitement and trepidation. We are leaving Matt at camp doing all the things he loves. My mind shifts through possible scenarios. I believe I have every imaginable option covered. My daughters have jobs and their own lives. Julia is staying at the cottage working in the beer store. Kathy, who is working in Oakville, will go up to the cottage on the weekends. They will visit Matt. Pickles will stay at the cottage. The years of teaching responsibility and care for belongings, as well as boat and water safety, must be trusted.

After I settle into the Air Canada's business class seat I accept a glass of chilled champagne. I marvel at my good fortune. Twenty-five years of marriage and this is what Jack chose to plan. He asked me about my preferences. I love having reservations in hotels with good dining rooms so that after a day of travelling and sightseeing we were not searching for a place to stay or a dinner spot. He has booked some hotels that boast great chefs. He kept control of many of the details, saying I had planned so many of our vacations, he wanted to make this special and do it his way. He told me to trust him. *Settle back, Marilyn, trust and enjoy!*

I am thrilled as we descend into Charles De Gaulle International Airport. It is 23 kilometres north west of Paris. The morning is clear and beautiful. My ears pop and I swallow repeatedly hoping not to have an aching ear for the next few hours. The flight was

smooth and after a tasty meal and some good wine, I had been able to sleep for a few hours. Excitement bubbles up inside. I hold Jack's hand for the descent and *we peer out the window hoping to see something recognizable. I love travelling well.*

Jack has rented a Mercedes 190E with air-conditioning and automatic transmission. Our luggage fits neatly into the spacious trunk. I would love to drive, but know he is eager too. Jack has excellent command of the French language and I have a smattering of poorly recalled high school lessons. He efficiently managed the car rental and the directions. He is in the role of the competent male and I am his wife. I am playing the role expected of me. I feel a little bit dumb and a little bit shy.

We navigate our way out onto the highway, both of us looking for road signs. Jack is driving on the right side of the road. We do not have to make the adjustment to driving on the left as we did in the British Isles. Roads are in excellent repair and the signs are clear. We are prepared with coins for the toll booths so feel confident and excited. I know paige means pay and peages are toll booths. The autoroute speed limit is 130 kilometres an hour, so we move quickly.

I point out the signs as we head first closer to Paris then northwest toward Rouen on the Normandie Autoroute. It is less than a two hour drive if we stay on the motorway but we want to start to explore.

We choose a road that follows the Seine River. Parts of it are marked in green on our map indicating a scenic route. We enjoy watching the working barges, pleasure boats and the activity at the locks. We reminisce about our trips up the Trent Canal in Ontario, with my sister Joan and her husband Paul. We laugh about the spiders and mosquitoes, the fishermen who woke us up before dawn in Hastings and racing to make a lock before it closed when there was a long run before the next one. Stopping at a lock because the lockmaster went off duty did not always leave us with time to spend in places we would choose to tie up for the night.

"Let's come back to do a riverboat trip someday."

One of the riverboats with fine cuisine appeals to me. There are so many rivers in the world that river travel could be a never ending pursuit. We can save riverboats for another day. For now we travel the roadways.

As I think of being seduced for two whole weeks of promised luxury, by the man I love, I know it is more than a dream come true. *Accept what you have Marilyn. Don't keep looking over the next hill and around the next corner. Stay in the present moment.*

I watch the scenery slide by with orchards filled with ripening fruit. My childhood memories have been stimulated. Just letting my mind follow whatever flows through is so relaxing. There is a part of me that would like to be a feminine, soft woman who is protected and cherished by my husband. I know I was not raised to be that way.

My country upbringing demanded that I be cautious and resourceful, resilient and strong. When I walked to and from school, often alone, I was told to appear like I have a sense of purpose. My body language must give the message: "Do not mess with me." I was told to stand up straight, keep my head up, be aware of my surroundings, and not to dawdle. Walking down our country road, tales of a wolf in the woods running through my head, I would swing my arms and often sing loudly. I am sure this is when I was first teased about my singing not being pleasant. I wasn't singing to be pleasant; I was trying to keep stray dogs of all kinds away.

I wasn't too sure what the warnings were about, but as I grew, I asked questions and listened to adult conversations. I learned that there were people who did bad things to children. I also learned that boys wanted to do bad things to girls, so I must not look too easily influenced. I was told: "It is always better to be safe than sorry."

I recall that sometimes my brother and I would talk things over and help each other understand the messages of adults. He was the one who told me about the summer farm workers and that some of them were not very nice, so to be very careful not to be too friendly. Mom and Dad didn't know we climbed the fence to pick the cherries, peaches and apples from Oak Ridge Farm that surrounded our property. If they guessed because of stained fingers and clothing, we were sure to be punished. I imagine stopping to pick fruit from the passing trees. It wouldn't be hard to get something. I giggle silently in childish glee. *Oh forbidden fruit!*

As we pass a young couple in a very little car, I comment on how that was what we were like when we first visited Europe twenty years ago. We had very little money. We referred to our tiny car as a sewing machine on wheels. We had toured Spain and Portugal with a day trip to Morocco.

The sleek automobile we now ride in is an outward manifestation of how far we have come in financial achievement and confidence. What a lot of water has passed under our bridge. Twenty-five years together. We are not counting the months of separation in 1988. Nostalgia swells through me and I feel a tear in the corner of my eyes. I reach across the seat to put my hand on Jack's thigh. He puts one hand on mine.

With shaky words I say: "I love you."

He squeezes my hand.

"No one else understands me the way you do."

I wonder how much I really do understand this man.

I really want this vacation and the uninterrupted time with my husband to help us become closer as a couple. I need time to just be a wife. I want to better understand the way he thinks and to have an appreciation for his expectations of our marriage. I'd like to redefine our roles and responsibilities. For now I am going to just sit back and calm down.

I have felt like Jack's caretaker for so much of our time together. I was the one managing holidays, the home, cottage and office and enabling him to have a closer relationship with his parents and children. I was the one who usually met with bankers, accountants, real estate agents, and the children's doctor, dentist and teachers. I even interviewed and recommended his staff. I have done the behind the scenes work, and allowed him to use me for many things that freed him to focus on building his career. I have been over responsible. *Let go Marilyn! Stop setting goals and looking for things to fix. Everything is fine. Relax!*

I pondered why Jack doesn't take command of our activities more often. He delegates tasks to his secretaries, receptionist, book-keeper, and to me. It is efficient to delegate responsibilities others can handle for us. I delegate to my secretary, my cleaning help, the lawn and snow maintenance people. Having people take care of our responsibilities is a luxury. I would rather work at something I really enjoy to earn enough to pay for chores I dislike, than save the cost of help by trying to do all the jobs myself.

I love the life we have created together. I would like more romance though. Romance is about leaving responsibility behind.

I so want to be spontaneous and carefree. I am hoping this trip will help us with the process of bringing more of the sparkle back into our marriage. I need to stop thinking so much.

ROUEN

As the countryside becomes more urban, we return to the motorway to follow the signs to centre ville, downtown Rouen, the capital of Normandy. It is the sea port for Paris and thousands of ships from all over the world come to load and unload their wares. Cruise ships plying both river and ocean routes dock here. The cast-iron spire of Notre Dame Cathedral, the highest in France, is easily seen on the skyline.

We find a spot to park the car near the tourist office. It is situated in a lovely old building. With all my art training, I never studied architecture. There is so much to learn and appreciate. I wish I had a better knowledge of so many things. I feel overwhelmed by the possibilities for exploration given our time limits. I look for brochures in English while Jack gets us a city map.

One of the attendants speaks to me in English and assists me in selecting material. She exclaims that it is too bad we were not here in early July as the tall ships had been in Rouen for the first time. It had been for the celebration commemorating two hundred years since the French revolution and the Declaration of the Rights of Man. The French Revolution was part of my high school curriculum too. I remember some of the vivid scenes from reading Charles Dicken's novel, A Tale of Two Cities. I remember the first line of the book. "It was the best of times, it was the worst of times...."

Seeing the tall ships would have been a magnificent sight. There were tours onboard. How wonderful to see those ships sailing off down the river in their final departure. If we had arrived without knowing millions of people would be gathering all up and down the riverfront to view the ships, we could have been unable to get into town. One reality of travelling is that one never knows when a local festival, holiday, renovation or celebration could close the museums, roads and access to what they travelled so far to see. Being prepared for changes in plans and unmet expectations is part of the reality of travel. It can be the best of times but with poor luck and sometimes poor planning it can feel like worst of times.

Wandering along old cobbled streets with timbered houses, we are reminded of the similarity to places in England. There really has been a strong shared influence between the two countries.

Joan of Arc was burnt at the stake in Rouen in 1431. She was charged with heresy as the Roman Catholic Church thought she was demonic. Men who don't like what women do or say, or do not understand women's unique gifts, are often quick to say the women are evil and crazy. Just because women think differently than men it does not mean we are deserving of death. The power of the priests has destroyed many women. The site of the burning is marked by a huge cross. Apparently her ashes were thrown in the river Seine. *What a horrid way to die. What inhumanity! And they call that the church of Christ!*

The Rouen market is filled with treasures from many gardens. I love the splendid flowers, array of meats and cheeses, succulent fruits and vegetables. We resist purchasing food that would only spoil, as I am sure we have no refrigeration in our lodgings and no cooler. The odd tables of old wares are interesting but we make no purchases. I love the crafts and marvel at the creativity. I smile and nod and say "Bonjour" to some of the vendors. If they try to carry on with a sales pitch, I reply with; "Excuse moi, je ne parle Français" When I find things that I would like to buy, I have to remind myself that we are sight seeing not shopping. I must not acquire too much "stuff" to take home.

We find a street side café. Since we are still jet lagged, it is hard to know if this is breakfast or lunch. It is five hours earlier at home. I think of my children starting their day and a desire to call slides through my mind. *Leave it alone Marilyn.*

A glass of cold local apple cider tickles my taste buds. I must remember to order this in place of a beer. It is much lighter and very thirst quenching. My quiche and salad are delicious. Jack orders something filled with a variety of seafood in a broth. He is a more adventurous eater than I am.

We explore quaint shops and admire window displays of items, both old and new, as we walk along the pedestrian only street, rue du Gros-Horloge. Seeing the 16th century astronomical clock that shows the time as well as the positions of the sun, moon and zodiac constellations is thrilling. The gold on its face gleams in the sunlight. Positioned in an overhead arch I marvel at the mind that created such a masterpiece. I love to contemplate how people create such things—both for their knowledge but also their ability to put that knowledge into something physical that lasts for so many years. It was heroically protected from damage during the Second World War by the people of Rouen. Modern buildings mixed with structures from the middles ages are indicative of war damage. Thinking of bombs dropping from the sky, I am saddened by the insanity of war. *Why do people have to try to destroy others for their own gain?*

A visit to Notre Dame Cathedral takes us into the magnificence of both styles of architecture and an array of stained glass windows. I take a few moments to sit alone, quietly marvelling at the splendour that surrounds me. I slide to my knees and place my face in my hands. I am overwhelmed with prayers of gratitude for all the blessings in my life. As my mind races through so many trials and heartaches, I know that finally I am in a place of happiness and peace. I feel an urge to weep but my tears do not come. Gradually I lift my face and slowly follow the line up the isle to the main alter then up to the highest peak above. *Glory to God! Thank you!*

Jack approaches and asks if I am alright. I smile with great joy and assure him I am very fine. He suggests we had better get on our way as we may have some difficulty finding our country chateau.

CHATEAU DU ROMBOSC - MOUNT CAUVAIRE

The sunrise is just starting to brighten the eastern sky. It is too early to rise. I roll over and return to sleep. Waking with the sun brightly shining, I know the day is well progressed. I feel lazy and refreshed. I lie still, quietly awake, and study the large pink roses on the black wallpaper. I hear birds twittering. I know I am alone in the room in this 17th century mansion.

I wonder where Jack is. A smile crosses my face as I know that wherever he is, I can relax my guard and not be paranoid that he has gone off to meet another woman. On the other hand, he could be chatting with a woman somewhere. It is not the casual relationship I fear; it is one woman and her influence. Better get up. I do not want to think of her here and now. I sure do not want to talk about my concerns. I must believe him when he says she is out of his life. *Will I ever get over this fear?*

It had taken us several tries to find this B&B. We had retraced our route following the directions we had been given, but some of the country roads had no signs. Jack had been able to ask a local farmer for assistance and finally we had found the long dirt drive through what seemed to be an overgrown lawn.

Once through into the courtyard, a variety of red brick out buildings, a carriage house and brick walls surrounded us. The chateau, three stories high with dormers in the roof and rounded rooms on each end was imposing in a number of ways. First it was huge. Second it was rather run down. Third it appeared deserted.

We had timidly approached the front door together. It was immediately opened and we were warmly greeted by the owners who must have heard our tires on the gravel drive. It is apparent that it is not a popular spot for tourists as there are only a few rooms available. We had been shown through them and were able to choose which one we wanted. There are no other guests. I wanted the one that would get the morning sun.

After putting our things in the room and chatting with our hosts, we briefly wandered about the property. It has a rustic charm and needs an immense amount of work if it is to be restored. Many of the sections looked unsafe and neglected for many years. Jack asked if I was alright staying here and I assured him it is an experience I wouldn't want to miss. This is a real French chateau. It is also a bigger project than I would want to tackle. These people have their work cut out for them. I hope they have a lot of patience, time and money.

We had driven into a nearby village and were enjoying a leisurely dinner. I had a delicious helping of mussels with white wine and saffron. I had soaked up the broth with wonderful fresh French bread. Jack had suggested a Muscadet, to accompany it. He does know his wines.

I crawl from the covers and head to the window. Jack is sitting on a white garden bench at the end of a straight gravel path, apparently lost in thought. A hay field with round bales of golden grass are speckled about. The entire field is surrounded by a red brick wall. This must have been the inner garden when this place was built. I can see the top of a much more modern roof over one section of wall. No one else is about. I do not want to shout and he does not look my way.

I quickly dress and descend the large stairway. I pause briefly to look at the portrait with the bullet hole in it. Our hosts had told us that American soldiers had been billeted in the chateau during the Second World War. When the property was returned to the family, there was a lot of damage. This was just one example and that was all they knew of the story. How horrid to have ones family home taken over. How horrid to think of the fighting, the pain and the sorrow this place has known. I do hope there has been a lot of pleasure as well. There is no sense of sorrow on this lovely morning.

The large, sparsely furnished dining room has a table right in the centre. It is not proportional to the room. Once this room must have been filled with lovely furniture as it is large enough for a banquet. The table is set with two places. Croissants in a napkin covered basket, a thermos of coffee, jam and juice have been left by our hosts. Apparently, Jack has not eaten. We were told when we arrived, that our hosts were planning a day of touring and they would be leaving breakfast. I was impressed that they trusted us, as total strangers, to have the run of their home. I expect their private space is locked.

Despite it being late in the morning, I pass by the food and go out to the back garden. The silence is profound. No noise of traffic, jets or machinery of any kind. A few bird calls then silence. I join my husband on the bench. I want to connect emotionally with him as well as physically. I ask what he has planned for the day.

As we sit quietly chatting I look toward the chateau. I can see our room because it has the only open window. There are no screens here. Some of the windows are shuttered. I'd love to explore the whole place. I recall poking about the old farmhouse behind our property before it was torn down for the subdivision. The farm had been sold and before the builders started to tear down the original brick farmhouse and farm manager's home, we had run freely where we had once been forbidden to go. Memories of seeing into abandoned closets and racing up staircases eagerly calling to each other to come look at this or that flood through my mind. There were more houses than just the ones on Oak Ridge Farm; there was the old barn across the road, and Mr. and Mrs. Hare's house, chicken coops and garages... A sense of sadness fills me as I think of the loss of those farms to be replaced with houses and lawns. I wonder what will become of this place. *Will they really be able to make it into the splendid place it appears to have been?*

DIEPPE

We consume our breakfast, then leave our lodgings and drive north to Dieppe. We drive straight to the beach, and park our car.

There is a wide boulevard along the waterfront with tall apartment buildings that face the sea. Then a park and the long beach that stretches for miles in both directions. Long rock structures reach out into the ocean to protect the beach from wave erosion. I walk across the stones on the sloping shore. As I dip my fingers in the English Channel, I imagine the fighting, the smoke and the noise of guns. It could have been a day like this in August 1942, just months before I was born. This beautiful summer day disguises the horror that those poor men endured.

I see an old chateau overlooking the beach with a Canadian flag flying beside the French flag. The Germans were up there sending bombs and bullets down on our men. Emotion grips my chest. The poor men, they didn't have much of a chance at all.

Off to the west the towering white cliffs would prevent escape. A huge cement German bunker, the Canadian Garden, the plaques to The South Saskatchewan Regiment, The Hamilton Light Infantry, The Royal Regiment of Canada and signs to the cemeteries all bring to life only a hint of the reality of history. Jack is obviously struck with emotion as he describes how the different forces arrived and were attacked.

Three thousand Canadians died, were injured or taken prisoner here. These were the Canadians our parents' age who came to fight the European war. My Uncle Peter Barnicke died somewhere during that war when his plane went down. My father used to watch the newsreels and the historical documentaries in hopes of seeing his picture or his plane. He was so young. I never knew him. His picture hung on Grandma's wall but once when I asked about him, she cried and I was told not to mention him again. I know his name is on a monument in Ottawa as I have seen it. There is a small island in Georgian Bay named after him. I wish my father's family had spoken more about our family history.

Thinking of war on such a lovely day gives the countryside a strange eerie aura.

We drive west along the closest road to the sea atop the cliffs. It is marked on our map in green, so it promises to be scenic. This reminds me so much of the white cliffs of Dover and our lovely trip along the English coast. Varengeville-on-Sea is a pretty village and it is understandable why artists have come to this area to paint for many years. The lovely scenery soothes my spirit. We continue west to Veules-les-Roses and find a lovely little cove. I'd love to stay and walk the beach, watch the tourists and perhaps swim. Jack says we will never get to our days planned places if we dawdle here.

We head directly south to connect with the motorway so we can head west again. Our route takes us over the mouth of the Seine, bypassing Le Havre. There are ships of all sizes and we chat comfortably about the riverboats and the huge ships that come in from the ocean. We speculate on what they might be carrying and I tease Jack about wanting to take a holiday on a cargo ship. He used to say it was one of his dreams.

BAYEUX

We are heading past Caen to Bayeux, to see the famous tapestry that depicts scenes from the battle between England and France. Jack loves history. I am fascinated by his knowledge and enthusiasm. He reminds me that William of Normandy, cousin to the King of England, was named successor to the throne because there were no closer heirs. There was a dispute about his right to the throne because he was illegitimate. William and his army attacked England at Hastings in 1066. I had to memorise that date in history class.

William later became William the Conqueror, and ruled England for twenty-one years. The tapestry we are going to see was embroidered, possibly in Kent England, to preserve the story of his historical right to the throne. Since we have been to Hastings and Battle in England, seeing the French countryside gives us insight into another part of the story. Learning history by travelling helps it make a lot more sense than the way we studied it out of books.

Jack suggests I drive and he will navigate us into town. He seems tense and constantly corrects my driving and gives me directions about turns on short notice. I ask him to calm down so we can enjoy our visit. Suddenly, after just turning a corner, I see the blue lights of a police car behind me and I pull to the side of the road. The gendarme speaks to me in French and I reply: "En Anglais, s'il vous plais?"

His response is spoken very quickly but I hear the "Non" clearly. Jack tells me to give him my driver's licence and passport. He looks at it briefly and starts motioning and explaining something. I have no idea what he is saying. He hands me back my documents as Jack says something to him in French. Studies show men prefer less intelligent women who they can impress with their powers. Jack is really trying to impress with his ability to speak French. I am impressed. I have been impressed by his abilities since I first met him. Why is he not willing to use that ability to ensure I have a good time? I get the distinct impression from the tones, laughter and wave from the officer for us to proceed, that it was something about me being a woman driver and Jack would explain the error of my ways to me. I ask him what it was all about and he says something about an improper right turn. I ask him specifically what I did wrong and he tells me he is unsure.

Jack had tried to get me to practice my French once we knew we were coming on this trip, but I had refused after he repeatedly corrected my pronunciation and I ended up in tears of frustration. I asked him to at least let me get the words right before I practice the pronunciation. He kept telling me he didn't know what I was saying if I didn't say it properly. When I finally said; "If I learn French, I will not choose you as my teacher" he stubbornly refused to help me any further. Now I think he is pleased to watch me struggle. I believe I will be able to learn better if I can use the words when I need them instead of in makeup conversations. We learn differently. We remember differently. I believe his good ear for music also gives him a good ear for accents and intonations.

I find a parking spot near our destination and stop the engine. Jack puts coins into a parking meter as I gather my purse and camera. I lock the car and turn to see a public phone. Calculating the time zone differences, I want to tell Julia or Kathy that we arrived and all is well. I am excited to share. After several tries to make a call with no success, I am frustrated.

"Will you please help me?"

"You don't need to call home."

"I am getting an operator or a recorded voice and I do not understand what it is saying. Will you listen and tell me what I need to do?"

"You don't need to call home."

"Why won't you help me? You are quick to criticise but not so quick to help."

"You don't need to call home."

"Why do you get to tell me what I do? I do not need to call home, I want to call."

He starts to walk away from me. I stay in front of the pay phone and watch him go. I am upset and surprised. *Why is he doing this?* I turn on my heel and stride off in the opposite direction. He is presuming I will follow him. I do not know where I am going and I do not care. I need some space from him. How can I hold onto Me when he is so stubborn? I must be true to myself. I find a small park and sit on a bench. *What have I done?* No one is about. *What did I do wrong that the police officer stopped me?* I wish there was someone I could just turn to and ask my simple questions. *Why was I stopped by the police? How do I phone Canada?*

The language barrier is like the Berlin Wall. I do not know how to get over it. I do not know where my husband is. I stand and think of heading back to wait at the car. I put my hand in my pocket and feel the keys. I have the only set of car keys. My devious mind starts to work. I could move the car. I could leave him stranded. I could pay him back for being mean to me. *Stop this nonsense Marilyn!*

I decide to visit the tapestry and I am sure we will meet. I have no idea if he has followed me. I cannot see any trace of him. I look cautiously about. The sign to the tapestry guides me where I want to go. Fortunately, there is no line-up. The ropes indicate that the lines are very long at times. I guess we are lucky.

The Bayeux Tapestry is 70 meters or 230 feet long. It is half a meter or 20 inches high. Embroidered on linen, it contains a series of pictures. My pamphlet tells me there are 626 people, 190 horses, 37 ships and 33 buildings. I do not bother to count. It shows the dress of the people and a great deal of information about what would have been worn for battle by the soldiers. I enjoy the story in pictures and marvel at the detailed work. I cannot make out all of the actions being depicted as there are people in sections that appear to have nothing to do with the story. *What a record of history!*

I watch for Jack but do not see him. I buy myself a light lunch and continue with my sightseeing. We always agree that if we get separated we will meet at a set time. Today it was to be at four at the car. I am a few minutes early and wait. By ten minutes after the hour, I decide to go to the sidewalk café just down the street.

> Traditional men want to be in a relationship where they are not challenged and where they are the one listened to. While they may like the financial advantages of a capable woman they do not want to deal with what she desires, her ideas and her success.

I think Jack expected I would just do as he told me to do. I leave a note on the windshield, tucked under the wiper.

"I'm having a beer down the street. If you face the front of the car and turn to look to your left, you will probably see me. Want a beer. I'll buy. Me"

I am just settled with a cold Carlsberg when I see him walking toward me.

"Excuse me sir. Can I buy you a beer?"

A few close patrons look from me to him. I wonder if they understand my words or are curious that as a woman sitting alone I dare to speak to an approaching man.

"Sure if you are paying, why not."

Neither one of us wants to keep the power struggle going so we enjoy our beer.

CAEN

Dinner in Caen is long and leisurely in a sidewalk restaurant. We took some time to poke about and see places from the car window but didn't do much walking. I feel tired and without asking just expect Jack to drive. It is over an hour drive back to Rouen then north to our lodgings. He insists I do the driving. *Why did I presume he would?*

Something in the way power is used in our relationship is unsettling. If I want something he gets to decide if he will support me in getting it. This means he has power, like with the call home. If he wants something, like me to drive, he decides and I end up doing it. *Am I giving in too much to prevent a fight?*

Fighting over not driving is useless. I quietly follow his directions out of town and head east on the motorway. I push the accelerator to take us to 10 kilometres an hour over the limit. The heavy car handles the challenge with ease. Traffic is light and other vehicles fly past me. I press harder on the peddle and test the feel of the car at 150 kilometres an hour. This is about 100 miles per hour and there is no sense of the engine working hard. Jack seems to have dozed off. I press harder again. I see headlights behind me and slow. Something fast speeds past. I press again and my excitement is high. *This is fun!*

"How fast are you driving?"

"Pretty fast." My foot eases up and I smile in the darkness. *It is so much fun to feel naughty!*

We find our way back to our Chateau without getting lost on the dark country roads. Jack has memorized the route and I let him direct me. His mood seems better since his nap. Arriving after our hosts had told us they retire, we feel like teenagers sneaking in so as not to wake Mom and Dad. I tease as we prepare for bed.

"This place could be haunted you know."

Jack teases back trying to spook me. He suggests he might have seen a shadow, something wispy white just across the hall. I cuddle close, suggesting whatever it might be, will get him first as he is closest to the door.

The Loire Valley

The Loire Valley is our next destination and we have a hotel reservation in Tours. It will be an all day drive. We want to see the countryside and not just by whizzing by at top speed. We take roads marked as scenic and travel south, meandering through small villages, avoiding Paris. We will be ending our trip with a few days there. We do take the fast route around some towns and for short sections to keep to the desired route. We travel south of Le Mans and see where the Le Mans auto race is run. The spectator seating, judges posts and barriers along the driving route stimulate conversations of driving and speed. What skill these drivers need to race on such roads.

Cyclists, individually and in large groups, are also a frequent sight. Care must be taken around blind corners and avoiding scratches to our car both on the road and when we park. The bicycles weave in and out of stopped traffic and riders assume we will avoid them. They seem to expect us not to be bothered by a hand on our vehicle or a sudden adjustment to their direction to avoid a pot hole on the road. At times I find it quite unnerving. Thoughts of touring by bicycle have run through our conversation. I am pleased to see more of the countryside from this comfort. I question Jack on his thoughts now that we are really here and see the touring cyclists if he would like to try that. He doesn't sound too enthusiastic about the idea.

There are long comfortable pauses in our conversation. My mind leisurely wanders over thoughts stimulated by the scenery. So many times, I return to memories of my childhood. I mention memories of an old tractor. Jack recalls the plough that was pulled by their horse on his grandfather's market garden. Seeing blackberries in a ditch, I ask to stop. Stopping by the side of a country road just to eat a few berries is delightful. We walk a way up a laneway that appears to go nowhere and inspect a crumbling stone wall with an old wooden gate securely fastened. *Oh the stories it could tell.*

I feel as if our energy is vibrating in sync and our thoughts and feelings are purely aligned. There is no opposition or distraction cluttering up our time or space. My Self is totally present. I am silently communicating to Jack a pure sense of who I am and what

I am about. Our eyes meet and love flows from me. I see his smile slowly appear and it is as if his thoughts flow into me. A slow shake of his head and deep wordless response tells me he is happy. Our eyes hold as we each move so our lips touch. I feel his arms encircle me and I move my hands to his back pulling him closer.

As we stand in a country lane, somewhere in the middle of the French countryside, I have complete faith that we can work on our relationship and have a marriage that lasts our lifetime. We have the ability to fight and make up with forgiveness. We have the ability to come close on so many levels. We need this time together. Just the two of us. We are in a very special shared moment. I want to hold it forever.

Love is not absolute, a fact, or a limited essence. It is not something you have or you do not have. It is a collection of feelings that ebb and flow depending on the way each person relates to another. It is an opening of the senses, an opening of the heart, an accepting without judgement. Reconnecting in memories and activities from the past can help the feelings come flowing forth, often stronger than before. Creating new memories built on trust and mutual acceptance enhance the magnitude of feeling lovingly toward another and feeling lovable as the Self. Trust is a vital part of opening to love.

Jack and I now have the chance to come together with a deeper love and a stronger commitment than we have ever had. Our love has changed, deepened and evolved with the trials we have endured. We are learning new ways to interact. We are experiencing new ways to be loving with each other.

The sound of an approaching vehicle and the cloud of dust behind it sends us scrambling for our car.

"Quick shut the door!"

We laugh at the fun of playing and the joy of feeling at peace. We drive on, holding hands in silence. The feelings are too deep for words.

The universal energies have smiled on us. Our guardian angels have conspired to help us celebrate all that we have created. We are discovering the power of using our thoughts to create our life together and the holiday of our dreams.

TOURS

We arrive in Tours and at the first site of our hotel, I exclaim how beautiful it is. The guide book claims the Jean Bardet Hotel, with only sixteen rooms, is the nicest hotel in Tours. It features a fine gastronomic restaurant as well. We will not have to drive after dinner here. We both go into the reception area. I marvel at the lovely décor while Jack checks us in. I hear his voice sounding annoyed and move to the counter. There has apparently been an error and we do not have a reservation. The woman at the desk has the initial request but says the confirmation fax with credit card information for the deposit did not arrive. Jack is very disappointed and wants to phone his office, or perhaps Karen, to see what happened. I know it doesn't matter what happened, they are fully booked. I ask for an alternate hotel and Jack asks if there is a table for us for dinner.

We are directed to L'Hotel de Groison, at 10 Rue Groison. It is an appealing white building with a pastel blue roof and when we enter it proves to be quite attractive. Our room is pretty with blue and white wallpaper very similar to what we had on

our bedroom in Georgetown. I am pleased and says it feels familiar. I suggest we have a glass of wine in the garden. I know Jack is disappointed about the reservation and he apologises repeatedly. I assure him I didn't have the expectations he had, so I am not as disappointed.

"This will be fine."

Why does Jack have to get so annoyed over an error he made? Everyone makes mistakes. The receptionist had the papers she exchanged with him and was able to clearly show that she had requested a deposit. He had insisted he be responsible for the reservations so he knows it was his error. *Why can't he accept he isn't perfect, apologize and move on?* I do hope he will get out of his mood before dinner.

Dinner is full of pretension and excellent food in an exquisite dining room. We choose the menu of the day. Jack wants the full effect of a fine French dining room with a renowned chef. It has many courses, some of them a total surprise to me. Even when I am eating, I am not sure what it is. Each is pleasantly presented and absolutely delicious. I try to eat only small portions of each dish but it is all so delicious, my will power is weak. I eat too much. I feel sleepy and we are not even at dessert. I want to forget the remainder of the meal but leaving would be too rude. Jack is having a fabulous time and converses with the waiter in French. Other diners present some interesting people watching opportunities. French women have such style. It certainly is an interesting experience.

Château De Chenonceaux

We approach Château De Chenonceaux along a magnificent avenue bordered by tall trees. It is about a half hour drive from Tours but we wandered along the Loire River valley, so we have taken several hours to arrive at Touraine. There were vineyards

271

and magnificent houses, riverboats, and flowers growing in brilliant profusion. We'd shopped for cheese, bread and wine and picnicked in a small park. It was very much like the way we travelled in England, Wales and Scotland, on our trips there, more or less following our whims but with general destinations in mind. I am glad Jack planned some unscheduled wandering.

The regular tales of historical significance and ways the places we pass fit into our lives, flow out of Jack's mouth with what seems like effortless ease. A vineyard here, where he reminds me of a special wine we enjoyed, or a type of architecture over there, that is reproduced in a Canadian building we know, keeps us entertained. He has an amazing memory and love of telling stories. He often said he wanted to be a history teacher rather than a lawyer. I am sure he would excel at whatever he chooses. I am so fortunate to have such a wonderful travelling companion.

After parking in the shaded space, we walk toward the magnificent grey structure with a soft blue roof. I imagine arriving by horse and open carriage, on a perfect summer day such as this, with a silk scarf billowing from my shoulders. I can almost hear the sound of the horses' hooves on the gravel drive.

Two round towers, one slim and the other just slightly taller and wider, mark the entrance. I presume they must be the footman's gate house. Perhaps one is waiting to escort us across the moat. This château is a romantic palace, created from the Renaissance onward by a series of aristocratic women. It stretches across the River Cher with a one hundred and ninety foot gallery built over a series of graceful arches. The water swirls gently underneath. The splendidly furnished rooms show of a time of grandeur. We wander through the bedchambers and admire fine paintings and tapestries. I excitedly ask; "Wouldn't it be fun to live here? It could be so private and romantic. Couldn't there be wonderful parties with beautifully dressed people dancing? Can you imagine the string quartet playing a waltz?" Jack smiles indulgently not really wanting to share my fantasies. *Do I seem like a romantic silly girl to him?*

My guidebook tells me that the women responsible for building and renovating Chenonceaux each left their mark. Catherine Briconnet built the turreted pavilion and one of the first staircases in France. Henri II's mistress, Diane de Poitiers, added the formal gardens and the arched bridge over the river. Catherine de Medicis transformed the bridge into an Italian Florentine style gallery. Louise de Lorraine, bereaved wife of Henri III, inherited the château in 1590 and painted the ceilings black and white, the colours of royal mourning. Madame Dupin, a cultured 18th century chatelaine saved the château from destruction during the Revolution and Madame Pelouze undertook a complete restoration in 1863. *Women after my own heart. I love renovating!*

The vaulted ceiling of the chapel is decorated with sculpted leaves and cockleshells. The stained glass windows were apparently destroyed by a bomb in 1944 and were replaced in 1953. My heart sinks as I imagine being here in the war. The thought of such beauty being bombed and used for army barracks is depressing. The thought of living here in grand style and coming here to this chapel to pray is a far happier thought.

I turn and realize I have been lost in my fantasies. Jack has gone. I wander outside and see a notice that visitors may rent a boat to ride on the river. I see my husband exploring the garden and ask if he wants to go rowing. He is not interested. I take his hand and we wander through the formal gardens admiring the roses. My energy is focused on the beauty of our surroundings. I feel light hearted. I am playful and flirtatious. I am trying to stimulate the loving feelings between us that we shared yesterday. I am not sure if he is laughing at me or with me, but it isn't the same closeness we shared so recently.

We return to our hotel dining room for dinner and order à la carte. Jack orders for both of us in clear confident French. Joy comes from successfully using our abilities. I see pleasure in his eyes. My meal is delicious. I enjoy having less food. I do not feel over fed.

As we sit in companionable silence, I know I like being married. Having a companion to share my life is very important to me. I feel better emotionally when we are happily sharing time together. I know our sexual relationship is good for keeping us connected, and not just physically. It relieves stress and I have a general sense of well being that flows into all areas of my life when we are able to be intimate with each other. It is normal for marital satisfaction to decline with stress and also that the hardest time to maintain closeness is when there are teenagers in the house. I recall my colleague who was presenting with me in New Orleans speaking about the later empty nest stages of marriage and saying that the years after the children leave home are often the happiest. They can be a honeymoon period. I smile at Jack. *Dear God please give us many more years together.*

BORDEAUX

Driving south from Tours on the A10 we are heading for Bordeaux. Our average speed is about 140 kilometres per hour. Our car certainly does travel well at high speeds and the traffic moves very quickly. We are frequently passed by Mercedes, Audis, Jaguars, Porches and sleek sports cars that are past us so fast we cannot even identify some of them.

The Reserve is a small three star hotel in Pessac, on the outskirts of Bordeaux. With just twenty-two rooms, the atmosphere is relaxed and friendly.

After we drop our suitcases in the room, we wander around the property investigating the amenities. Situated within a nature preserve, with a pond for Mallard ducks and swans, it has a feeling of being in the country. The pool is deserted. I think of having a swim. Jack is anxious to go into Bordeaux. He has made dinner reservations for eight o'clock so we have several hours available to sightsee.

We drive through town in busy traffic until we get to le centre ville.

Bordeaux, the fifth largest town in France, is over two thousand years old. The world's finest traditional wines come from this area known as Aquitaine. As a port town, it is recognized as a vital cultural hub. Built on a curve of the Garonne River, it has been a major port since pre-Roman times. There is little visible evidence of the Romans, or the Wars of Religion that have marked its past.

Driving slowly along the Allées de Tourny and along the waterfront, we notice the long sweep of elegant Classical façades. My guidebook tells me it was first built to mask the medieval slums behind. It reminds me of the park in Bath and for a moment, I recall being there on my own. It was free time and other group members were off independently as well.

So much has changed both for me and in me, since I went Questing Marilyn. I have learned to trust myself, my suspicions and my reality. I can now feel more comfortable with myself and to have trust and confidence in my abilities to think, plan, perform and live with the consequences of my decisions.

Travelling to California and then to the Bahamas with my children demanded that I accept all of the responsibility. This helped me hold onto my Self. I had to trust myself to not only make decisions for me but to make decisions that impacted on other people who depend on me. They at times wanted something I didn't want to give. I had to resort to my own judgement and my own sense of what risk I could tolerate for all of us. Making the decision to purchase the cottage (where I am the one both deciding to make the purchase and the one who must live with the consequences), was a big step for me.

> Some decisions have short term consequences and others have long term responsibilities. Some choices have big risks and others are only my fears. Growing is about stretching beyond our fears.

Now I am experiencing a new adventure. This adventure involves holding on to my Self when I am closely involved with my husband. It is one thing to feel comfortable and confident as my Self but it is another to hold onto the same sense of Self when in relationships with others. The more accepting the other is of individual differences the easier it is to maintain our selves. Sometimes I think Jack wants to see me as he wants me to be, rather than how I am. Presenting my Self to him day after day without breaks in our time together is challenging. Thoughts of the terrain we will be covering and his careful planning and set expectations gives me some concern.

I gave up my wants when he wouldn't help me call home. I could have found another way to make that call if it really mattered. The camp and the girls have our schedule and the numbers of our hotels. There were no messages for us at the Jean Bardet Hotel. It was a whim to think of calling. I was annoyed and felt it better to have some space in our time together rather than smoulder. *Time to get over it Marilyn.*

Jack manoeuvres the car along the unfamiliar streets with confidence. We pass the Grosse Cloche or Great Bell, in the old Town Hall's belfry. It is one of the symbols of Bordeaux. It is fun to see the real places that have tempted us from the guidebooks. I suggest we visit the Jardin Public but instead we drive over and back across the Pont de Pierre Bridge, commissioned by Napoleon, and finished in 1822. This magnificent stone bridge is almost five hundred meters long. It used to be a toll bridge, but in 1861 the town bought it and it is now free. It is a beautiful bridge!

One reality of touring when not in the driver's seat is that suggestions can be made but the driver has control of the car. Sometimes, the decision of where to go depends on what lane of traffic we are in at the time. Other times it is a conflict between two options and the driver can choose and make it happen. Fortunately, we are usually able to compromise and find a way that we both get a chance to see what we desire.

Jack makes no reference to my request. I choose not to repeat myself. *Am I giving in to avoid conflict?* This is what I do repeatedly. *Is he trying to start something?* He could at least acknowledge that I spoke out of general politeness. *This is no time to be teaching manners.*

It is a lovely evening and we park the car to walk. I am relieved to be able to move. I love le Monument des Girondins built at the turn of the 19th century, with its tall single column rising into the sky. A winged angel sits on top. To me it is saying "Yes!" to the world. The magnificent fountain at the base is so large that as I walk around it, I lose sight of Jack on the other side. I walk around it several times taking pictures and marvelling at the wildness portrayed in the horses. The shooting water has such energy. Something deep

inside me is touched by the message of strife and hope. Suddenly I get sprayed when the breeze blows the mist unexpectedly toward me. I laugh out loud and run from its reach.

We follow the guidebook suggestions for a walk through the quaint, narrow streets of Quartier Saint Pierre. Our time runs out before our interest and we decide we want to return again tomorrow for at least part of the day. We also want to visit some chateaus where we can sample the local wines. We have travelled through many fields of grapes and Jack has explained the differences in the wines that depend on the grape chosen by the vineyard owner, the soil type and the ways the grapes are pressed and fermented. He knows wines by taste and enjoys the subtleties in flavour.

Le Rouzic at 34 Cour de Chapeau-Rouge, in downtown Bordeaux, with Michel Gautier, maître cuisinier of France is our destination for dinner. The elegant decor intimidates me. I am not nearly as stylishly dressed as the other women present. Our waiter seems not to notice and is attentive and helpful. I am delighted with a salad filled with both ingredients that I recognize and some I don't. Jack is helpful in explaining the main portion of the meal and I choose salmon with a to-die-for delicious sauce.

Everything is presented like a work of art, almost too nice to touch, but the aroma is so enticing and my appetite whetted. I cannot resist. Fresh raspberries served in a crystal bowel with a silver spoon and a separate dish of whipped cream for me to help myself is the perfect dessert to a wonderful meal. *Oh how I wish we could come back here!*

AUCH

Two hundred and three kilometres from Bordeaux, our day's destination is Auch and de France Hotel. It is in the centre of the Gascon capital and a former coach house. It is also advertised as being one of the best restaurants in France. Situated near the cathedral, with boutiques around the square, it promises to be another treasure.

The town, under the protection of the Counts of Armagnac, managed to stay calm and prosper throughout the rambunctious Middle Ages. The old part of the town is lined with narrow streets that centre on Place Salinis. I spy a ladies wear shop and would love to glance through inside but it is closed. We ramble through quiet streets and enjoy the soft pastel colours of the sky as the sun sets.

Visiting the charming hotel restaurant, with its Napoleon the Third decor, stained glass windows, and opulent comfortable chairs, is somewhat intimidating. Thankfully it is not too busy. I am fearful of my ability with the language and not sure how help-ful Jack will be. He seems to resent that I have not put more effort into working on my use of French. The chef visits our table before we order. He asks what we would prefer for dinner. Jack asks questions about the featured dishes and the suggestions are discussed. His French is superb and his delight in the conversation obvious. I do not understand it all but I feel a very special welcoming atmosphere. After some consultation, I let Jack order for both of us. He is charming and helpful and I relax and greatly enjoy the food and wine. I feel cared for and loved. Surely this must be what heaven is like.

Before leaving town, while stowing the bags in the car, I request a few minutes to visit the ladies wear shop. Jack suggests he will accompany me. I am surprised but pleased. I enjoy his opinion on what I wear and he is often complimentary on how I look. I love it when he flirts with me.

We are the only ones in the shop. I try on several jackets and par-ticularly like a grey plaid traditional styled one that the sales woman tells me is from a well know Paris designer. I do not know Billevesee as a designer, but then I do not know a lot about expensive clothing manufacturers. Is says it is made in France and the name Paris is on the label. I love it. I am sure my eyes are dancing with delight. Jack has told me I must pay for my own purchases on this trip. I decide to decline.

Suddenly, as the woman is hanging up the jacket, Jack suggests he will buy it for me. I am charmingly surprised. I look into his intense blue eyes and ask if he is sure. He smiles shyly and nods. I feel as if I am his mistress taken out for a treat. What a treat! The sales woman suggests slacks or a skirt and I decline. I want the jacket. I am very satisfied. She suggests a shirt to go with it and shows me several lovely ones. Jack encourages me to pick one. I choose a very silky white blouse with pleats down the front and pretty gold buttons. I am delighted with the quality. *I wonder what came over him? Why did I not just put it on my American Express card the way I shop at home?* I know it is the price. Even though I wanted it the amount is well above what I can afford given my other financial responsibilities. *I like feeling this way.*

High self definition allows high intimacy. I can trust that if I let someone really know me, I will not lose myself in them as I have a strong sense of Self. I can hold onto Me while I am with the other person. I feel I just experienced another part of myself— rejecting the independent woman and allowing my husband to be the generous giver. I accepted and said thank you. Over the months of uncertainty in this relationship I have often been able to say: "I love the Me I can be when I am with you." It is an independent me. Being the recipient of Jack's thoughtfulness and being appreciative feels more like the way we used to relate. When I changed so dramatically over the years, and took on more personal power, I set the relationship out of the old balance. I set raising my children, getting my education and building my career as a high priority. I lost the dependent woman role. Now it feels familiar.

THE CAVE AT LOMBRIVES

We are blessed with lovely days. Jack has carefully marked the map and I look for road signs and posters directing us to a wine cellar or Roman ruins and examples of ancient architecture. I am not concerned with which way we turn or even where we are going. Jack has the route generally memorized and only occasionally consults a map. It is as if he doesn't want my help. I am relaxed and happy to go along on the tour.

Travelling along pretty winding country roads, through pastured valleys, medieval towns and villages, enjoying the wonderful changes in the countryside, our conversation is relaxed. Questions circle in my head but I choose to leave them unspoken. At some points there are picturesque views of the Pyrenean peaks. We are climbing steadily.

Jack has chosen for us to tour Lombrives, a cave that is noteworthy because it is the largest cave in Europe. We ride a small train from the car park to the entrance. Our assigned group heads into the underground passages. We see markings on the walls that date back centuries. Some are names and dates while others are markings thought to be made by cave dwellers. The small group allows the guide's words to be easily heard. We are also told that the caves of southern France held criminal fugitives and those hiding from religious persecution. During times of war caves were also places to find shelter and avoid capture. The temperature remains a constant thirteen degrees Celsius. I am glad I have worn a warm jacket.

Lights are turned on in the area we visit and turned off behind us. We are walking in what appears to be a moving puddle of light, surrounded by deep blackness. The floor is uneven and I am mindful of where I place my feet. I am wearing sturdy walking shoes yet still feel cautious in sections. Massive rock formations of various colours and shapes are everywhere. Some are thin, fragile and stringy while others are fat and solid. Some look like ugly growths and others are beautiful. There are stalactites and stalagmites in beautiful shapes. I know the ones that hang down are called stalactites. They are formed by acidic water dripping, depositing the minerals it contains, just like an icicle. I remember this because they remind me of holding a pair of tights. Stalagmites are upward growing mounds, grown from many layers of deposit, much like dripping wax from a candle. After many years they grow into a column and then the deposits widen it. Each area has different minerals that create the underground formations so they can be many different colours and shapes.

As we explore deeper into the underground passage, I feel more and more confined. I lag to the back of the line and can barely hear the guide's words. I consider going back out alone. *Could I find the light switches?*

I am summoned to stay with the group. I am sure I could not find my way back alone even if I dared to try. The walls close in and the ceiling dips. We are guided through a very narrow opening in the rocks and I resist. I can feel my heart pound and my breath quicken in shallow gulps. I do not want to go through. I suggest I wait here for the group to come back. My thoughts turn to an earthquake and I imagine a crushing roar of rock. Jack asks if I am alright and I assure him I am not. Our guide guarantees me that it is a short confined passage, and the huge vaulted room beyond is worth the visit. Like a small child, I clutch Jack's hand, and allow myself to be manoeuvred through. Tears sting at the corners of my eyes. I feel so silly and so frightened.

A huge cavernous room spreads before us. Spotlights illuminate the rock formations and cast eerie shadows. Concerts are held in this vast area called the cathedral. I imagine the soft sound of a harp but doubt

it would fit through the narrow passage. Perhaps a guitar or wind instruments like the flute and oboe. My thoughts pull musical memories and I find I am humming softly. The echo of sounds would be very interesting to hear. I am pulled from my imaginings when our guide suggests we retreat. I am again fearful of the narrow passage. I know I must pass through. I plead with Jack to be among the first through. He agrees. We easily make our way to the head of the group. Some want to linger but we are cautioned that the lights will be turned off, so we must follow along. Knowing I am on my way out, I easily slide between the tight rock walls and want to run to the entrance. We are cautioned to stay together. I impatiently wait.

We took the shortest tour. I was not sure how I would be as sometimes I feel claustrophobic while at other times in tight places I am not bothered at all. Soon I see the natural light of day and my heart soars. Finally outside, feeling the warmth of the sun on my face and the glare in my eyes, I breathe deeply. I am glad I went. I am even happier to be out.

"Can we just walk for a few moments?"

My sense of being trapped lingers with me. I stretch my arms and shake my body then stride across the parking lot. Something happened in the cave that frightens me. I cannot place what it is but I feel something is stirring just below my consciousness. *What is trapping me? Is it my own fears? Is it something between Jack and me?*

FOIX

Château de Foix is a stunning medieval castle perched on a high point. We visit the Musée de l'Ariège and see displays of armour, stone carvings and artefacts from the Roman Empire to the Middle Ages. We wander through the narrow streets of Foix and eat our dinner in a small restaurant.

While Jack is happy to search for Roman history I am finding the stories of the Cathers fascinating. Before being taken to England, legends tell of the Holy Grail being kept in this part of France. People who were disenchanted with the Roman Christian church followed their own spiritual beliefs that were less rigid and more feminist. Tales of bloody persecutions and secret societies fill the guidebooks in the shops but I am not able to really read them. I get the message from the pictures and the few words I do understand. I haven't found any in English. I wish I'd paid more attention in French class in high school.

FROM THE PYRENEES TO PROVENCE

Our day starts early. It will take us several hours to get to our next destination near St. Remy de Provence. Jack starts the driving. At first we travel through the countryside descending out of the mountains. There are lovely vistas and quaint settlements. As we join the autoroute near Carcassonne we get our toll money ready and I assume driving. We head straight east toward the Mediterranean.

"Oh let's go down to the sea!"

"We cannot take the time or we will be off schedule. That is planned for another day."

We can see the sun sparkling off the water in the distance and I am drawn to it. I resist the temptation to just take a short detour to the coast. I am in control of the car. I could do it. *Behave Marilyn!*

I marvel at the pleasure of having such a lovely car. I tell myself to enjoy what I have and not wish for more. I love to drive fast and continue to be amazed as cars appear in my rear view mirror as if I am standing still. I try to stay out of their way, before they put on their turn signal to let me know they want to pass. At times the lane to the left is not clear and I have an expensive vehicle with an impatient driver practically in my trunk.

During our drive I have time to think. It is also a time where we can talk without being interrupted. It is difficult to avoid something as we are captured in our vehicle. My mind settles naturally on my marital relationship. We have been together through a number of different experiences and over a week of days and nights. I feel an unsettled agitation but cannot define what it is. I believe I am on the edge of another insight. Something is about to change. I can feel it coming but cannot identify what is shifting. *Is it some awareness in me? Is Jack about to do something that will alter our relationship?*

"Are you happy with the tour so far?" I ask.

As we discuss some of the highlights and several disappointments, I am aware that Jack is talking about practical things. Matching our memories from our unique perspectives reveals how we process the same events differently. I use so much emotion in my memories. I recall how I felt as well as what I did. Neither view is right or wrong. We are different and understanding our differences can lead to greater closeness. I learned the roles of memory keeper and gatekeeper in my family of origin. I passed messages between my parents and often from my parents to my siblings. I was also the record keeper. I became accustomed to holding memories and reminding others of past events. While I don't memorize well, I hold onto the process of occurrences. Our children sometimes argue with me that I have forgotten specific amounts or dates because I do not remember numbers well. I can however, recall the story line and enjoy telling "remember when" accountings. Doing this helps keep continuity in the line of events of our family story. I want to ask Jack if he is happy being with me.

A marriage is an evolving process. Every couple sees their marriage from their own perspective. To create and maintain a satisfactory marriage requires time and energy. Each partner needs to nurture the relationship as a separate entity from their individual wants and needs. I know it is sometimes hard to give up what I want in order for the relationship to stay balanced. Knowing what to give up and when to give in and when to stand my ground for what I want is a challenge. Sometimes I feel as if I give in too often.

I have had clients where I meet one partner first and then when I meet the other, and they describe their view of their relationship, I am so surprised by the differences in perception. Other couples easily identify their differences and come into work on them specifically. They are clear that they want to work on anger management, parenting or money management. Sometimes, one partner thinks everything is fine while the other is very unhappy. What we expect of our marriage also has an impact on our sense of satisfaction.

I do not speak my question. I am not sure enough that I will get the answer I want to hear. I love this man. Not just as an emotional feeling but I am deciding to keep my heart open to him. It is my choice. I sometimes wonder if it is a foolish choice but I choose it in awareness that with risking there is danger. For now I choose love.

PROVENCE

We exit the highway at Nimes. We are hunting for the Roman aqueduct that was built before Christ and went from Uzes to Nimes. It carried spring water by gravity and was built without the use of mortar. The nearly 50 mile long three story structure is in ruins for portions of the route. We are able to see sections of it from several vantage points. Amazing how it has stood for so many years. It is a real tribute to Roman architecture.

Lunch on the sidewalk under bright umbrellas delight me. I feel as if I am again in a travel poster. Jack is a wealth of information and tells the history of the Romans in this area as if he were a professional travel guide. My fears evaporate as I watch his enthusiasm. I so wish I had many more weeks to explore like this. Time for us to enjoy where we are and who we are as individuals with each other.

Jack is eager to see the Roman amphitheatre in Nimes said to be the best preserved one in France. It is used for bull fights and concerts. The splendour of the images from movies like Ben Hur swirl in my head as we first see the massive two stories of stone arches and curved walls. I know he is thrilled to explore, taking time to read the signs and speak with others who have also come here as tourists. I do not understand all that is said but know he is being told about other places worthy of visits in this area. The Maison Carre is another magnificent example of Roman architecture. It is a free standing building with columns all around. I feel as if I am in Italy not France as I walk around the outside. It is still in use as a museum.

From Nimes, we drive on small country roads east. Crossing the Rhône River, we stop briefly to watch the river traffic and inspect our map to agree on our route. The Rhône is a major transportation route and has been for centuries. It drains south from the centre of France and the French Alps. I'd love to sit and watch the boats but since we are again staying in the countryside we agree to find our lodgings before too late in the day.

Turning off the main road, we slowly enter another world. The long tree lined drive takes us between open fields. The Chateau Roussan, is our home for two nights. It is a large beige structure with brown shutters and old tiles on the roof. It looks rather run down. I am filled with fascination. I raise a questioning brow and ask Jack if he is sure this is the place. He is sure. We follow the drive around to the back. I feel like an invader in someone else's private space. It is charming and rough, with tangles of vines and unkempt looking gardens. It was built at the beginning of the 18th century as a farmhouse for a small farm by the Marquesses of Ganges. At one time the Mas de Roussan was Captain Bertrand de Nostredame, brother of the astrologer and seer Nostradamus, over 400 years ago. I feel an exciting thrill.

Château de Roussan
Route de Tarascon

We are greeted by our host. Jack speaks in French and I nod and smile, only understanding the general message of the communication. The foyer is painted bright pink and the curved ceiling is white. Fancy plaster mouldings and fine antique furniture give the feeling of faded elegance. *I love it!* Our room is spacious, bright and clean. We have a large window opening over the back garden. The grounds are gorgeous in a wild old world way, with tall trees creating a canopy over a barely moving stream. Ducks are paddling lazily and song birds are singing. *What a soothing scene!* There is a sense of the proprietors being barely able to keep up with the repairs and maintenance. It is like something from a story book. I love the authenticity.

ST. REMY DE PROVENCE

After exploring just enough to know our way in and out and where breakfast will be served, we take the short trip into St. Remy de Provence. We park in the town square then start to explore on foot. I love all the flower baskets and planters. One sight we enjoy is the astronomical clock. It isn't as fancy as the one in Rouen. I am sure the town clock has always been an important place in people's lives. Fountains and flowers, churches and old buildings. I am feeling overwhelmed with so much information and I am ready for a glass of cool white wine. There are a number of restaurants as possible choices for dinner. We take our time poking into shops and wandering the centre section of the town before we make our decision.

The evening is warm and calm and couples stroll arm in arm. We explore more narrow streets and admire the intricate facades on the buildings. So much is so old and has such wonderful colours and textures.

Sitting in the Chateau Roussan garden, in the soft evening light, with glasses of vin de pays, "wine of the countryside" that we bought in town, a lovely summer evening is interrupted only by the cicadas and tree frogs who noisily sing their hearts out. We are the only guests in the garden and it is a relaxing romantic way to end another wonderful day.

ROMAN RUINS

I am up and out before Jack. I wander the garden with my camera. As I pause beside the slowly moving water, a duck approaches me for food. I have nothing to offer. It soon sees me as not worth the begging and waddles to the shore and swims away. I wander out the pathway to the back of the chateau past weathered statues, overgrown gardens and flower containers filled with weeds. A murky swimming pool does not tempt me at all. As I snap pictures, I wonder if anyone is watching from a window. No one appears to be about.

Our breakfast is served in a charming room. While it looks and feels like this place could be haunted, I have a sense that the spirit would be friendly.

Jack has a day of touring planned. We start with the lost Roman city of Glanum. It sits in an area of farmland which was created when a vaulted dam was built in the 1st century. Lac de Saint Remy was created by an aqueduct believed to originate in the Greek era two hundred years before Christ. There was a vast irrigation system that supplied water to this area. Unfortunately, enough water was not available to douse the grass and forest fires before they swept through here earlier in the summer. Vast patches of charred earth and stumps mar the landscape. It must have been very frightening to be here when it burned.

The Arc de Triomphe and the Mausolée des Jules, known as Les Antiques, marked the monumental entry to the ancient town. It is situated on the Via Domitia, a travel and trading route that ran from Spain to Italy. For a long time, before the discovery of the lost city, they were the only visible monuments of Glanum. They are among the most famous Roman monuments in Europe.

Mausolée des Jules is a well preserved monument in honour of the father and grandfather of an important Roman family. It is famous for its unusual structure which is quite unique in Roman architecture. I ask Jack what he would like as a marker on his grave someday. He suggests he would like to be cremated and his ashes scattered on the wind. I push to see if he really wouldn't like a monument like this for posterity and he emphatically refuses to be drawn into my teasing with a loud "No."

We poke about the ruins and I am amazed to see in real physical form, how the buildings were structured so clean water could come into them and dirty water drain away. It would be equivalent to modern day indoor plumbing.

The ancient Greco-Roman city of Arles is another must-see on our quest for Roman history. The day is very hot so we decide we can take time to see it tomorrow before we start our trip north as the mornings tend to be cooler. I am relieved when Jack agrees we can head for the coast.

COTE D' AZURE - FRENCH RIVIERA

I want to at least dip my toe in the Mediterranean before we leave. Thrilled by the thought of visiting the Cote d' Azure on the French Riviera, my spirits are high. I do hope we will have the opportunity to swim. The traffic is moving fast and I follow along on the map as we pass signs bearing the names of places I wish we had time to explore.

Jack is in high spirits too and is trying to recall French songs that go with the names of places. He sings a few bars then finds another. His imitation of Maurice Chevalier singing Thank Heaven for Little Girls is funny. The laughter stops when I ask if he thinks the song could be that of a pedophile. I talk about the acceptability of the French for men having mistresses and men wanting virgins and young women for sexual activity. The miles slide by as we discuss monogamy, affairs, mistresses and sexual abuse. It is a serious discussion that includes our teenage daughters and the role parents need to take as protectors. At one point, he jokes about the desirability of being French and having a wife and a mistress. I assure him if I had the chance, the role of mistress certainly sounds advantageous to the role of wife, in a number of ways.

We were headed for St. Tropez. We wanted to see the place that has so much glamour associated with it. We have decided to forgo that ambition even though we are only 12 kilometres away. Jack had mentioned it at the petrol station and was warned that it will be very busy. It would take us several hours in slow traffic as it has narrow streets and gets very congested. It is a harbour without a beach and we'd be lucky to even find a parking space. He is also warned that it is very pricy. He suggested we go over on the ferry but we decide a relaxing few hours at the beach is more to our liking. It is too hot to spend any more of the day in the car. It is busy but not crowded.

The sea is as blue as the travel posters promised. Driving slowly along the shore road, we explore our options. We have decided that having lunch at the seashore will be divine. We choose a place then wait briefly for a table to be available. I feel as if I am in a dream. I do not want to wake up. The menu has English descriptions. I order a prawn and mussel salad with a crusty roll and a selection of cheeses. Jack orders us each a glass of wine.

Walking along the enclosed beach, I carry my shoes in my hand and wade at the water's edge. Because we ate at the restaurant we have use of the beach. There are open sections of beach for public use and fenced off sections where the beach is cleaned and chaises and chairs with umbrellas are available for rental.

We decide to swim as the water is refreshing. The buoyancy of the salt water allows me to tread water with little effort. I tease Jack about looking at the topless women on the beach and he teases me right back by suggesting that I have been curiously watching the skimpy suits on the men. We are used to much more conservative beach wear in Canada. He dares me to take my top down and swim topless. I do, then dare him to take his suit off. With much giggling and joking we are swimming naked well out from shore. I am reminded of the times we have gone swimming naked on a hot summer night when we had a swimming pool in the yard or at the cottage. He swims close then grabs my suit. He teases that he will keep it and make me walk out of the water naked. In half an instant fun turns to fear. I change my tone.

"This isn't fun when you talk like that."

I plead for my suit. I am beginning to be upset. He apologises, swims close and hands it to me. He hugs me and kisses me, then asks me not to ruin a lovely day.

I wonder at my immediate shift from feeling relaxed and playful to fearful. I know my brother would lure me into something and then suddenly turn and trick me, and think my reaction was funny. I have a deep distrust from being hurt by being too trusting. *Why is it that men do not seem to have respect for my vulnerability? Surely they must know they are stronger and can physically intimidate me. What is it in a man that he gets a sense of power by having a woman be frightened? Could I have asked for help from someone on shore if Jack had kept my suit? Would everyone just laugh at my predicament and blame me for taking off my bathing suit in the first place?*

I wonder if I would be best to laugh at myself and make a joke of my fear. I do not want to ruin our day. I do not want to appear bitchy.

What is it about my time with this man that we can go from shared fun to something that I feel is almost sinister? Is he angry that I really took off my swim suit? Does he get delight in seeing how sensitive I am? Does he do it just to feel powerful? I hate the feeling of distrust. I hate it when he turns it around to make it look like I am the spoiled sport. Sometimes I think he is afraid to get too close to me.

On our drive back to the Chateau Roussan there is no singing. Fearful that I will cry, I keep my voice as even as possible and explain to Jack that it is difficult for me to trust him by allowing myself to be vulnerable, when he uses my trust to frighten me.

"How would I know you would get so upset?"

In becoming a therapist, I learned to trust others with information about myself. This is a very scary form of trust. It involves risk because I had to learn that by revealing myself I was trusting that, at a later time in the relationship, the other person would not use what I shared against me or to harm me. Because of the strict code of confidentiality that is part of my professional code of ethics, I learned that telling my truth to a trusted other was accepted. I learned that the stories I felt ashamed or fearful about were common experiences of life that many people go through. I was not belittled for revealing vulnerability, I was supported. When I met my supervisor or other therapists in my supervision group, I was accepted and asked how I was managing with my problems. I was given encouragement and taught new life skills.

I explain that when I was raised there was a lot of family shame because my father was only educated to grade six and there was shame about the ethnic heritage—not pride. I was told to keep secrets and not let others know about what happened in our home. Denial and avoidance of real issues was the norm.

"I know all that." His tone is sharp.

"Yes, but do you understand how it has affected me as an adult?"

I want him to try to understand things from my point of view. I try to explain.

"It is still hard sometimes for me to really talk about what is deep inside my thoughts and feelings. I am afraid I will be abandoned by you if I do not always appear happy and nice. I have been trying so hard to please you. You seem much nicer to me when I am accommodating and submissive. I want us to develop the skills necessary to establish a deeper positive emotional intimacy based on mutual trust. It is a critical developmental task of adult life that leads to a sense of personal security. Intimacy is not possible if we are on guard because we fear being rejected. At the heart of intimacy problems is the basic fear of abandonment. I am afraid that you are going to leave me again."

My throat is tight and my breathing is shallow. Tears flow down my cheeks. He takes my hand and squeezes it gently.

"Did it ever occur to you that I am afraid you will leave me?" His voice is now soft and quiet.

"Yes. I know you thought I was going to leave you a number of times. You were right. I have thought of leaving our marriage. I have had a very hard time with the lies and all your times with Beth. I do not want to separate but I also do not want to live a life constantly feeling afraid, on the alert and worried that I might be missing some clue. I want to trust you so I can be free to be my Self. I do not want to live a life in a role without a sense of honesty. It would be like play acting. My purpose in life is not to meet someone else's expectations, yours, our children's or anyone's.

I want to live with integrity. This means I am accepting responsibility for my own life. I am not blaming you or anyone else for myself as an adult. I can understand the influences my upbringing had on me but I am not bound by it. I can grow and change. At first I thought it was disloyal to my parents, then to you, to do things in new and different ways. I now know that I can grow beyond what I was taught and still love and respect you and my parents. Can you understand this?"

"Yes, you are a very determined woman."

"I have worked hard to change parts of myself. I have learned to like who I am. I enjoy exploring new ideas and concepts and creating a belief system that works for me. I continue to work on improving my concept of my Self. It may feel like I am abandoning you when I change my beliefs about some of the old ideas that we shared when I am trying new creative ways to be my Self that are new to you but I am not abandoning you. I am finding Me. I am breaking my dependence on you for my thoughts and beliefs. I can do this and still love you very deeply. I can separate from you on some levels and still respect you and want to grow old with you. I am not here just to orbit you. You are not the sun and I am like a moon only surviving on reflected light. I have a destiny of my own. I love you. I want you for my husband and life partner. I say this not because I have to be with you. I want to be with you. It is a conscious choice. I am happy being me with you. I also want you to choose to be with me."

"I'm here aren't I?"

I squeeze his hand and let go. I blow my nose and dry my tears.

I sit quietly, and know that I can observe Jack and keep my boundaries intact. I hoped he would have said more about being committed to our marriage but I will not push the issue. I am no longer absorbing his every word, feeling and attitude, and taking it as acceptance or rejection of me. I do not feel as overwhelmed by him as I have in the past. I have tended to get over involved in his issues and ignore my own. I have reacted too much to his wants and expectations of me, always hoping that someday if I was good enough he would love me, be faithful to me and stay.

By taking my time and observing him, I have been able to evaluate what is happening, see his actions more clearly, and watch how he seduces and manipulates me to get his own way. Then from a position of greater clarity, I can think before I react, so hopefully I act more appropriately.

There have been times on this trip when I have felt myself giving up what I might have felt or wanted to compromise and keep the flow of what we are doing. There are also times when I have given up too much of myself to give into what he wants. The night in Tours when I ordered the huge meal to share the experience with him. I really didn't want that much food. Funny how I can see that now, but when I accepted his suggestion I wasn't as aware of what I wanted. I don't think it really would have made a difference if I had ordered less.

As I watch and analyse how Jack is relating to me, I collect the experiences and store them away. My journals help me to identify patterns, as does having an excellent memory for social interactions. This is a real asset in my work. I am also adaptable and can switch my actions and reactions as the situation shifts. I am sometimes amazed how I feel as if I am sitting on my own shoulder directing my words and actions with purpose and intent. This is what living in my own life rather than just reacting is all about.

I know as I detach, become more objective and aware, I will never feel so hopelessly in love with this man again. There have been so many hurts, disappointments and lies. I hope some day I will not be so watchful and wary. *Will I ever be able to truly trust him?* Trust is so vital to a relationship of any kind, but especially in a marriage.

I no longer see my marriage as something that just happens because we love each other. I know we have chemistry between us as well as sexual energy. We have so many areas where we are compatible. We have built so much worthy of keeping.

It is also very important that we give beyond ourselves and consider what we give to the next generations. How we deal with life not only affects our children and their lives but our grandchildren's lives and beyond. To be effective parents, we must take into account how our behaviour and words impacts others. I frequently think about how our marital dynamics and my reaction to them impacts my ability to be a healthy parent. I am working hard at becoming the kind of person and parent I really want to be. I chose to be a parent. I want my children to be able to create themselves to their own ideals.

ARLES

Arles is at the top of the Rhōne Delta and is linked to the Mediterranean by a canal. It is also famous as a home of Vincent Van Gogh who painted many scenes here in the late eighteen hundreds. The Roman amphitheatre is newer than the one in Nimes having been built just after the birth of Christ. Part of the old stone walls that surrounded the city still stand.

The Church of St. Trophime is named in honour of the first bishop of Arles, and is built on the foundations of an 8th century church. The structure that is currently there dates from the 12th century. The main portal has been added as an afterthought to the otherwise unadorned facade. It is where some say the Holy Grail was secretly kept for many years. I walk quietly along the cloister hallway and try to imagine what it would be like to reside here knowing the secrets of The Holy Grail.

I have seen enough ruins for awhile and I am anxious to be on the road. We have a good four hours of driving and all of it is not on fast roads. We are heading up into the French Alps. Jack has a passion to walk in the Alps.

We head north choosing a route that will take us to Pont du Gard to see another part of the aqueduct. It is not far off the A9 that will allow us to move quickly north to Valence then head north east to Grenoble and on to Annecy. There are lots of green roads that would take us through picturesque countryside but we will have to save that for another trip.

After a short stop we are on the road and moving quickly. We cross the Rhône and then follow it closely for quite awhile. I enjoy my turn at driving and just watching the scenery as Jack takes the wheel.

I am very aware that the Romans were filled with masculine energy and power. Throughout my visit here I have had a recurring vision of how it must have been in the time before they came with their power to transform the landscape. How gentle a countryside this must have been. It is as if they raped the land, building their roads and monuments and bringing their lifestyle with such force that it overtook everything in its path. Then the Christian churches were built on old pagan places of worship. It is as if they were trying to stamp out old beliefs and insist on their way as the one true and only way to connect with the forces of the universe. The feminine energy and goddess worship were stamped out with both of the invasions. So many examples of men taking control, fearing the power of the feminine and needing to crush it. There is such a difference in energy when the two forces work together in harmony. I do hope our world is moving more in that direction with so many more women using their power.

> I know it isn't as cut and dried as that. There are many men who are gentle and nurturing and who know that co-operation is more important than having mastery over another. There are also powerful controlling women who only want to have authority over others. They are not looking for co-operative relationships. Like good sex the hard thrust with the soft reception can be mutually pleasurable and satisfying and used to create new life or it can be abusive and destructive.

I am stunned when after a considerable silence Jack asks:

"Why would someone consider suicide?"

After a pause I ask; "What are you really asking?"

"What makes someone want to take their life?"

"People who commit suicide are usually depressed and feel their life is meaningless. They cannot accept that people love them and want to have them in their life. Sometimes they feel they have no friends and their family has rejected or abandoned them. Feelings of hopelessness and helplessness can be present. People, who lose the people or things that are the most important to them can sometimes think of ending their own life. "

Since I know more men commit suicide than women I ask if he is thinking of suicide. He tells me that he isn't but that he is convinced a client's spouse who had a motor vehicle accident may have committed suicide. I ask about the implications for the estate, life insurance and such things, then ask if he wants to talk about that client. He avoids my question and asks me why I sometimes say my mother committed suicide with her alcoholism.

"My mother felt trapped in a life with little meaning especially after her children were grown. She didn't have a way to support herself and she wanted to move to the city from the country. Dad wouldn't sell the house. He loved coming home to his country estate from work in Toronto and puttering about the yard and his garage. She saw no future for herself. She was also depressed and had been treated for depression."

"Have you ever thought of suicide?"

His question is blunt and I take a few minutes to respond.

I recount times I have been sick or felt trapped and wanted the pain to end.

"I have never seriously thought of killing myself. That time in Jamaica when I had such a bad time with a tummy upset was pretty bad. I thought dying would be easier than that. I was sad and sick in Dublin but not so desperate that I'd end my life. Once when you were being really awful about me cooking a turkey dinner in the summer then not showing up, I thought if I tipped my canoe and drowned perhaps it wouldn't be so painful. I have been so deeply hurt by some of your behaviour."

He is silent and the air is filled with tension.

I know I hurt so much because I care so deeply. The more I disengage from him the less pain his words and actions can cause me. Caring too deeply for him is sometimes dangerous to me. I do not believe I really would end my life over him though. I have too much joy and happiness that has nothing to do with him for that. I have places I want to go, things I want to do and people with whom I want to share my life. I would never leave that as a legacy to my children. Suicide is such a selfish act.

I have an eerie sense of apprehension and ask him if we can talk about something else. I am quiet for a long time, deep in thought. *I wonder if he ever wishes me dead.*

Ville La Clusaz in the French Alps

Ville la Clusaz is in the east branch of the Rhône section of the French Alps. Its name stems from the words God's Narrow Place as it is in a valley between two mountains. It is a lovely drive up into the mountains then back down into valleys, as we wander toward our next destination. The town sits picture perfect in the valley, we descend. A tall church spire is dwarfed by the majesty of the mountains. It is hard to believe we are just an hour from Geneva, Switzerland.

Le Vieux Chalet is a small, rustic, cozy hotel on the edge of the ski slopes. We pass through the town then up the far slope. It is a good walk back down to the town, but in winter it would be possible to take a lift to the hotel and ski right to and from the porch. There is a summer bobsled ride where people ride the chair lift from the town, up to just outside our hotel, then ride a single sled back down a twisting track.

Built into the side of the mountain, the dark wood is a perfect fit for my fantasy of an alpine chalet. Baskets of bright geraniums line the entrance and are placed around the patio that overlooks the valley. The beamed ceiling and wooden tables are rustic and in keeping with the character of the chalet. Our room is comfortable and our window looks right out to the top of the lift. As we settle in the clanking of the lift suddenly stops. Silence, then a few voices and laughter. *I wonder what time that thing starts in the morning. It will wake me for sure if I am still asleep.*

We are on the dinner and breakfast included plan. Our table for two is in the centre of the wall and I seat myself on the bench. This allows me to survey the dining room and watch the other guests. It appears the hotel is filled with visitors but I cannot discern another English speaking couple.

I survey the menu and can not identify anything that I am sure of what I will get. There are no descriptions in English. I ask Jack what he is ordering and he tells me he hasn't decided. I ask if he will tell me what some of the dishes are that he knows might meet my tastes. He is annoyed and tells me I should have polished up my French. His words sting me. *Why does he do this?*

Menus are one of the hardest areas to translate as so many descriptive words are used mixed with the names of sauces and herbs as well as ways to cook. I cannot even tell what some of the ingredients or preparation styles are in English speaking restaurants. I review the menu, but now as I am more nervous, none of them make any sense.

I already know from when we were checking in that the staff does not speak English. I hold tight to my self-control and in an effort to appear calm, close my menu. Traditionally, this is a signal to a waiter that I am ready to order. I have no idea what to do. Jack closes his menu as the waiter brings the bottle of wine he has ordered. Just as my glass is being poured, steaming plates of mixed seafood over rice are deposited on an adjoining table. I recognize crayfish and shrimp. As the waiter asks: "Vous avez choisi?" I know this is asking if I have made a choice. I smile and say: "S'il vous plait." and point to the dinner which is now being eaten beside me.

Thank you dear guardian angel for giving me just what I needed.

My dinner is delicious. I sense Jack was surprised that I carried that off so well. *What were his intentions?*

I recognize citron for lemon on the dessert menu and enjoy a lemon tart.

After a full breakfast, lingering over second coffees on the deck, we drive to the village. We take the cable car up the massif Beauregard to the plateau at 1690 meters. It is exciting to see the buildings dwarf in size as we ascend. The air is thin and bright and the view magnificent from the top. I want to enjoy the vastness of it all and take my time. Standing overlooking the valley we marvel at the distance we can see. We point out farms and churches, other ski slopes and lifts. I am reminded of the story of Heidi that my mother read to me when I was a little girl. I am so glad it is a clear day.

Jack starts to move away from me. The others who rode up with us have started to scatter.

"Can we just take a few more minutes here so I can get some pictures?"

Jack tells me to take all the time I want. I turn with my camera at my eye and snap a picture. Suddenly I hear him announce from behind me that he is going hiking alone. He puts emphasis on the word alone. I am shocked. It is obvious by his tone that I am not welcome. I turn and watch his retreating back as he quickly strides off with purposeful intent as if he knows exactly where he is going. *Why was this not discussed? Why does he not want me along? How long will he be gone?*

I want to race after him and ask for an explanation but I know I would have a hard time keeping up with him. His legs are so much longer than mine and he seems determined to leave me behind. Tears sting my eyes. I gaze off in the distance not seeing anything through the blur. Gradually, I settle myself down and decide that I must make the best of this. The cable car has gone back down and will not be back for some time.

A family is standing at the railing overlooking the valley below. I wait until they are all looking away from me and take their picture. My heart aches for my children. *How many times have I found solace in my children when I have been heartbroken over Jack?*

I wander away from the top of the lift and see a young girl with a walking stick, gazing out over the valley. I take her picture from the back. Her long hair held back with a band, flows down her pink shirt. Like her, I am alone. I cannot see her companions and she remains still for quite a long while. I wonder what she is thinking. *Is she from this area?* She doesn't have a backpack like many of the others who came up with us.

As I move along the path, I stop to consult my map. I know this is the top of one ski lift but the trails lead to other lifts that go even higher into the mountains. There is also a sign to a ski hill back down to the village. Standing alone on a lovely summer day, I imagine putting on my skis and skiing back down. It would be a long run, longer than any I have ever been on.

Fear immediately grabs my chest. My knees feel weak. I have been a skier for many years. I am a cautious skier. I enjoy the gentlest to medium slopes, preferably without moguls. I love the exercise and fresh air. I breathe deeply. Memories of being taken down Mt. Tremblant in Quebec in a ski patrol sled with badly torn tendons cause me to shiver. The scrape of the patroller's skis on ice and the people looking at me is not a pleasant recollection. I ended up giving my presentation to a conference in Montreal the following week on crutches. It took months and months for my knees to heal.

I had been on the chair lift with Jack and Matt. My right boot was hooked on Jack's ski binding as I got off the lift. I fell hard. *I do not like this memory one bit!*

Moving further from the edge of the slope, I notice a large hill covered in wildflowers and grasses. Jack is nowhere to be seen. A few couples and the family in the distance, heading away from me, are the only sign of people. I cannot see the girl with the braid. I am alone. I think of the scenes from The Sound of Music. Imaginary music fills my head.

I want to climb that hill.

I survey my surroundings and know that from up there I should be able to see Jack if he returns before I come down. I am fearful he will return and descend the mountain without me. He has the car keys. *He is so passive aggressive! Is he angry with me?*

I had no sense that he was. He seemed normal at breakfast. Yet he must have planned to leave me. I know I could get back to our hotel. It might be a bit awkward not speaking French though. I do have money with me. I put my passport and one credit card and some cash in my deep Tilley pants pocket. I won't go too far. I have no desire to play power games or to do anything that could be seen as starting something.

Slowly I wade through the grass climbing the uneven ground, watchful for animal holes or rocks. I do not want to fall. I look about to see if anyone is watching me. The people who came up with us have all disappeared.

This feels like so many other points in my relationship with my husband where he does something very unexpected and sudden and I am left wondering what is happening. Part of me wants to confront him and ask why he didn't tell me before we got up here that he wanted to walk in the mountains alone. *Why just stride off and leave me?*

This man has been suddenly leaving me and returning over and over again ever since we first met. Our relationship gets very good, very intimate and close and then he does something to put a wedge between us. I used to plead and seek him out, questioning what I did to make him withdraw. He would tell me I was too something and hadn't done this or that and I would try to repair whatever he complained about. Then I learned that sometimes he withdrew for reasons that had nothing to do with me and I didn't have to assume responsibility for his behaviour. I am so glad we have had this time away from our responsibilities together. It is a perfect time to reflect on the personal aspects of our relationship and for me to look again at my life. I have some uninterrupted time right now to explore my feelings about this marriage and my life, and some time to explore some ways that I can work so that I can be happy. *What do I want right this very moment?*

Climb every mountain ... the music flows into my mind..... ford every stream... I hum....'till you find your dream. ...follow every rainbow.... I do not know all the words in the right order but I do know it will take all the love...every day.... as long as I live.[1] My vision is blurry so I stop to regain my self control. *I want to live as long as I live with love.*

As I wipe my eyes and can see clearly again I resume my climb. *What are my dreams?*

I let my mind ramble about my life. *So many wonderful adventures, so many loving happy times. So much insecurity with this man. Is he really true to me? Does he really love me? He makes so much money convincing judges and juries with his smooth style. Is he lying to me? Why am I standing alone on a mountain top, surrounded by vast peaks covered in snow, questioning my husband's motives?*

My mind returns to Tintagel and standing atop the castle ruins. I was homesick then because I was missing him. Now he is here physically but I sense he is far away. I think of my children and my heart lurches in sadness. I wish I could bring them here. They'd love to explore with me. They'd love to ski here. Perhaps a family ski vacation ...

You really must let go of the children as the focus of your life. What do you want Marilyn?

While individual differences are normal, keeping score and blaming the partner for not meeting our needs is not productive. I can see that this much time together is too much for him. We used to travel together and want the trips to go on forever. We didn't have this awkward space in our togetherness. We had differences and separated while we cooled off. This isn't like that. *Was he thinking I would have started a fight over the ordering of dinner last night and he could have gone off in a huff today to walk alone?*

It isn't really the time apart that is bothering me, it is the way he suddenly just left. It wasn't negotiated. I wasn't given any choice or warning.

I know Jack could change if only he would accept that he is responsible for his happiness and often with his behaviour he is the cause of his unhappiness. If he would stop blaming me or the challenges of the children, his workload or his relationships with others, he would see he has the power to change his life. It is his attitude that needs to change first. He could lower his stress in many ways. First he needs to see that his way of coping needs to change. Running away is not going to solve the problems he has with me. It will only add new ones.

Stop thinking about him! You spend entirely too much time worrying about pleasing him when he will not allow himself to be pleased. This is my 25th wedding celebration too. I have survived life with him too.

I reach the top and look all around. I am so high I must be over the rainbow. Somewhere over the .... The music swells in my head. Oh how I wish I could sing on key. One wish I had recently was to be able to sing. I turn all 360 degrees in a circle. Not another soul in sight. I start to sing softly, then stop and try a little lower in my throat. As I sing "bluebirds fly" I stretch my arms high above my head and imagine I can fly. The sky is blue.[2] I get lost in the lyrics and breathe deeply. I smile and thank God for the wonderful experience of being Me. My life, not our life, my life, is filled with so many gifts and treasures my heart expands and I feel a tingling throughout my body.

Oh dear guardian angels of mine, for surly there must be more than one to help me create such a life filled with wonderful experiences and people who help me learn and grow, thank you. I am truly blessed. I know I am not alone.

I stand silently, breathing gently and turning slowly. Everywhere I look there are vistas and peaks, valleys and…out there is the world! *Dear God, please let there be peace on earth. Take the wonder of our world and give every human being a sense of wonder and a touch of love.* My heart expands and I have a sense that I have no boundaries. It is as if I am vapour and can spread throughout the cosmos spreading the wonderful way I am experiencing this moment as if I am the scent of a flower on a gentle breeze. Time is gone, I am everywhere and I am here. A breeze passes my cheek. I am suddenly solid again.

"When you walk through a storm…" as if there is an orchestra playing in my head …"hold your head up high" …the words softly play on my lips …"and don't be afraid"…

The memory of music and the heightened sense of healing energy flows through my being, filling me with a sense of complete trust and love …"you'll never walk alone." [3]

I turn and see Jack returning along the same path where I saw his back disappear.

"Walk on through the storm…the rain…I wipe tears from my eyes. He turns and sees me above him and I wave.

"Though your dreams be tossed and torn…"

I am surprised how calm and at peace I feel. I am filled with an inner sense of joy. Nothing he does will disrupt it. The words "with hope in your heart" sit gently in my awareness but the music has disappeared.

As I watch him climb toward me, I know I will go with this man into the next phase of our lives. I care deeply about him but I am in control of my Self. I am again filled and my cup is running over. I am in the state of my Holy Grail.

As he nears I start to sing. "Climb every mountain…" I cannot carry a tune very well. At first he looks sheepish. He knows he has acted with a lack of consideration. I even think he is surprised to find me greeting him by singing. Or perhaps he thinks my singing is his punishment because he has such a good ear for music.

I now feel quite silly and my emotion is showing through. I hold out my arms for a hug and he moves close. I ask if he is alright and he says he is but he is thirsty.

"That wasn't very nice of you to just desert me."

"You're right it wasn't. I just wanted to be alone."

"OK, for your punishment I want you to sing with me."

"What?"

Standing on top of the hill together, arms around each other we sing as much as we know of Climb Every Mountain. His voice is steady and deep and it helps me keep better in tune.

We turn and see a couple climbing the hill toward us. They explain that it looks like a good vantage point and apologise if they are interrupting. This is all spoken in French but I read their body language and know "excuse" and "s'il vous plais." I ask them to

take our picture and we exchange cameras. I take theirs. A lot can be said with a gesture if people want to communicate.

We leave them and walk down the slope toward a snack bar. We had agreed to skip lunch as we had a large breakfast but I want something.

Sipping a cold pop and munching on chips, while sitting on a small terrace, I am dismayed that Jack invites the couple we just met to join us. They move chairs to form a circle. It is as if I am being purposefully ignored and he is intentionally bantering on with them in French. I try to join in but the woman keeps getting the giggles over my poor pronunciation—she speaks no English. Her attention returns to the conversation with the two men. I sit in silence. I consider wandering off but I have no desire to go anywhere. The sun is dipping toward the horizon. I am ready to go down. It is almost time for the cable car. I suggest we start back.

Slowly Jack ends his conversation and we walk toward the cable car. I am annoyed but I do not want to start a fight. I am quiet. Just before the departure platform, Jack hands me the car keys, tells me to meet him at the bottom and informs me he is walking down. I am shocked.

"How? Why? Where will I meet you?"

He points to a narrow dirt roadway and tells me to meet him in the centre of town. I caution him that it is a long way down and the light is fading. He turns. I again see his back retreating from me.

Stunned, I ride down in silence. The couple he was chatting with look at me and say something I do not understand softly to each other. I turn to the window, ignoring them. Soon after we depart I see Jack far below. There are cows on the hillside behind him. He waves. I take his picture.

The village grows in size. My heart has lost all its song. Sadness sits in me like a heavy lump. *What is he doing? Why is he doing this? Is he trying to get me upset so he can say I am ruining this holiday?*

I arrive back at the car and take time before I start it to consider what could be his motive. I look on the ski map I picked up on my way up and see the Ancienne route des Aravis comes out from Beauregard in the centre of the village of la Clusaz. It isn't a very detailed map.

He might come straight down the ski hill but the grass is long. There are cows grazing so there are sure to be cow droppings and animal holes. He could meet a fox. I wonder if there are bears. He could also take the road but it switches back and forth so it is a longer trip. The attendant from the snack bar is on our gondola so he is not likely to be driven down. I didn't see a vehicle up top. There are no ski patrollers to do a last sweep of the hill like they do in ski season. Some of the roads have chalets on them but not the one he is on. What a reckless thing for him to do. What if he falls? He doesn't have hiking gear, probably not even water with him. He is not accustomed to so much walking.

I am reminded of his comments about suicide. He sure has been strange today.

I drive the car to the centre ville. Finding a place to park is easy. I wander through shops not really looking for anything. I keep an eye on the car as I am sure he will be exhausted when he arrives. I can see the sun on the mountain but it is all in shade here.

Finally I see him. He looks horrid. His face is scratched and his pants are dirty. Mud clings near his knee and he has smears across his face. His replies to my concerned questions tell a tale of falls, encounters with brambles as short cuts down forested slopes to shorten the route, much as I had imagined. He admits it was further than he thought and closer to nightfall. Even though it was all down hill, it was harder than he imagined. He is exhausted and very glad to be driven back to our hotel.

Flopping onto the bed with a groan, he looks like he could sleep for hours. I suggest a bath to soothe his muscles and in a stern controlled voice tell him I will not tolerate him deserting me for dinner. I pour two glasses of wine and hand him one in the tub. I stand at the open window looking out over the valley. Somewhere I hear a bell then the sound of a cow mooing.

We are both quiet during dinner. I order the same dish I had last night as I can now point it out on the menu. It is delicious but I have little enthusiasm. I ask Jack what is wrong. He says nothing is wrong. He won't explain. I won't ask again.

From la Clusaz it is just 60 kilometres to Geneva. We are up and out early as we went to bed soon after dinner.

I had stayed up alone and watched the moonlight on the mountains. I considered joining the people who I could hear laughing in the bar or quietly talking on the patio but didn't want to venture out on my own. I didn't want to do anything I would be questioned about in the morning and conversation would have been impossible because of the language barrier. I felt lonely and sad. I tried to recall the wonderful feelings of the mountain top but they eluded me. Only one solution—sleep.

Once the bags are in the trunk, I try to lighten the mood by suggesting Jack take the bobsled down and I'll drive. I am a little surprised that he agrees since he is complaining about sore legs. His mood is lighter today. I snap several pictures and laugh at his looks of horror as he releases the break and moves away from me, quickly down the slope. I have no desire to ride and happily meet him at the bottom with the car.

Vineyards lay across the rolling hills and majestic mountains fill the horizon. Huge white billowing clouds cast shadows on the slopes that are dotted with cows. I am nervous as we approach the border into Switzerland but Jack is confident with his mastery of French and our Canadian passports, we will have no problem. He is right again.

Sometimes referred to as the Capital of Peace, Geneva is the European headquarters of the United Nations. We walk along the lakeside promenade, watching the boats and gulls, and the famous water jet. Jack's legs are tired but I offer no sympathy.

Our tourist information tells us that the jet was created in 1951 to replace the former jet created in 1891. The present jet reaches a maximum height of 140 meters. The water reaches a speed of 200 kilometres an hour. The exhaust pipe has been carefully designed so that the water jet is hollow and filled with microscopic drops of water to ensure it remains opaque and white. I love the energy and the sparkles and rainbows created when the sun hits the mist.

Spray from the jet soaks the pleasure boats tied at their moorings like continual rainfall. I can see that as a disadvantage of having a boat slip there, especially in breezy weather.

We wander along Bastion Park on the south side of Lake Geneva. It is a glorious morning. Exploring alleyways in the old part of town, window shopping in antique dealers, art galleries, antiquarian booksellers, souvenir shops with postcards and Swiss knives, fills our morning. Not bothering to go into most of them we absently walk and talk. Our time is our own and we can follow our whims. Jack asks if I want to visit St. Peter's Cathedral and I decline. We ponder what it would be like to live here.

"Do you want to take a boat cruise on Lake Geneva?"

"Not really. I'd rather stay close to the people than see the shore and long views. Perhaps on our next visit."

The Alps seem close enough to touch. This is so calm and relaxing. I feel quietly happy and catch Jack's hand to walk hand in hand for awhile. I am prepared for rejection but he returns my smiles and we share interest and laughter over things we see. *This is really wonderful! What is the difference between yesterday and today? I do not believe it is in my behaviour or my words.*

Jack asks what I want to do for lunch. I suggest a drive out the shore looking for a restaurant on the water. This time I blurt out just what I really want to do with no hesitation or deference to him. He asks if I know of one.

Sometimes I have read a part of the guidebook he hasn't or I have seen a sign or pamphlet. Sometimes I have an instinctive feeling or hunch that proves to be correct. I assure him I don't have any specific information. It seems like a good possibility. I ask if he is willing to explore. He seems sceptical but says he is alright with at least looking as long as I agree to return to town if we cannot find a place in a reasonable time. I agree.

Retrieving our car from the car park we leave downtown Geneva. Driving slowly along the Route du Lac in the brilliant sunshine, I hope my hunch is correct. We pass through Bellevue and Versoix and I see several spots but they are not quite up to my fantasy. As we pass through Coppet, a village that sits astride the lakeshore Route Suisse, I see more plain eating places. I ask Jack to drive as slowly as possible. There is hardly any traffic. I hope to see something nice.

The Hotel Du Lac catches my eye but we are past before I have a chance to open my mouth. I ask to go back and Jack skilfully turns around and we stop in the hotel car park. I do hope they serve lunch! We are just 12 miles from Geneva but I am ready to stop.

Entering the hotel together, we are assured lunch is now being served and we are welcome. This wood beamed inn was built in 1628, and was apparently lodging for people arriving by coach or on horseback. It doesn't look as if it has changed and the atmosphere delights me. We follow through a magnificent dining room, antique laden drawing room and are escorted onto a shady lakeside terrace that runs across the back of the inn.

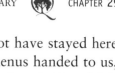

Common foot travellers would presumably not have stayed here but at simpler places. As we are seated and menus handed to us, I am able to appreciate what a gem we have found. Our drink order is taken and I browse through the menu looking for familiar words. I sip a glass of chilled crisp Sauvignon Blanc while our waiter makes suggestions for our lunch. I am delighted that he explains in English. I know what I want to order. I smile in satisfaction, but I sense Jack does not want to see my delight.

Boats of all sorts churn up the water on Lake Geneva, just steps from our table. Guests arrive by boat, both personal yachts and what appears to be small ferry boats or water taxis. This is so beautiful. I am so pleased my intuition is working today and Jack trusted me.

The Château de Coppet was built by Jacques Necker, a Genevois banker and Minister of Finance to the French king Louis XVI from 1776 until the Revolution in 1789. I ask Jack if he wants to visit it. He is happy to take our time here, then he wants to go by the United Nations building and then on to our lodging for tonight. It is about a two hour drive from Geneva. He wants us to arrive in daylight as we are travelling unknown roads in the mountains. I agree.

We are off to Beaune near Dijon. It is in the heart of the Burgundy wine region. It is our last night before Paris. Our tour is nearing its end.

As we exit Switzerland, I am sorry we didn't have a longer visit. This is one country I know I will return to someday. The words from a well loved song flow in my mind.

"We'll meet again, don't know where, don't know when ….."[4]

I don't know where I will be in my life or when but I do want to return and see more of Switzerland.

After the border, I drive. As we travel north I am struggling to hide my true feelings. I know doing so is not necessarily in my best interest. Suppressing feelings creates stress and can cause blood pressure readings to climb. Thinking of sharing my true emotions with the man I love evokes feelings of fear. I feel vulnerable, open to criticism. I also know suppressing feelings can inhibit a relationship. Talking about feelings calmly can help foster a supportive environment between people. I waver with my choice but decide to stay quiet. I should be able to feel calm and trusting. Confidence is feeling accepted and capable. I do not feel very confident. Is *this me? Why is it so hard to hold on to Me when I am with you?*

We arrive at Le Cep Hotel in Beaune. The advertisement says it is part of the small luxury hotels of the world and was once a private residence. This 16th century gem is everything and more for a romantic evening. We need romance. *I want romance!*

It is in the centre of town and has just been remodelled. Our room is lovely. We have a small balcony that overlooks the centre courtyard and dining area. We have made reservations for dinner here but that is not for awhile. Given the choice I want to eat in the courtyard as it uses the same menu and the tables are set just as exquisitely as the indoor dining room.

I want to stay awake so I suggest we explore the hotel and its gardens. I do not want to visit a church or go shopping. Soon I suggest I return to our room as I know I will not be able to enjoy my dinner without a rest. Jack is more than accepting as his legs are sore. We set the alarm for one hour and crawl into the soft bed for a nap. The pillows are like a cloud. I have no problem getting to sleep. I am emotionally exhausted and physically tired.

When the alarm wakes us, we quietly chat for awhile then share our sexual energy. While I shower, Jack pours us a glass of local Chardonnay that we bought from a cave along the route.

The Chardonnay grape is the most famous white grape. It is a native of Burgundy. I sip the delicious wine while I dress. Jack showers then joins me on our little balcony in intimate companionship.

The ringing of the phone startles us. I am not very happy to hear my daughter's concerned voice on the phone. She assures me they are all fine but there is a problem she wanted our opinion on. It isn't serious and soon the conversation is a sharing of news. Jack says a quick hello and she is gone.

When I return to the balcony, I can sense he is disturbed. In answer to my inquiry, he tells me I change when the kids are involved. I assure him I know I go into parental mode, but that I can also leave it behind once the issue is solved. He says he wants my undivided attention. I think there is something more. I avoid speaking about our children and make every effort to return to our romantic evening.

"So what was so important?"

"Do you really want to know?"

"Yes."

"There is a plumbing leak at the cottage and the hall carpet is all wet. Julia has been taking her usual long showers and I do not think the tub surround can take all that water. Don't worry. I'll attend to it when I get home. I told her to take a swim instead of a shower."

"She won't do that. You know teenagers."

"Enough. We can deal with this later. We are powerless to do anything about it from here."

Dinner in the open is divine. Candles flicker. Soft music plays. Laughter and the gentle scent of flowers float on the air. Stars twinkle in the sky. Jack is attentive and calm. We linger over a fabulous meal and wonderful wine. I do not want this evening to ever end.

"Aren't the garden statues attractive? I'd love to have a private garden filled with roses and alyssum. One where we could eat out on the patio in candlelight like this without bugs."

"You have a private garden with roses and alyssum and a lovely stone patio, Marilyn"

"Could we get some statues to put in it?"

We banter about naked women statues as opposed to naked men. We giggle at a statue that is commonly seen with a little boy peeing into a fish pond and how silly some of the statues really are. The wine and the sense of being protected and well served are giving us the freedom to be silly. This is what I dreamed our tour would be like.

Jack spends what I consider a rather too long time chatting with the waiter who is off duty soon and seems eager to complete his night. I do not like the interruption in our time together.

We stroll the softly lit gardens then return to our room. I suggest another glass of wine from our pre-dinner bottle. Jack tells me he wants to sleep. I put on a negligee and sit alone on our little balcony with a glass of wine. The waiters have gone and the bus boys are clearing the tables. One by one as the candles are blown out, I think of our trip. One by one the days passed and are forever gone. I have my notes. I have my pictures. I have my travel brochures and I will have the postcards I sent home. I ask people to save them for me rather than throw them out. They are a memento to me. I

have them for many trips and from many people. They document my life and my family ties and friendships.

We tour the medieval city of Beaune briefly by car after a lovely breakfast on the terrace. Taking the A6 north through hills and valleys covered with vineyards and chateaus our conversation is focused on the scenery and the Burgundy wines.

Stopping for fuel and to change drivers gives me an opportunity to stretch. Jack gets involved in a discussion with a fellow who has admired the car. He is asking about a place where we might buy some wine that is not too far from the highway. We take a short drive and stop at a cave where we can taste wines, purchase them and go back into where they are stored. It is a small winery and Jack enjoys chatting with the winemakers. I wander back to the car and see a pleasant restaurant not far away. There are flowers overflowing from boxes and baskets and chequered table-cloths on a patio. Jack accepts my suggestion that this would be a good spot for lunch. We are not disappointed and we linger over our food enjoying our last day in the French countryside.

My excitement builds as we enter Paris. It is said to be the most romantic city on earth. It is late afternoon but prior to rush hour so traffic isn't too bad.

The A6 enabled a fast trip right into downtown Paris. We have had good directions provided by the hotel and we are able to follow them easily. We hit red traffic lights often enough to check street signs. We turn left and travel right along the banks of le Seine and we can see tour boats and commercial barges moving past. Lovely arched bridges span the water. I'd love to see Paris from the river.

Passing Notre Dame, which is on an island along with the Palais de Justice, I am eager to get out and walk. Street vendors with post cards and candy, pieces of artwork and cold drinks line the sidewalks. We have agreed we would go directly to our hotel, hoping we can check in. If our room is not ready we can leave our luggage and return our car.

The Hotel Relais Christine is a small luxury hotel several streets back from the river and within walking distance to Notre Dame and le Louvre. It has been converted from an old abbey of the 16th century and I am delighted by the enclosed cobblestone courtyard surrounded with flowers. I feel very special to have the chance to enjoy such a marvellous place. We are warmly welcomed and shown to a fabulous room filled with antique furniture. We over-look the garden and I can hear birds singing.

Since we are returning the car today, we take all of our belongings into the hotel. There is no point in paying a rental for the car to sit parked at the hotel.

I like to explore a hotel just enough to have a feel for where the amenities I might want to use are located. Heavy oak banisters and furniture as well as lovely décor surround us. The dining room is located in a stone cellar. It is painted white and has fat columns holding up a vaulted ceiling. Tapestries and suits of armour as well as the fabrics and decorative touches create the illusion of being somewhere in the past. *I love it.*

Jack is eager to get the car back but I suggest that while we have it we drive past the Eiffel Tower. I am excited to see it. I also suggest driving around the Arc de Triumph. The Hertz return is about four miles away and it wouldn't be too far out of our way. Jack complains about it being rush hour and not liking to drive in an unfamiliar city with the crowds. I go along with him just to see more of Paris. He drives directly to 73 Blvd. Victor and they drive us straight back to our hotel. I am disappointed but understand. We had such a lovely car and it would be silly to take a chance on an accident now.

We venture out to explore on foot. I am immediately horrified to see the extent of dog excrement all over the sidewalks and in the gutters. Walking takes great care. It looks as if no one scoops their dog's poop. This would never be tolerated at home. It is unsanitary. *How do the shopkeepers, hotels and residents keep their floors clean? Who cleans it up?*

In some places, especially on the narrow street near our hotel, the smell is revolting. They never showed this in the travel posters or movies I saw. *How do they keep it off the dog's feet?* No one seems to notice. The pedestrians seem to have developed a way to avoid it without looking at it.

We walk along the sidewalk close to the river and stop to look at some drawings, watch an artist sketching and identify that there are numerous river tours available. For now we want to wander and soak up some atmosphere.

We haven't researched a spot for dinner. I wish we'd asked the hotel staff for some recommendations. I am not good at making a choice as many of the menus are only in French. When I find one with an English version I ask if we can eat there. It is on the second floor and reminds me of some of the more touristy restaurants in Toronto. Jack agrees. I am sorry once we get seated and have our wine as it is obviously very much geared to the sightseer. The food is not at all as good as what we have been having even though the price is comparable. I apologize for my choice but I also know that Jack could have told me what was on the other menus. He isn't concerned and says his dinner was just fine. Mine was just fine too.

The streets are busy when we come out from dinner. We wander along the streets enjoying the warm summer evening. We browse in shop windows and stop to watch other people with no agenda and no rush. I suggest we visit the Eiffel Tower but Jack suggests we explore more in the area closer to our hotel.

We turn onto a busy street with many people walking and a good selection of restaurants. There are tables in front on the sidewalk and large widows that are folded back so the interior is exposed. These look more like where we should have come to eat.

I am frightened by the sudden burst of shouting and breaking glass. I am sure we have come across a fight in a bar or restaurant. As we draw near the window, a group of laughing onlookers catch our curiosity. Looking inside, the floor is littered with broken white china and people are laughing, eating, toasting and drinking. Waiters are delivering food and clearing tables. Jack enquires to discover what is going on. We are told it is a Greek wedding custom to dance a circle dance then throw the dishes on the floor. They also throw money at the musicians. So the party is a wedding party and a happy shouting not one in anger. I am relieved.

It is a dull overcast sky that mutes the colours as we walk from our hotel on Rue Christine to the Musée le Louvre. It isn't that I'd wished for rain, but being inside on a summer day in Paris is easier than if it was a glorious sunny day. I hope it will clear so we can go up the Eiffel Tower later.

Crossing the Seine, we again stop to watch the canal boats whisking tourists and cargo in both directions. I could watch the passing parade all day. We had seen them last night with their lights glowing. They looked so romantic. I hope we have time to take a boat tour. I picked up some brochures with times and distances but Jack wouldn't commit to going. It would be best on a nicer day. I can feel my enthusiasm bubbling up. *I want to do everything!*

As we walk across the expansive courtyard and around the splashing water of the fountain in the middle of the Cour Carree, my feet are light with anticipation. I feel as if I am in a movie as the pigeons flutter about. Soft music tickles my ears as we progress toward the archway under the Sully section of the museum. We pass by a woman harpist and my sense of being in a dream heightens. The Pyramid of glass surrounded by dancing fountains looks like a magical entrance into the underground reception area, straight ahead in the centre of the cour Napoléon.

"Isn't this amazing!" I stop and turn all 360 degrees around and feel like I need to pinch myself to know I am not dreaming. Jack tells me I look like a kid filled with excitement. As I look directly into his eyes, mine fill with tears.

"You know how many years I have studied art and how wonderful it was for me when we visited the Prada in Madrid on our first trip to Europe. It is as if the wonderful paintings and sculptures that I know so well from pictures are coming to life right before my eyes."

He smiles and grabs my hand as we stride across the courtyard. The large glass pyramid that is now the entrance sits amidst fountains and is a dramatic contrast to the more traditional architecture. I pause a moment to survey the scene barely able to really accept that I am here. This modern entrance caused considerable controversy right from the outset. I am surprised at how attractive it is, surrounded by traditional French architecture with bedecked turrets and flounces. There are statues of full sized or larger people up around the rooftop. Just looking carefully at the architecture would be a study in itself.

We descend down the escalator under the towering ceiling of glass. *I'll bet this is magnificent in the sunlight!* I have seen pictures of the pyramid illuminated in the evening. I wonder if we will be back this way after dark.

The new reception area is below ground level. Established in 1793 by the French Republic, the Musée le Louvre, originally designed as a palace, is divided into seven sections. A succession of architects and decorators have left their mark on it. The expanse of white marble flooring and recessed ceiling lighting of the reception area is functional and a dramatic change from what I expected to meet.

Jack pays our admissions. I can see he is enjoying his fluency in French. He suggests we start with the Greek and Roman exhibits. He majored in Greek and Roman history in university and just as I studied art and am eager to see what I want, he has an agenda to follow his avid interest.

I suggest we split and meet in an hour. He seems disappointed but agrees that I will probably want to see things he isn't really interested in. I am able to get an English version of the guide and happily wander through gallery after gallery enjoying myself. The size of some of the pieces startles me. The Mona Lisa is far smaller than I'd thought and the Winged Victory and Venus de Milo much larger. Wonderfully expressive carvings and deep thought provoking paintings evoke a smorgasbord of emotional reactions in me. When we meet after an hour we agree to separate for another hour and a half as we are both enjoying ourselves. We agree we will meet for lunch then take each other to see the most spectacular pieces we had enjoyed.

After a light lunch we take turns acting as guide and return to our favourite pieces. It is evident to me that ones we choose are the ones that evoke emotions in us. We build stories and share our enthusiasm and for awhile I feel the missing closeness between us return. We browse through the gift shop and I purchase several postcards and a small piece of costume jewellery as a souvenir. I take Jack's hand as we pass through the entrance foyer and ascend the long escalator up to street level.

Tired and overloaded with artistic input we decide to visit Notre Dame. I seek out a spot close to the front left side of the magnificent cathedral and sit quietly. Jack wanders. My feet are tired and my mind bursting with information. I just want to sit. I do not want dates and names. I turn and look around the vastness of this structure and the beauty of the stained glass windows. Letting my eyes linger on the detail of the altar, the ceiling and the carvings, I feel a sense of peace come over me. The longer I sit the more calm I feel.

Sliding to my knees I say prayers of thanks and ask for guidance and support in my life. I ask for help in dealing with the challenges of being married. Marriage is not for everyone. Those who prefer a series of romantic adventures would not appreciate the harmony that can occur between two people who are committed to sharing their lives. I like the idea of having one life partner with whom I can share goals and experiences. I wonder where Jack is.

Time to move. I feel a little stiff as I stand. Exploring the small alters and alcoves I find my husband sitting quietly alone. He turns as I approach him. I smile and motion that I am ready to go. He nods and follows me outside. I suggest a river boat ride and he suggests a beer. He wins.

With the recommendation and reservation made by our hotel we enjoy a wonderful meal in a good French restaurant. We are both quiet and our conversation is light. I have asked to visit the high fashion district of Paris. I want to see where the haute couturier fashions are sold and I want to people watch. I have noticed many well dressed stylish women but in the tourist areas people are more casually and comfortably dressed.

After breakfast I ask if Jack will get directions for us. I believe we are going to the Eiffel Tower, to the fashion district and perhaps on a boat tour. Jack has been vague and distracted. He suggests we start with a walk around Notre Dame as we were tired yesterday. It is a better weather day and I agree.

The large flying arches off the sides and the massive stone walls are very impressive. Having seen many pictures I thought it would feel more familiar. Perhaps it is a tension in the air that is distracting me.

"Do we need a cab to get where we are going next?"

"I don't know where you are going but I am going to look for some stamps."

"Stamps! For what?"

"I want to see if I can find something for my collection. Perhaps a stamp collector in Paris has something that would be a rare find and he doesn't know it's real worth."

"But what about what I want to do?"

We have been walking along the street away from our hotel and away from the cathedral. He points to a small cafe and tells me to meet him there at four o'clock. He strides away leaving me dumbfounded. *You bastard! You led me to believe that this was our celebration and repeatedly told me that the last day in Paris would be whatever I wanted to do. I followed you around all those ruins thinking ....Oh shut up Marilyn.*

I do not know what to do. I wander slowly along keeping my head low so no one will see the tears streaming down my face. I guess I should have predicted something like this. Gradually I stop crying and dry my eyes. I don't know where I am but it is a busy street and there are shops. I look in windows and gradually gain my self control. *I will not let him ruin my day!*

Do I want to go to the Eiffel Tower alone? I could. There are cabs about and I could just get in one and go. Perhaps I should get a cab and say: "Christian Dior" or "Chanel" or "Armani" and see where I go. I start to laugh at myself because I really do not know much about any of them and certainly could not afford to shop there. I just wanted to see where it is and what the people shopping there are wearing. I'll bet there are fabulous jewellery stores too.

It is a fun fantasy but one I soon abandon. I step into a clothing store and poke through the clothing. It is all for much younger women. I look in one store after another at shoes and bags, jackets and blouses. I had planned to spend some money on something special and it is as if it is burning a hole in my wallet.

"Je ne parle Français."

In broken friendly English a young woman tells me she is studying English in school and would love to practice. By the time I leave the store I have made several purchases. I have a wonderful red wool cape with black belt and edging for myself and cute tops for my daughters. I buy a fine collarless white shirt for Jack. I have seen them on many men here for casual wear and they are in the stores at home. Perhaps he will enjoy wearing it on the weekend as he wears court shirts and suits with ties every day. It is expensive but fun. There is nothing suitable for Matt but I am sure I'll find something he'll like.

By the time I meet Jack I am tired and ready for a cold drink. I happily show him my purchases telling him about the woman who wanted to practice her English. He isn't too thrilled with the shirt and I suggest I return it. It isn't really very far away. He insists I keep it. He shows me several stamps he has bought as we decide to order something to eat. Neither of us had lunch. I keep my feelings hidden and know that I will only end up upset if I confront what I feel is another broken promise.

We arrive back at our hotel knowing we must pack. We have arranged for an early taxi as our flight departs at 10:20 in the morning. It is a struggle to fit all my belongings into the cases I have. I do not want to crush my new jacket so decide to wear and carry it.

I am sad to leave Paris. I am disappointed Jack tells the cab driver there is not time to pass the Eiffel Tower. I plead to go as it isn't very far. The driver says: "Oui madame." Jack's determined voice tells him not to take the time as he fears we will be late. I understand both his tone and intent very clearly. So does the driver.

Our business class return flight is uneventful. I enjoy the chance to listen to music. There is an interesting movie ... I eat. We don't talk much. I am tired. Not in a physical way but at a deep emotional and psychic level. It is a place too deep for tears.

I know people will ask me about my trip and how I liked Paris. They will ask where we went and what we did. I have stories I can tell and some that may never be told. I will keep them hidden in my memory. They will colour my future decisions. Perhaps some day I'll dare to tell. *What have you got yourself into Marilyn?*

1   Oscar Hammerstein, Richard Rogers, *Climb Every Mountain* from The Sound of Music (motion picture)

2   Harold Arlen and E.Y. Harburg, *Somewhere Over the Rainbow* from The Wizard of Oz (motion picture)

3   Oscar Hammerstein, Richard Rogers, *You'll Never Walk Alone* from Carousel (motion picture)

4   Ross Parker, Hughie Charles, *We'll Meet Again* recorded by Vera Lynn,

EPILOGUE

I have never been back to Paris. Perhaps someday I will climb the Eiffel Tower, drive round the Arc de Triumph and ride on a river boat. I'd like to go back to le Louvre. Actually, I'd like to go back to Switzerland too. I love to travel.

This trip to France has given me a chance to see how my husband and I relate—how we use and abuse power, and how we repeatedly separate and come back together. Without the distractions of our usual responsibilities we have shared ourselves with each other and discovered more about each other than we might have noticed when all the busy activities defuse our intensity together. I know more firmly that my life must be what I choose to create and not living out the role someone else writes for me. This is my Quest. It is also my responsibility.

Our celebratory trip has also revealed more of what each of us expects of our relationship and ways that we do not meet each other's expectations. Our struggles were not played out with loud physical confrontations but with subtle power plays. Each struggle forced me to confront my Self and to decide how I wanted to behave. I have learned new skills of observation, listening and self protection. I have also gained greater self-control.

I learned a lot about holding onto my Self and not just reacting to others in my life, no matter how much I care for them. I can hold onto me in new ways without just reacting to what is happening around me. I not only moved through France, I moved through stages of adult development.

I am not as brave as I'd like to think and not as irrational as I have been accused of being. I am capable of things I once never thought possible for me. I now have a different perspective on my marriage and on my Self.

I know with all certainty that I am not the sole cause of our relationship difficulties. I cannot repair what is wrong on my own. I cannot create the marriage I want by myself. We must work together.

I want to have a partner who shares my desires for an intimate relationship filled with honesty and personal accountability. I don't believe I have that.

I did not hold Jack accountable for his broken promises and rude behaviour. To avoid conflict I have not been honest with my feelings. We never resolved my walking away when he wouldn't help me with the phone. I never did call home. I let some of my wants go unmet. I must hold myself accountable for that. I could have found ways to make the call. I can meet many of my own wants.

In spite of what I might have done differently, I have grown deeper as a woman. I know I can choose to keep an open loving heart no matter what happens. It is my choice. I can reject bitterness, self-pity and resentment and choose to keep an open mind. I can meet my own expectations of my Self. I can hold onto my Self while in a committed intimate relationship. While I struggle with these issues, when I persist, the result is worth the effort. I end up liking my Self and enjoying my own company. I am in the process of creating the woman I want to be.

The Holy Grail that is my Self is now much richer and more varied than ever before. I am thankful to have had the opportunities these trips with my family members have provided. They have given me many chances to see who I am and how I interact with others. I have turned out to be different than my previous self perceptions led me to believe. Confronting my Self has been interesting.

Once I returned from my Quest to France, my personal and professional responsibilities invaded my time and consumed my energies. I continued with my parenting responsibilities, deepening my relationships with my children in more ways than just playing the role of mother to them. Through my travels with them and their maturing we have learned to have times when mutual trust, playfulness and respect for each other as people has flourished. They are such a special part of my life. I hope they always will be.

Many years have passed since this trip to France. There have been more vacations and I have encountered many challenges with my Self, my husband and my children. Some challenges were created by my choice but others were as unexpected as finding myself alone on the last day in Paris.

I continue to meet each new experience knowing I am the one person with whom I must spend every moment of my life. Thankfully, I have learned to trust and enjoy my Self.

Looking back, I am pleased to have had these experiences as they have contributed to the development of my Holy Grail, the vessel that is my evolving Self. I have gained wisdom, tolerance, confidence and deep respect for those who have the abilities and determination to create loving respectful lasting relationships. The people who I love and who love me in return give me my greatest joy even though at times they bring me my deepest sorrow.

Sharing my learning is important to me. I know I risk the sting of criticism by revealing such intimate details of my life. Some people have difficulty with this much intimacy.

I glow in the knowledge that by sharing my stories, readers have found new hope for growth and change in their own lives. I also know that the search for the true Self is a journey worth taking.

I have achieved in new directions and dimensions both personally and professionally and experienced dramatic changes, more than I could ever have guessed .... well that's another story for another time.

This closes the second book in the library of my life. Thank you for travelling with me. I do love to share what I have learned. I hope you had some new insights that will be useful in your life. I look forward to meeting you again soon.